D1452812

From Flintlock to Rifle

OTHER BOOKS BY STEVEN ROSS:

European Diplomatic History, 1789-1815
The French Revolution: Conflict or Continuity?
Quest for Victory: French Military Strategy, 1792-1799

From Flintlock to Rifle

Infantry Tactics, 1740-1866

Steven Ross

Rutherford • Madison • Teaneck
Fairleigh Dickinson University Press

London: Associated University Presses

Associated University Presses, Inc.
Cranbury, New Jersey 08512

Associated University Presses
Magdalen House
136-148 Tooley Street
London SE1 2TT, England

bur
UD
/5
· R 6

Library of Congress Cataloging in Publication Data

Ross, Steven T
    From flintlock to rifle.

    Bibliography: p.
    Includes index.
    1. Infantry drill and tactics — History — 18th century.
2. Infantry drill and tactics — History — 19th century.
3. Armies — Europe — History — 18th century. 4. Armies — Europe —
History — 19th century. I. Title.
UD15.R6   356'.1   77-74397
ISBN 0-8386-2051-5

To my parents, Michael and Ruth Ross

Contents

Illustrations

Acknowledgments

In the preparation of this book many people gave me valuable advice and assistance. I would like to thank the following individuals for reading and commenting on the manuscript in its early stages: Col. John Keeley, USA; Col. Frederick Mathews, USMC; Professor Kenneth McDonald; Professor Richard Megargee; Col. Wendell Morgenthaler, USMC; and Lt. Comdr. Benjamin Simpson, USN. Their criticisms, though painful, were very useful. I would also like to thank my father-in-law, Fred Schlessinger, for his help in translating nineteenth-century German military manuals into modern form. My thanks also go to Mr. Tony Sarro for drawing the maps and diagrams. Finally, I would like to thank Mrs. Barbara Campbell, who with great patience and diligence made sense of my rough drafts and typed the manuscipt.

Introduction

Infantry in the mid-eighteenth century fought in rigid linear formations. Armed with smoothbore muskets, soldiers advanced in line and traded volleys at point-blank range. Parade-ground drill and battlefield tactics were virtually identical. But by the second half of the nineteenth century, infantrymen, armed with rifled weapons, were learning to advance in open order and to use aimed fire. The introduction of breech-loading rifles increased the importance of skirmishing techniques and precision fire.

The transition from inflexible linear tactics to open-order fighting involved social and technological change as well as military innovation. Recruited from a narrow social base and armed with slow-firing, short-range, inaccurate weapons, Old Regime armies relied upon harsh discipline and formalized evolutions to attain tactical proficiency. The French Revolution shattered the traditional social structure, and, in the military realm, it created new problems and opportunities. The Royal Army collapsed, and the French replaced it with a mass citizen army. The Republican army retained many elements of the old tactical system but placed a new emphasis on mobility, flexibility, and individual initiative.

Napoleon Bonaparte inherited well trained and experienced troops. Throughout his career he adhered to Republican tactical methods, making no drastic innovations, since his genius lay in battlefield execution rather than in the realm of basic reforms. Thus, Imperial armies were deadly imitators of their Republican predecessors.

Napoleon's rivals had to counter French tactics while avoiding the upheavals that had helped produce them. Some rulers were satisfied to imitate particular aspects of the French system; others sought to copy the spirit of the new tactics engineering social reforms from above and creating their own citizen armies. These reforms were reasonably successful and at the same time, there was a gradual decline in French tactical proficiency because of the loss of veterans and the constant influx of new recruits. Consequently, Europe's other sovereigns were finally able to use their improved armed forces to defeat and depose the emperor.

After 1815, generals and politicians continued to develop tactical doctrines that embodied the lessons of the Napoleonic wars. Technological developments, however, created a host of new problems. Industrialization had a swift impact on weapons technology, and firearms improved in range, accuracy, and rate of fire. As a result, military men had to modify their drill and battle tactics to cope with increased firepower. Armies gradually allowed greater small-unit flexibility and initiative for junior officers and enlisted men and placed a growing emphasis on aimed fire. Thus, a process initiated by the French Revolution was accelerated by the Industrial Revolution.

From Flintlock to Rifle

1

The Old Regime Army

Eighteenth-century Europe's social structure and weapons technology dictated the basic organization and tactics of the armies. The deadly minuet of battle drew its form and content from these preconditions.

Society still bore an aristocratic imprint. Despite the growth of the royal bureaucratic state and the development of commerce, the nobility preserved and even expanded its privileges and power. The Ségur Law, the Russian Charter of Nobility, the Prussian General Code, and Louis XVI's capitulation to the nobles in 1788 demonstrate the tenacity, ability, and power of the aristocracy in the Age of Enlightenment.

Armies reflected noble preeminence. In France great aristocrats with court connections dominated the highest military posts. Lesser noblemen filled the lower commissioned ranks. Commoners did manage to enter the officer corps and comprised about a third of the total. Bourgeois officers could attain high positions in the artillery and engineer corps. In these service arms proficiency outweighed concern with status, but high rank in the cavalry and infantry remained an aristocratic preserve.[1] Noble influence was so strong that the government often created new posts for such men even though the army was overloaded with officers. In 1740 there was one officer for every eleven men. In 1758 there were 364 generals and 389 brigadiers for fewer than 300,000 men, and in 1789 1,156 general officers for fewer than 200,000 troops. Despite efforts to reduce the

17

number of officers, the French army in 1789 employed 9,578 officers, of whom 6,633 were noblemen.[2]

A similar situation prevailed in other armies. Younger sons of the aristocracy and gentry dominated the British army's commissioned ranks. In Sweden in the 1760s, two-thirds of the officers were of noble extraction, and 89 percent of the generals were aristocrats. In Prussia by 1789, there were 379 field-grade infantry officers; only 2 of them were commoners. Frederick II preferred to employ foreign nobles rather than to allow native commoners to enter the officer corps. In Russia about 90 percent of the officers were aristocrats.[3]

Aristocratic officers were not professionals. They did not regard themselves primarily as military men, but, rather, looked upon their commissions as an adjunct to their hereditary status. Aristocratic military men were reliable in battle and personally courageous, but few of them studied war on a systematic basis. Some individuals did become proficient commanders. Some even contemplated the fundamentals of strategy and tactics, but states had no effective means at their disposal to provide a minimum level of training for the officer corps as a whole.[4]

Officers frequently left troop-training duties to their non-commissioned officers and took extended leaves. In the French army of 1775, for example, there were about five times as many officers on leave as there were on active duty. Commanders in the field lived in great luxury. The government, in an effort to improve the army's efficiency, tried to limit the number of horses, coaches, and servants that an officer could take along on a campaign.[5] Success was marginal, since aristocratic officers tended to regard war as part of their special life-style rather than as a distinct profession.

Venality in grade up to the rank of colonel served as a further detriment to professionalism. For a man lacking money or influence, promotion was excruciatingly slow. In 1760, for example, a poor officer became a lieutenant colonel, but only after he had served thirty-two years on active duty. Governments did try to force prospective purchasers of commissions to demonstrate a minimum level of ability and sought to provide for advancement based on demonstrated talent, but purchase and influence remained the dominant road to higher rank.[6] Thus the officer corps remained in the hands of the nobility.

The enlisted men provided Old Regime armies with their professional component. They served from six to twenty-five years, and, in practice, most common soldiers stayed in the ranks until released by death, wounds, desertion, or old age.[7]

The Continent's economic structure dictated in large measure governmental recruiting policies. Europe was basically agrarian, and the vast majority of the populace either engaged directly in agriculture or depended upon it for their livelihood. Moreover, most farmers pursued subsistence rather than commercial farming. The middle classes were relatively small. In western Europe the bourgeois existed in substantial numbers, but in the east the middle classes were weak in both numbers and wealth. Governments typically encouraged business enterprise in order to provide themselves with strategic goods and an increased tax yield. States, especially those in the east, sought to exclude the bourgeois and productive peasantry from military service. Their role was to produce wealth and taxes. States, therefore, searched among economically marginal groups for recruits. Consequently, the unemployed, poorly paid workers, vagabonds, and even criminals filled the enlisted ranks. Many governments hired foreigners. If volunteers and mercenaries were insufficient, rulers might conscript peasants or serfs, but they always preferred to fill their armies with the economically disadvantaged.

With limited access to foreign recruiting grounds, the Russian czars usually resorted to conscription and drafted serfs for twenty-five-year terms.[8] The Hohenzollerns used a combination of conscripts and mercenaries. The Prussian monarchs preferred to hire foreigners rather than draft their own subjects. In 1740 Frederick II commanded 50,000 Prussian and 26,000 foreign soldiers. In 1751 his army contained 50,000 natives and 82,000 foreigners, and Frederick even instructed his officers to try to have two-thirds of each company composed of foreigners. The number of mercenaries shrank during the Seven Years' War because of the closing of foreign recruiting grounds, but by 1786 Frederick had 110,000 Prussian and 80,000 non-Prussian soldiers.[9]

When foreign recruiting failed to fill the ranks, Prussia resorted to conscription. In 1733 Frederick William I established a canton system whereby he divided his kingdom into districts, each with sufficient inhabitants to fill a regiment and to supply replacements. In theory the cantons made the regiments immortal since they could perpetually replace losses.[10] Burghers, laborers with fixed abodes, and newly established subjects from abroad received exemptions. Consequently, conscription fell almost exclusively upon the Prussian serfs. The draftees served for twenty years, but, after two years with the colors, they received furloughs in order to return to labor on their master's estates. While on leave, the soldier-serf continued to wear his uniform and had to return to his barracks for drill every spring.[11]

The French monarchy also relied upon the enlisting of native subjects and the hiring of foreigners. In wartime the government had the option of activating the militia, composed primarily of conscripted peasants. French volunteers signed up for six-year terms and constituted 60 to 70 percent of the army's total. The northern and eastern provinces furnished more recruits than any other regions, and urban areas were heavily represented in the French armed forces. In 1763 32.9 percent of the army's total came from urban environments. In the time of war, the rural percentage rose significantly, but even in wartime the proportion of recruits from cities was markedly higher than the percentage of France's total urban population.[12]

Whether from city, town, or rural village, most volunteers, over 80 percent of the total, came from the lower classes. Occasionally, an aristocrat fleeing debts or a rich bourgeois seeking adventure joined the ranks. Some criminals, vagabonds, and beggars also joined up to avoid a worse fate at the law's hands or simply to obtain food, housing, and pay, but most French troops came from the lower middle classes. In the 1760s, artisans supplied 35.9 percent, agricultural laborers 39.2, and common laborers 13 percent of the army's manpower.[13] Unemployment, low wages, lack of economic and social opportunities, and desire for adventure led young men to don the king's uniform. These were not the scum of popular legend. Indeed, they formed a fairly representative cross section of the state's lower orders.

The peasant militia furnished large numbers of soldiers in wartime when the government used militiamen as replacements in regiments that had lost heavily in action. In 1710 Louis XIV mobilized 50,160 militiamen to reinforce 318,000 regulars. In 1744 Louis XV had 93,800 militiamen on active service, and in 1785 Louis XVI had available 76,320 provincial troops.[14] The peasants regarded militia service as an unfair and arduous obligation, and lack of training and low morale reduced the militia's efficiency. French rulers, therefore, tried to avoid using the militia and turned instead to the hiring of foreigners.

Mercenary units constituted a substantial portion of the French army—anywhere from 12 to 35 percent. In 1710 foreign soldiers composed 12 percent of the army's total. In 1733 Louis XV had ninety-eight French and sixteen foreign regiments, and in 1746 ninety-seven French and thirty-three foreign regiments. In 1789 Louis XVI had seventy-nine French and twenty-three foreign regiments.[15]

Great Britain and many lesser powers also hired mercenaries. During the American Revolution, England hired whole regiments of German soldiers. In 1776, for example, the British gathered some 32,000 men near New York City. Of this total, hired Hessians accounted for 17,775 men. A total of 29,875 German mercenaries served George III between 1775 and 1783.[16] The Spanish, with an army of 133 battalions in 1751, employed 28 foreign battalions, and the Dutch maintained a Scottish brigade.[17]

Standing armies were expensive, and governments spent a

remarkably high percentage of their revenues on the military. Every continental power used over half of its annual budget on the armed forces.[18] Despite large expenditures, armies remained fairly small. Governments simply did not have the money to create larger standing forces. Europe lacked the taxable wealth and credit institutions to produce more money for the military. Aristocratic resistance to royal efforts at fiscal reform further restricted governmental fiscal options. And, given the prevailing social structure, monarchs could not realistically plan to create a reserve system or a citizen army. Desertion, a problem common to all armies, made it impossible to establish a ready reserve, and no monarch would willingly arm the lower classes. Governments therefore had to maintain standing forces at levels approaching full strength and had little choice but to trust their armed security to small standing armies led by aristocrats and staffed by long-service enlisted men from society's lower orders.

By devoting most of its financial resources to the military, the Prussian crown created one of Europe's largest armies, despite a relatively small population. Moreover, the Hohenzollern armies grew steadily beause of the rigorous exploitation of state resources and territorial expansion. Prussia had a 63,000-man army in 1729 and 186,000 men by 1786.[19]

Although the Hapsburg monarchs ruled more provinces and people than the Hohenzollerns, Vienna's army was usually smaller than its Prussian rival. Extensive provincial autonomy made it difficult for the crown to exploit fully its human and economic resources. Nevertheless, the Austrian army did grow during the eighteenth century. In 1740 Maria Theresa had about 82,000 men under arms. During the Austrian Succession War, the Hungarians supplied an additional 100,000 men, mainly light infantry and cavalry. By the start of the Seven Years' War, the regular army numbered 144,000, and in 1774 it contained 164,000 troops.[20]

The Russian army after the reforms of Peter the Great was Europe's largest. It numbered about 200,000 regulars and

100,000 Cossacks in 1724, and thereafter remained at about this figure.[21] By conscripting serfs and spending about three-fourths of their annual revenue on the military, the Romanovs created a large, well-trained fighting force.

The French army during the eighteenth century at times matched the numerical strength of the armed forces of the eastern powers, but between 1700 and 1789 the overall size of the Bourbon army tended to decline.

In 1706 Louis XIV had over 400,000 men under arms, and even in 1711 he had about 387,000 troops.[22] The army's size declined rapidly after 1713. During the various wars of the mid- and late eighteenth century, there was renewed expansion,[23] but at the end of the hostilities the army's strength again declined.[24] The overall trend was downward, and in 1789 Louis XVI's army contained about 170,800 men, of whom 74,500 were ill-trained militia.[25] The crown's inability to reform its fiscal apparatus, plus the necessity of spending about half of the military budget on officers' salaries, led to a gradual but steady decline in the army's size.

In the 1750s, Spain had a 109,000-man army, of whom some 76,000 were ready for active campaigning. Bavaria fielded about 15,000 men; Piedmont, 40,000; Saxony, 23,000; and the Dutch Republic anywhere between 30,000 and 80,000 men.[26] Because of their geographical security and naval supremacy, the British maintained a small army. After 1763 the army numbered about 39,000. In wartime, the British could count upon a Hanovarian force of 34,000, an Irish garrison of about 12,000, and mercenaries.[27] Wealth, geography, and naval dominance enabled Great Britain to act as a major power without the financial burden of a large standing army.

Statesmen did not build small armies because of any philosophical predilection for small, limited wars. Rulers often launched wars with grandiose political objectives. In the 1740s, for example, France and her allies tried to partition the Hapsburg Empire, and in the 1750s a coalition sought to dismember Prussia. One basic reason for the failure of these and similar schemes was that statesmen asked too much of their military machines. Social and economic conditions placed severe restrictions upon the size, composition, and effectiveness of Europe's armed forces.

Once in uniform, most soldiers felt little loyalty to the state they served. Aside from ties to comrades, reinforced by isolation from society at large, troops felt little sense of obligation to their superiors. Rulers recognized this fact of military life and relied upon rigid discipline to prevent desertion. Desertion, however, remained a common and unsolved problem in all armies. Between 1713 and 1740 Prussia lost 30,000 men by desertion, even though there was no war. During the Seven Years' War, Frederick lost 80,000 deserters. In the same war, France suffered 70,000 and Austria 62,000 desertions. Despite isolation from Europe's main population centers, Russia in 1732 had 20,000 desertions.[28]

Harsh discipline was the most effective and perhaps the only means of holding armies together. Frederick II believed that soldiers should fear their officers more than the dangers of combat, the Prussian drill regulations in 1748 contained fourteen rules for preventing desertion. The regulations even prohibited night marches and movements through wooded or hilly terrain.[29] Military men generally agreed with Frederick's attitude. Harsh punishment was the rule.

Extensive use of the lash was common. Officers could in many states force soldiers to run the gauntlet, ride a wooden horse with muskets strapped to each foot, or drag a cannon ball chained to one ankle. In infrequent, but by no means rare, instances, soldiers were flogged to death or beaten to death with gunstocks. Officers regarded draconian codes as essential both for discipline and for proper tactical proficiency.

The fundamental tactical problem in Old Regime armies was to find the forms and evolutions best suited to the effective use of the smoothbore, flintlock musket. The infantry musket was basically an inaccurate weapon with short range and a slow rate of fire. Rifles had an even slower rate of fire and were more fragile than smoothbores. Armies, therefore, rejected rifles for general use and issued them only to a few specialist units. The British Short Land Musket of 1768, for example, was four feet eleven inches long, weighed ten pounds eleven ounces, and fired a .75 caliber lead bullet. It had no rear sight, took twelve motions to load and fire, and had an effective range of about 125 yards. The French pattern 1777 musket was four feet two inches in length and had an effective range of about 100 yards. It suffered about one misfire out of every six rounds. A trained soldier could load and fire his weapon two or three times a minute under optimum conditions. The Prussian pattern 1782 musket was so heavy and poorly balanced that no soldier could aim it. With a range of about 120 yards, it could hit a stationary target less than half the time.[30]

The solution was to employ linear battle formations, since the line was the battle order that brought the most weapons to bear and produced the greatest volume of fire. Commanders felt that the force that deployed most rapidly and that attained fire superiority usually won its battles. Consequently, troop training emphasized rapid deployments and volley firing. Soldiers fought elbow to elbow. They were forbidden to show initiative or independent judgment even to the extent of aiming their weapons. Officers trained them to direct all of their attention and energy toward the rapid and precise execution of commands to deploy, load, and fire.[31]

During the early years of the century, French troops fought in a five-deep line, although on occasion the number of ranks fell to four or even three. After 1713 France adopted a four-rank line and in 1754 introduced a three-rank line already used by the Prussian army.[32]

A deployed Prussian battalion of some 800 men occupied a front of 150 yards. By the 1740s Prussia had already adopted the iron ramrod and cartridge to facilitate loading and rate of fire. Other powers followed suit. Spain and Piedmont adopted the cartridge in 1738, and the French introduced cartridges in 1744. Constant drill, however, enabled the Prussian army to deliver the heaviest volume of fire of any European army. A single soldier could fire four shots a minute, and a battalion could deliver five volleys in two minutes.[33]

A Prussian Battalion Volley - Flickering Fire

I	2	3	4	5	6	7	8	Platoons
I	3	5	7	8	6	4	2	Firing order

A French Battalion Volley - Rolling Fire

I	2	3	4	5	6	7	8	Platoons
I	2	3	4	5	6	7	8	Firing order

Prussian battalions used a flickering fire wherein some units fired while others reloaded. With eight platoons on line, the Prussians had the platoon on one flank of the battalion fire followed by the platoon on the opposite flank. Alternate platoons would take up the firing, working inward. When the two center platoons fired, the flank units would have reloaded and could then start a new volley.[34] Other armies used a similar system, often delivering a rolling fire wherein companies fired in order from left to right. In combat after the first few rounds, noise, smoke, casualties, and the confusion of battle made it very difficult for soldiers to hear commands. Troops then loaded and fired individually, thus continuing the firefight automatically.[35]

Armies marched to battle in open platoon columns — each platoon occupied in column the same space it would hold on a battle line. To deploy from column to line, the column usually moved to a position marking a flank to the projected line. The soldiers then made a quarter turn and marched until the flank of each platoon was on the line. Finally, the troops wheeled and faced front.[36] Several hundred yards to the rear of the first line, generals usually placed a second line of deployed battalions.

A field army deployed for battle occupied several miles of front. At Mollwitz, 10 April 1741, Frederick deployed 22,000 men in two lines. The front extended for about two miles. At Prague, 6 May 1757, 65,000 Prussians occupied two and one-half miles of front. At Fontenoy, 11 May 1745, some 60,000 French held two and one-quarter miles, and at Torgau, 3 November 1760, 45,000 Prussians covered a mile of front.[37]

Armies deployed in flat terrain, and commanders tried to rest their flanks on impassable obstacles. At Prague, for example, the Austrian line rested on a swamp at one end and a river on the other, while at Fontenoy the French covered their flanks with fortified villages, a river, and a wood. The opposing armies would then advance to close, sometimes point-blank, range and begin to fire. At times, the front rank knelt to allow the rear ranks to bring their muskets to bear. Most generals, however, felt that it was difficult to get the front rank to rise and advance and directed their men to fire while standing. With all three ranks standing, the third rank could not usually bring its weapons to bear. Consequently, the third rank often acted as replacements and as a sustaining element for the front rows.[38] The opposing forces would trade close-range volleys. Some generals would direct their troops to alternate forward movements with volleys. Usually, one side would break under fire, and leaders would on occasion order a final bayonet charge against a wavering foe.

Cavalry played a supporting role. Horsemen composed a fifth or sixth of an army's strength. Commanders typically placed their cavalry on the wings. At the start of the eighteenth century, the practice followed was for horsemen to advance at a walk or trot in a three-rank line. Frederick II turned his cavalry into a shock arm by ordering it to advance in column and attack at a gallop. Other powers then imitated the Prussians. In addition to heavy cavalry for shock action, many armies contained light horse units for scouting and raids. British, French, and Prussian cavalry excelled in shock action, while Austrian and Russian mounted arms emphasized light cavalry roles. French cavalry at Fontenoy charged the British infantry three times; Prussian horsemen played an important role at Rossbach, and Austrian light cavalry raided and occupied Berlin in October 1757.[39]

Artillery also played a supporting role in battle. The heavier guns, placed in front of the battle line, provided a preliminary bombardment and then fell silent as the infantry advanced. Since the guns were too heavy to move rapidly, they generally played no further part in the engagement. Light field guns often advanced with the foot soldiers, and, on occasion, artillery, both heavy and light, played a significant part in combat. At Fontenoy French guns helped stop a British advance, and Prussian artillery did great execution at Zorndorf, but in most battles artillery was rarely decisive. Military men recognized the artillery's limited value, and in 1758 the French field artillery contained only 636 officers and 5,520 men. In 1763 France had 1,097 officers and 10,638 gunners. The Prussian artillery corps in 1762 numbered 6,200 men, and the Austrians in 1791 had only 13,500 gunners.[40] Lack of mobility of all but the smallest fieldpieces forced commanders to relegate the artillery to infantry support and siege warfare tasks.

Most powers also employed light infantry formations. Light troops performed special tasks—scouting, harassing the foe, rounding up prisoners and deserters, and patrolling rough terrain. The light foot often worked with the light cavalry but remained functionally separate from the line infantry.

Frederick the Great had little respect for light troops and never exploited their full capabilities. During the Seven Years' War, he raised twenty-three "free battalions" of light troops.

They were levies raised in haste and were poorly trained. Frederick often employed them to proceed his line infantry and to absorb the first enemy volley. The Prussian army also contained a few rifle-armed jaegers, who, along with free battalion troops, performed scouting missions and executed raids into hostile territory.[41]

By contrast, Austrian light formations performed important functions in the Hapsburg armies. In 1740 Vienna had 45,000 Croatian border troops, 20,000 of whom accompanied the field army. In 1741, along with Hungarian light cavalry, the Croats harassed the French and Saxon armies operating in Bohemia. In the following year, Austrian light troops raided Bavaria and participated in the capture of Munich. Light units participated in the Seven Years' War. At the Battle of Kolin, 14 June 1757, the Croats so effectively harassed the Prussian infantry that they diverted Frederick's army from its planned march and forced it to attack on disadvantageous terms. In 1758 Austrian light troops captured a huge Prussian supply convoy, thereby compelling Frederick to abandon his siege of Olmütz. In the same year, Croat and Hungarian light units screened the night march of the regular army to the Hochkirch battleground.[42]

French light infantry resembled the Prussian rather than the Austrian model. The royal government raised light formations for each war and disbanded them upon the cessation of hostilities.[43] French light troops lacked training and discipline, and, consequently, they often failed to carry out their assigned tasks. At Krefeld, 23 June 1758, for example, the Duke of Brunswick surprised the French army because the light infantry failed to discover the Duke's approach.[44]

British light infantry did useful, if limited, work. At first the British used Highlanders as light infantry and, in 1755, formed a special light battalion for combat in America. The colonials raised additional light troops. At Quebec on 15 September 1759, General Wolfe used light troops to silence French batteries, but ten years later the crown disbanded the light companies. In 1770, however, the British added a light company to each line battalion, but field commanders used them as regular infantry. At Bunker Hill, for example, Howe gathered his light companies into a single force and ordered them to advance in linear array against the American left.[45]

All armies had contingents of light infantry but rarely used them as part of the main battle force. With rare exception, light units performed accessory duties, and major combat fell to the regular line infantry.

Given the weapons and tactics available, Old Regime battles tended to be infrequent, tactically rigid, strategically indecisive, and resultant in heavy casualties.

It was extremely difficult to compel an unwilling foe to fight. Deploying from a marching column into a battleline was a time-consuming process, and it was difficult to force combat upon an unwilling opponent. Occasionally, a commander could achieve surprise. Frederick surprised his enemies at Leuthen and Rossbach, and Austrians surprised Frederick at Hochkirch, and at Leignitz both sides came upon each other unexpectedly. Such instances were the exception, not the rule, and armies usually fought only when both commanders desired a battle.

The most effective means of forcing an enemy to fight was to threaten or attack one of his garrison cities. Standing armies were housed in and supplied from fortified cities located at strategic points near frontiers. Such cities represented both an economic and military prize worth defending, and generals who would not ordinarily risk combat would fight to protect or relieve a major garrison. Fontenoy, Roucoux, Lanfeldt, Prague, Kolin, Leuthen, and Quebec form but a partial list of major battles fought to take, protect, or relieve a garrison city.

Once joined, battles were marked by rigid tactics. Most states organized their armies into two battalion regiments. The regiment was the largest permanent tactical unit. Two regiments often served together in a brigade, and, on occasion, two or more brigades acted under the orders of a superior officer. Brigades and divisions were, however, temporary formations for a single campaign and were dissolved at the conclusion of a specific operation. Moreover, brigades and divisions were units of march, not combat.[46] Once on line, a battalion, brigade, or divisional officer had no other responsibility than to keep his soldiers properly aligned.[47] Neither the soldier, noncommissioned officer, nor officer had any combat initiative, and only the field commander exercised any battlefield discretion. Consequently, battles were decided more by volume and continuity of fire than by maneuver. Generals could, of course, employ parts of their second line to strengthen a weakened portion of the front or mount an assault. Saxe at Fontenoy threw forward his reserves to halt the British advance, and the Austrians at Leuthen tried to feed in reserves to the first line. At Kunersdorf Austrians from the second line helped the Russians reform their left wing.[48] Linear formations made more extensive maneuvering impossible, and the volley remained the deciding factor in most battles. Prussian fire at Mollwitz, Leuthen, Leignitz, and Torgau, and Wolfe's volley at Quebec provide examples of the dominance of volley fire on eighteenth-century battlefields.

Delivered at close range by serried ranks, volley fire produced heavy losses among victors and vanquished alike. Casualties could, in fact, reach as high as 40 percent. At Mollwitz the triumphant Prussians lost 4,850 men out of 21,600 effectives, while the Austrians suffered 4,400 casualties out of 19,000. At Fontenoy the British disabled 700 Frenchmen with a single volley, but they lost the battle, with 7,000 casualties of a total of 50,000 men. At Prague the Prussians, with 64,000 men, lost 13,000, while the Austrians, with 70,000 men, lost 14,000. Zorndorf witnessed astounding casualty figures. The 30,000-man Prussian force lost 12,000 men and 21,500 Russians out of 52,000 fell in this battle. At Kunersdorf Frederick lost 20,700 out of 48,000 soldiers, while the Austro-Russian army suffered 16,000 casualties out of 80,000 men engaged.[49]

Despite heavy, even staggering, casualties, battles were rarely decisive. Even the most badly battered army could escape to

fight again. Frederick fought on after Zorndorf and Kunersdorf, as did other powers after equally devastating battles. A defeated army could escape total destruction because victors rarely pursued. Fear of desertion restricted aggressive pursuit, night attacks, and night marches.[50] After Fontenoy, Saxe sent light troops to harass the allied retreat, but they were too few in number to inflict serious damage. After Frederick's victory at Rossbach, there was no pursuit at all.[51] Thus, no Old Regime army collapsed under the combined impact of combat and relentless pursuit.

Battles were also relatively rare. Their inability to produce decisive results, combined with high loss rates, made generals and statesmen reluctant to risk their limited stock of expensively trained troops in battles producing marginal gains. Commanders rarely fought more than one major battle per campaign. Frederick did fight two battles in the space of two months twice in his career, but he was exceptional. In some campaigns there were no major clashes. Military men preferred to avoid expensive, indecisive field engagements and relied instead on marching and sieges. Logistical considerations further limited mobility and aggressive conduct. In peacetime, governments maintained their standing forces in garrisons. In time of war, generals maintained their troops by means of supply columns to avoid the necessity of foraging and its concomitant problems of desertion and damage to civilian property. Reliance on supply trains severely restricted an army's radius of action and increased commanders' reluctance to seek decisive engagements. Thus Old Regime warfare witnessed much marching, few battles, and indecisive results. Frederick the Great noted that "great enterprises but rarely produce such effects as might be expected."[52]

Even the outstanding generals of the Old Regime worked within the limits imposed by their milieu. Saxe and Frederick made the most of what they had. They perfected an accepted system but did not radically alter it. Saxe, for example, ordered his troops to march in step, a simple reform that facilitated rapid deployment. In battle, Saxe made good use of fieldworks — at Fontenoy his defensive position contained five redoubts and two fortified towns. He continued to use a four-rank firing line, but at Fontenoy, Roucoux, and Laufeld he introduced assault columns for attacks against fortified positions.[53]

Frederick's major innovation was the oblique order, a method of attack whereby Frederick pulled back one wing and maneuvered his line across an enemy's by extending a flank. He then advanced in echelon against an exposed wing or brought his force into action against a portion of the enemy force.[54] At Prague, Frederick struck his main blow against the Austrian right; he tried, but failed to execute, an oblique attack at Kolin; at Rossbach he struck the head of an undeployed force; and he struck the Austrian left at Leuthen. At Torgau the Prussians tried to hit both enemy flanks.[55] Both Saxe and Frederick functioned within a given system. They used what they had with dash and brilliance but did not transcend the social and military realities of their era.

Not all military men were satisfied with linear warfare. Several French officers, dissatisfied with their army's performance in several wars, tried to devise tactical changes in order to add flexibility and shock to the line's firepower. The Chevalier de Folard (1669-1752) wrote works in 1724 and 1727 calling for the introduction of massive assault columns. Folard's column had a variable number of battalions, but individual battalions measured sixteen files by thirty to thirty-six ranks. The column could not deploy. It was in essence a maneuver and shock element. Folard even suggested arming half the men in each column with pikes. In action, Folard called for the use of numerous shock columns, with the intervals between them covered by cavalry and line infantry.[56]

Maurice de Saxe (1696-1750) also sought heightened mobility and shock power. Saxe called for an army divided into legions consisting of four infantry regiments and half a regiment of light troops. In contrast to Folard's massive formations, the legion was to operate in small, flexible columns covered by light troops which were to direct armed fire at the enemy and prepare the way for the columns to deliver a bayonet assault. Another officer, Mesnil-Durand (1729-1799), added his voice to the call for assault columns. In 1755 he designed a column composed of two subordinate units, each of twenty-four files by sixteen ranks. In action, light troops would by aimed fire prepare the way for the column's bayonet attack.[57]

Calls for change together with actual experience, ultimately moved the Bourbon regime to undertake some limited reforms. After 1748, the government began to issue standard drill regulations to replace the system wherein each regiment trained according to the whim of its colonel. In 1753 the French army sanctioned the use of the Folard-type column, and the regulations of 1754 introduced marching in step and a three-rank line, in addition to retaining the large assault formation. The 1755 regulations, used during the Seven Years' War, emphasized linear combat but introduced a two-battalion column six ranks deep and kept the established deep column.[58]

For France, the Seven Years' War was an unmitigated disaster. France "entered the conflict without enthusiasm, fought without distinction and emerged from it without victory."[59] Despite the flexibility allowed in the 1755 regulations, French commanders usually adhered to rigid linear tactics. At Rossbach the French tried and failed to advance in columns. At Minden, 11 August 1759, the French employed a few columns, and at Bergen columns acted as a reserve for the deployed front line.[60] The French, however, fought most of their actions in linear order, and the army's failure produced numerous demands for reform. The intellectual ferment after 1763 led to extensive tactical debate and experimentation.

Impressed by Prussian tactics, the army issued a new drill manual in 1764 in an effort to copy Prussian methods. The regulations emphasized instruction for linear combat but kept the single-battalion assault column. New regulations, issued in 1766, retained emphasis on linear combat, introduced a two-rank firing line with the third rank loading muskets for the men in front, and added a two-battalion column in addition to the single-battalion assault formation.[61]

In 1772 the Comte de Guibert (1743-1790), the son of a professional soldier, published his *Essai général de tactique*. He presented a new system of warfare designed to improve the army's tactics and make military operations more decisive.

Guibert argued that warfare brought no significant results because governments could not afford long conflicts. If, he argued, a vigorous people with a national militia arose in Europe, they could sweep all before them. Such a force would make war support war by subsisting upon its enemies' resources. Freed from reliance upon magazines and supply trains, the militia army would not have to halt operations because of monetary problems. An enlightened French king could create a loyal, well-governed populace from whose ranks could arise an aggressive, mobile citizen militia capable of winning meaningful victories.[62]

Guibert then turned his attention to military tactics in an attempt to provide guidance for the future and to improve the existing army's combat capabilities. He tried to eliminate useless evolutions and to establish a multipurpose infantry with the ability to act in line or column, according to circumstances. He believed that the habitual battle order should be the three-rank line, with the column serving as a maneuver element and, in some cases, as an assault force. He sought to provide infantry formations with the properties of speed, firepower, shock, simplicity, and depth.[63]

Perfect alignment was not necessary on a battle line. Kneeling and firing while advancing prevented maneuver and accuracy. Guibert, therefore, advocated aimed fire and fire at will from three standing ranks. Drill in general, he argued, should be simple and related to actual war.[64]

In action, Guibert asserted, the necessary evolutions were doubling ranks, wheeling in line, forming in column, and deploying into line. Doubling produced a six-rank line, useful against cavalry. Efficient wheeling was more complex. The standard method called for movement on a fixed pivot. Each rank had to wheel successively, and a rank could not move until the one in front had completed its conversion. To avoid this time-consuming process, Guibert proposed wheeling on a moving pivot. Each rank moved and turned simultaneously, thereby saving time.[65]

To move from line to column, Guibert provided two methods. The first involved a simple quarter turn. The second served to create a column perpendicular to the line. If, for example, a commander wished to establish a column on the right of his line, the first platoon remained in place. The others made a right turn and marched off together on a diagonal. When the left file of the second platoon arrived behind the right file on the first, it halted, executed a turn, and moved into position behind the first platoon. The other platoons followed the same procedure. To form on the center platoon, the most rapid technique, the officer in charge would order one group of platoons to move diagonally to the rear and the other group to move diagonally forward.[66]

To deploy from column into line, Guibert called for the use of quarter wheeling or the employment of the same method used to get from line to column. The deployment could be executed from a closed column, which meant that columns did not have to keep distances equal to their projected front, thus facilitating maneuvering speed.[67]

For battlefield maneuvering and assaults, Guibert believed that a column with a two-company front, the column by division, was the most efficient. He advocated using several columns covered by light infantry for attacks on fortifications, trenches, or salients. The double-company column could maneuver, deploy, or attack, according to specific tactical conditions, and its use gave commanders increased mobility and flexibility.[68]

Guibert also dealt with the functional separation of light and line infantry. He advocated the abolition of specialist light for-

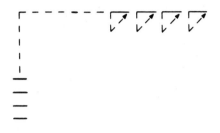

Standard Deployment
from column to line

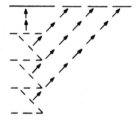

Guibert's method of
deploying an open
column into line

Guibert's method of
deploying a battalion
by division into line. The
deployment is based on
the second division. It
could be based on any
of the divisions

From J. A. H. Guibert, *Essai général de tactique.*

mations. Instead, he wished to train all foot soldiers to perform both line and light infantry roles. He also called for the reduction of heavy guns and the substitution of light field cannon with better-trained gunners, who could work closely with the infantry.[69]

Guibert believed that the fundamental battle order should be two lines of infantry with cavalry on the wings. The basic order should not, however, degenerate into mere routine. Generals should always consider the tactical specifics and be willing to modify the standard array according to circumstances. An army should operate mainly by fire but should also be prepared to use assault columns, either alone or in conjunction with the line.[70]

The concept of a small, well-drilled army equipped with flexible tactics did not win immediate approval within military circles, where advocates of either line or large-column tactics continued to propound their own ideas.

Baron de Pirch, a Prussian who entered French service in 1773, advocated strict linear tactics. The 1774 drill book adopted Pirch's tactics and retained the standard full-distance column and wheeling on a fixed pivot. Regulations issued in 1775 and 1776 retained the emphasis on linear tactics.[71]

Proponents of the column were also vocal. In 1766, 1767, and 1773, Joly de Marzeroy, a veteran of Saxe's campaigns, called for an army based on columns of eighty files by eight ranks. A force of 120 light troops and 64 grenadiers would cover the column. Other officers also called for the use of assault columns.[72] In 1774 Mesnil Durand reentered the debate and, in *Fragments de tactique,* renewed his call for large columns as the basic battle order. In 1775 and again in 1778, the army tested the column against the line in actual maneuvers. The results were far from clear. Marshal Broglie professed satisfaction with the large columns, but others present felt that Mesnil Durand's formations were difficult to maneuver.[73]

In 1779 Guibert published *Défense du système de guerre moderne* as a refutation of Mesnil Durand and other advocates of massive columns. He asserted that large columns could not take advantage of terrain because they were not sufficiently flexible. The smaller column by division, however, could operate in rough terrain, cover rapidly spaces swept by artillery fire, attack posts and trenches, turn an enemy flank, and bring forward reserves to a firing line.[74]

The *Défense* went on to argue that the deployed order was the fundamental battle formation. Guibert was not, however, dogmatic about the use of lines and columns. Linear firepower was decisive, but columns had their place in combat. The column, because it was composed of individuals, was not a solid battering ram and had limited shock power, but it did give individuals a sense of solidarity and could often intimidate an enemy.[75] There were times when a general should employ deployed battalions and columns in the same line. The columns could advance against an enemy covered by fire from the deployed units. Guibert took a pragmatic approach and argued that, although the deployed order was fundamental, columns could usefully supplement and strengthen the lines.[76]

The second volume of the *Défense* reiterated Guibert's flexible approach to tactical problems. Rarely, he argued, did nature permit the deployment of two infantry lines. Generals, consequently, had to modify the basic battle order, and the better a leader, the more he would modify the linear order. Guibert then went on to renounce his earlier plea for a citizen army and stated a belief in a professional army fighting wars of limited liability as the best guarantee of peace and prosperity. Within this system, he wished to improve the French army by creating more flexible tactics.[77]

Other officers also demonstrated a growing appreciation of the possibility of using column and linear formations in mutually supporting roles. Marzeroi in 1777 called for the employment of columns for attack and of lines for defense. In battle, lines and columns would be intermixed. The Marquis de Castries and Baron de Traverse came to favor the use of small columns for maneuver during battle and for bayonet assaults. A provisional drill book issued in 1778 continued to emphasize linear tactics, but the regulations of 1787 and 1788 provided rules for the formation of battalion columns.[78]

After 1763, many military men accepted the need for tactical reforms. Some desired to copy the Prussians; others wanted to adopt columns as the fundamental battle order, and a third faction sought to combine the deep and thin orders for the purpose of utilizing the advantages of both systems. The Royal Army did not, prior to 1789, find a definitive solution, but the war of books and pamphlets among the partisans of different systems did serve to heighten awareness throughout the military of the possibilities inherent in the various tactical methods.

Whatever their views on the merits of columns and lines, all factions in France agreed that light infantry should play a greater role. Other powers also displayed an interest in improving light infantry tactics. After 1776, the French ceased to rely on volunteer legions to supply light troops in wartime and began to create permanent light formations. By 1784 there were twelve battalions of *chasseurs à pied,* and each line battalion had a small contingent of marksmen.[77] In 1773 Frederick the Great raised the number of jaegers to five companies, and in 1786 he established three light infantry regiments. In 1787 his successors abolished the light units and in their place created twenty-four fusilier battalions. Ten men in each battalion received rifles, while the remainder carried a ligher version of the standard infantry musket. Although most fusilier training was the same as line infantry drill, the light troops received some instruction in open order tactics.[80] In the line companies, ten men received rifles. Although the Prussians did not vigorously develop flexible, open tactics, they did manifest a growing interest in light infantry techniques.

British, Hessian, American, and French soldiers fought on the North American continent during the Revolutionary War. The New World environment did not, however, produce any startling tactical innovations. The belligerents, while making some adjustments to rough terrain and great distances covered in campaigns, usually fought in traditional linear formations.

At the start of hostilities, Washington and Congress sought to create a regular army using European tactics. In September 1776 Congress authorized an eighty-eight-battalion regular force. In 1779 the American army consisted of 38,600 regulars supplemented by 26,800 militia.[81]

Regulars and militia alike tried to fight with muskets in linear formations. Only a small minority used rifles. Congress in March 1779 adopted a set of drill regulations written by Baron von Steuben. The field manual was a modified version of Prussian tactics, and Continental line regiments used it to face British regulars in European-style engagements.[82]

There were, of course, some deviations from formal Continental tactics. British and American forces occasionally used a two-rank line. Since many of their troops could not fight in linear order because of insufficient training, American officers resorted to field entrenchments and individual aimed fire. At Bunker Hill (Breed's Hill), for example, the Americans constructed fieldworks and detailed marksmen to pick off British officers. Americans used natural or artificial cover at White Plains and Bemis Heights, and at Freeman's Farm and King's Mountain, they employed aimed fire with great effectiveness. The Americans also learned how to combine militia with regulars. At Guilford and Eutaw Springs, General Greene directed his militia units to fire and retreat, leaving the rest of the fighting to his deployed line infantry.[83]

The British, for their part, occasionally used their light troops effectively. Hessian jaegers drove in American outposts at Long Island, and at Paoli British light infantry, using only bayonets, conducted a successful night assault on an American camp. The Americans did the same thing to the British at Stony Point.[84]

Most fighting, however, conformed to the European pattern. At Monmouth, English and American troops traded volleys at forty yards, and at Camden, Maryland and Delaware line regiments employed volleys and bayonet charges.[85] Thus the American Revolutionary War, though marked by a few tactical innovations, had little influence on European tactics. Both sides tried to fight in formal linear order, and the Continental military, reformers and conservatives alike, paid little attention to the distant colonial conflict.

In Europe military leaders demonstrated a growing interest in transforming the artillery into a more mobile branch of service, better able to give close support to the line infantry. Austrian artillery remained relatively unchanged after an initial effort to create light, mobile fieldpieces in the 1740's. Frederick II, however, displayed a growing interest in artillery. He created a horse battery, where guns and gunners rode to battle, and used it during the Seven Years' War. After 1763, he enlarged his artillery service, and by 1787 Prussia had four foot-artillery regiments with 8,000 men and 970 horse artillerymen.[86]

In their overall effort to reform the army after 1763, the French made significant efforts to improve their artillery. In 1763 the French used fieldpieces designed by Jean Florent de Vallière (1667-1759) in 1732. There were seven different gun calibers plus a howitzer. In 1737 the army added a light gun designed to operate with infantry battalions and produced an even lighter battalion cannon in 1757. After 1763, however, officers began to complain that field artillery pieces were too heavy and immobile. A force of 120 field guns required a train of 618 carriages and 2,743 horses.[87]

In 1764 Jean Baptiste Vacquette de Gribeauval (1715-1789) introduced improved fieldpieces. The new guns had standardized parts to facilitate production and repair. They had elevating screws, improved sights, and prepackaged rounds. Gribeauval reduced the number of calibers to three plus a howitzer, and the new guns were lighter than the Vallière cannon.[88]

The army accepted the new guns in 1765 and reorganized

the artillery corps into seven regiments, each with its own school. Supporters of the old system, led by Vallière's son, struck back, claiming that the new guns were too expensive and inaccurate. The Royal Academy of Science supported them. The *Encyclopédie*, dominated by the philosophes, backed Gribeauval, but in 1772 the Crown restored the Vallière system. In 1774 the Crown changed its mind and readopted Gribeauval's new guns.[89] In 1778 the government created seven artillery militia regiments, and by 1789 the artillery corps contained 11,000 regulars, 9,940 militiamen, and 2,106 colonial gunners armed with 1,300 field and about 8,500 fortress guns.[90]

French officers also developed new tactics to enable their guns to work effectively with the infantry. The Chevalier Jean du Teil argued that a mobile field artillery used in large concentrations against infantry, rather than in counterbattery work, could play a major part in future battles. Du Teil's elder brother commanded an artillery regiment and trained his cadets according to the chevalier's doctrine.[91] Among the cadets was a small Corsican destined to become Europe's most famous artilleryman — Napoleon Bonaparte.

By 1789 the French possessed the best artillery corps in Europe. The government also undertook in the name of efficiency a series of measures to improve infantry organization and to increase interarm coordination. In 1762 the war minister standardized battalion strengths at eight fusilier and one grenadier company — a total of 584 men. In 1775 the ministry declared that regiments would have two, or in special cases, four battlaions. In 1776 each regiment created a depot company to give recruits preliminary training. The government also reduced the number of officers from 35,000 to 9,578 by 1789, and, despite the Ségur Law, which restricted commissions to the nobility, the Crown was able to insist that noble officers spend a minimum amount of time on active duty before obtaining promotions.[92]

To improve coordination among the service arms, the

government began to create formations containing combinations of infantry, artillery, and cavalry. In 1776 the war minister created permanent infantry brigades and divided France into sixteen military divisions. A military division was a territorial region with a permanent garrison. Garrisons varied from region to region. The First Division, for example, was located in Flanders and contained four infantry and a light cavalry brigade. The Second Division in Hainault had four infantry, one cavalry, and one light cavalary brigade, plus a light infantry battalion. The Sixth Division in Lorraine contained two infantry and two cavalry brigades and a light infantry battalion. Artillery regiments, depots, and schools were part of the division in which they were located. In 1788 the government raised the number of military divisions to eighteen and created twenty-one two-brigade infantry divisions. Inspector generals of the military divisions could hold combined arms maneuvers and, for special missions or campaigns, create units containing two or more service arms.[93] Although the interarm formations were temporary and disbanded at the termination of a specific mission, the Crown had begun the process of training men from the various branches to serve together — a first necessary step toward increased tactical flexibility.

The decades after 1763 witnessed a general surge of military reforms. The French, because of their disastrous performance in the Seven Years' War, made the most sustained effort to improve their armed forces. Some wanted to remodel the Royal Army along Prussian lines. Others wanted to replace the line's firepower with the shock impact provided, theoretically, by massive columns. A third faction sought to combine the strengths of the line with the shock effect and mobility of small battalion columns. Increased awareness of light infantry's importance, improvements in artillery material and tactics, and efforts to improve interarm coordination further emphasized a growing concern for tactical mobility and flexibility. Though by no means complete in 1789, the Bourbon military reforms paved the way for continued innovation by revolutionary regimes.

NOTES

1. L. Kennett, *The French Armies in the Seven Years' War* (Durham, N.C., 1967), p. 57.

2. Ibid., pp. 66-67; L. H. Bacquet, *L'Infanterie au XVIIIe siècle* (Paris, 1907), pp. 133, 210-11; A. Dussauge, *Le Ministère de Belle-Isle Krefeld et Lütterberg (1758)* (Paris, 1914), p. 264; S. Wilkinson, *The French Army Before Napoleon* (London, 1915), p. 101; A. Duruy, *L'Armée royale en 1789* (Paris, 1888), pp. 83-84.

3. P. Paret, *Yorck and the Era of Prussian Reform, 1807-1815* (Princeton, N.-J., 1966), p. 266; R. R. Palmer, *The Age of the Democratic Revolution*, 2 vols. (Princeton, N.J. 1959), 1:101; J. S. Curtiss, *The Russian Army under Nicholas I, 1825-1855* (Durham, N.C., 1965) pp. 176-77; J. Luvaas, *Frederick the Great on the Art of War* (New York, 1966) p. 91.

4. Kennett, *French Armies*, p. 67.

5. Wilkinson, *French Army Before Nepoleon*, p. 86; L. Dussieux, *L'Armée en France histoire et organisation*, 3 vols. (Versailles, 1884), 3:301-2; R. Waddington, *La Guerre de Sept Ans* 3 vols. (Paris, n.d.), 1:393.

6. Dussieux, *L'Armée en France*, 3:313; Kennett, *French Armies*, p. 55.

7. Kennett, *French Armies*, p. 72; Bacquet, *L'Infanterie*, pp. 73-74.

8. M. S. Anderson, *Europe in the Eighteenth Century, 1713-1783* (New York, 1962), p. 136.

9. T. E. Griess and J. Luvaas, eds., *Regulations for the Prussian Infantry Translated from the original (1759)* (New York, 1968), p. 373; Luvaas, *Frederick the Great*, p. 31; G. Ritter, *Frederick the Great: A Historical Profile*, trans. P. Paret (Los Angeles, Calif., 1968), pp. 133-34.

10. Luvaas, *Frederick the Great*, pp. 12, 76; R. Ergang, *The Potsdam Führer: Frederick William I, Father of Prussian Militarism* (New York, 1941), p. 77.

11. Griess and Luvaas, *Regulations*, pp. 371-389.

12. A. Corvisier, *L'Armée française de la fin du XVIIe siècle au ministère de Choiseul*, 2 vols. (Paris, 1964), 1:373, 390, 392, 394, 406, 427.

13. Ibid., pp. 468-69, 483, 522-24.

14. Lieutenant Colonel Belhomme, *Histoire de l'infanterie en France* 5 vols. (Paris, n.d.), 2:466, 3:100, 249, 403-4; C. Pajol, *Les Guerres sous Louis XV*, 7 vols. (Paris, 1883-91), 7:66.

15. Belhomme, *Histoire de l'infanterie*, 2:466, 3:100, 164, 208, 271; Dussieux, *L'Armée en France*, 3:357.

16. C. Ward, *The War of the Revolution*, 2 vols. (New York, 1952), 1:209; E. J. Lowell, *The Hessians and Other German Auxiliaries of Great Britain in the Revolutionary War* (Port Washington, N.Y., 1884), pp. 61-63.

17. Anderson, *Europe in the Eighteenth Century*, p. 137.

18. H. Holborn, *A History of Modern Germany, 1648-1840* (New York, 1964), p. 197.

19. E. Carrias, *L'Armée allemande son histoire, son organisation, sa tactique* (Paris, 1938) pp. 6-7; C. Jany, *Geschichte der Preussischen Armee,* 4 vols. (Osnabrück, 1967), 2:83; Waddington, *La Guerre de Sept Ans,* 1:2, 280; Luvaas, *Frederick the Great,* pp. 96-97. Prussia's total strength included garrison troops and separate detachments. In active campaigning, field armies were only a fraction of the total — anywhere from 22,000 to 65,000 men.

20. Waddington, *La Guerre de Sept Ans,* 1:3-4; Pajol, *Les Guerres,* 7:17, 84; C. A. Macartney, *The Hapsburg Empire, 1790-1918* (London, 1968) p. 18.

21. V. O. Lluchevsky, *A History of Russia,* 5 vols. (New York, 1960), 4:65.

22. Belhomme, *Histoire de l'infanterie,* 2:42-23, 470.

23. Ibid., 3:507, 115. In 1735 the army numbered 240,000, and in 1748, 334,000.

24. Ibid., pp. 156, 174, 184, 232, 271. In 1740 the army declined to 198,000. In 1773 it numbered 150,000.

25. Ibid., pp. 282, 303, 403-4; Pajol, *Les Guerres,* 7:105; Bacquet, *Infanterie,* pp. 210-11.

26. F. Rousseau, *Règne de Charles III d'Espagne,* 2 vols. (Paris, 1907), 1:23; Pajol, *Les Guerres,* 3:370; Waddington, *La Guerre de Sept Ans,* 1:5.

27. Between 1715 and 1763 the army's strength ranged from 16,000 in peacetime to 67,700 during the Seven Years' War. See Pajol, *Les Guerres,* 2:27-30, 46-57; B. Williams, *The Whig Supremacy, 1714-1760* (London, 1962), p. 214; R. Glover, *Peninsular Preparation: The Reform of the British Army, 1795-1809* (Cambridge, 1963), p. 6.

28. Anderson, *Europe in the Eighteenth Century,* pp. 137-138.

29. Luvaas, *Frederick the Great,* pp. 72, 78, 121-22; Jany, *Geschichte der Preussischen Armee,* p. 248; Ritter, *Frederick the Great,* p. 135.

30. H. L. Blackmore, *British Military Firearms, 1650-1850* (London, 1961) pp. 61, 277; D. G. Chandler, *The Campaigns of Napoleon* (New York, 1966), p. 341; Paret, *Yorck,* pp. 14-15.

31. Luvaas, *Frederick the Great,* pps. 13, 79; Paret, *Yorck,* p. 19; Wilkinson, *French Army Before Napoleon,* pp. 26-27.

32. J. Colin, *L'Infanterie au XVIIIᵉ siècle: la tactique* (Paris, 1907), p. 27; Belhomme, *Histoire de l'infanterie,* 3:199; Dussauge, *Le Ministère de Belle-Isle,* pp. 105, 112; G. Duroisel, *Historique du 93ᵉ régiment d'infanterie* (LaRoche-sur-Yon, 1893), p. 41.

33. Jany, *Geschichte der Preussischen Armee,* pp. 305-6; Paret, *Yorck,* p. 15; Luvaas, *Frederick the Great,* pp. 31, 90; Griess and Luvaas, *Regulations* p. 2; Bacquet, *L'Infanterie,* pp. 24-25.

34. The Prussians used the company for training. There were six companies in a battalion. In combat, however, the Prussians divided the battalion into eight platoons or four two-platoon divisions. See Griess and Luvaas, *Regulations,* pp. 50-51.

35. Jany, *Geschichte der Preussischen Armee,* p. 306.

36. Colin, *L'Infanterie au XVIIIᵉ siècle*, p. 56.

37. Luvaas, *Frederick the Great*, p. 3; T. Carlyle, *History of Frederick II of Prussia Called Frederick the Great*, 10 vols. (London, n.d.), 7:111; F. H. Skrine, *Fontenoy and Great Britain's Share in the War of the Austrian Succession, 1741-48* (London, 1906), pp. 151-54.

38. Colin, *L'Infanterie au XVIIIᵉ siècle*, p. 255; Griess and Luvaas, *Regulations*, pp. 47-48.

39. L. E. Nolan, *Cavalry: Its History and Tactics* (Columbia, S. C., 1864), pp. 18-19, 260-61, 268, 274; G. T. Denison, *A History of Cavalry from the Earliest Times with Lessons for the Future* (London, 1913), pp. 216, 255, 281.

40. M. de Saxe, *Lettres et mémoires choisis parmi les papiers originaux du Maréchal de Saxe*, 2 vols. (Paris, 1794), 1:174, 188; Pajol, *Les Guerres*, 3:380; J. M. White, *Marshal of France: The Life and Times of Maurice Comte de Saxe (1696-1750)* (London, 1962), pp. 157-58; Carlyle, *History of Frederick II*, 8:49; E. Picard and L. Jouan, *L'Artillerie française au XVIIIᵉ siècle* (Paris, 1906), pp. 17, 21-22; M. Lauerma, *L'Artillerie de campagne française pendant les guerres de la Révolution* (Helsinki, 1956), pp. 54-55.

41. Luvaas, *Frederick the Great*, pp. 148-49, 167; Paret, *Yorck*, pp. 22-23, 29, 32; C. F. Gumtau, *Die Jäger und Schutzen des Preussischen Heers*, 3 vols. (Berlin, 1834), 3:18-23.

42. Paret, *Yorck*, p. 26; Pajol, *Les Guerres*, 2:97, 137-38, 188; Luvaas, *Frederick the Great*, pp. 241-42; Carlyle, *History of Frederick II*, 7:151-61, 8:71; Waddington, *La Guerre de Sept Ans*, 2:234-38.

43. Pajol, *Les Guerres*, 2:58; Dussauge, *Le Ministère de Belle-Isle*, pp. 178-79; Belhomme, *Histoire de l'infanterie*, 3:164, 174, 224, 249; Bancquet, *L'Infanterie*, p. 57-60.

44. Dussauge, *Le Ministère de Belle-Isle*, pp. 160, 182, 242-43: Waddington, *La Guerre de Sept Ans*, 2:101-2; Colin, *L'Infanterie au XVIIIᵉ siècle*, p. 30.

45. Skrine, *Fontenoy*, p. 168; J. F. C. Fuller, *British Light Infantry in the Eighteenth Century* (London, 1925), pp. 88-89, 92, 112, 124.

46. Kennett, *French Armies*, p. 29; Bacquet, *L'Infanterie*, p. 51; Wilkinson, *French Army Before Napoleon*, pp. 45-46.

47. Griess and Luvaas, *Regulations*, pp. 63, 227. The Prussian army placed great emphasis on keeping battalions aligned with neighboring units at all times.

48. Carlyle, *History of Frederick II*, 7:278, 8:158-65; Skrine, *Fontenoy*, p. 181, White, *Marshal of France*, p. 162.

49. Skrine, *Fontenoy*, pp. 188-90; White, *Marshal of France*, p. 163; Carlyle, *History of Frederick II*, 7:244, 281, 8:54; T. A. Dodge, *Napoleon*, 4 vols. (New York, 1904), 4:750; J. W. Fortescue, *A History of the British Army*, 13 vols. (London, 1910-30), 2:119.

50. The Austrians at Hochkirch did launch a night attack and lost 2,000 men by desertion on the approach march. They never repeated their performance. Carlyle, *History of Frederick II*, 8:70, 78.

51. Skrine, *Fontenoy*, 225; Waddington, *La Guerre de Sept Ans*, 1:627; Pajol, *Les Guerres*, 3:386.

52. Luvaas, *Frederick the Great*, p. 45.

53. Duroisel, *Historique du 93ᵉ régiment d'infanterie*, p. 39; Colin, *L'Infanterie au XVIIIᵉ siècle*, p. 32; White, *Marshal of France*, pp. 156, 159-60; Fortescue, *History of the British Army*, 2:154, 160-61; Saxe, *Lettres et mémoires*, 1:166, 212.

54. Luvaas, *Frederick the Great*, pp. 210-11.

55. Carlyle, *History of Frederich II*, 7:118, 153, 241-42, 271; 9:80.

56. Colin, *L'Infanterie au XVIIIᵉ siècle*, pp. 36-38.

57. Ibid., pp. 44, 47-49; Dussauge, *Le Ministère de Belle-Isle*, pp. 106-7.

58. Duroisel, *Historique du 93ᵉ régiment d'infanterie*, p. 41.

59. Kennett, *French Armies*, p. 82.

60. Colin, *L'Infanterie au XVIIᵉ siècle*, pp. 74, 113.

61. Ibid., pp. 87-89, 93-94.

62. J. A. H. Guibert, *Essai général de tactique*, 2 vols. (Liège 1775), 1:13-15, 40-47.

63. Ibid., pp. 21, 29, 30-35.

64. Ibid., pp. 57, 79, 81-85, 89.

65. Ibid., pp. 91, 94, 105, 107-9.

66. Ibid., pp. 110-116.

67. Ibid., pp. 130, 160-61.

68. Ibid., pp. 119-20, 124-25, 129.

69. Ibid., pp. 215, 221, 224, 228, 231, 236, 248, 250.

70. Ibid., 2:13, 39-41, 114, 214-15.

71. Colin, *L'Infanterie au XVIIIᵉ siècle*, pp. 150, 158-59.

72. Ibid., pp. 185-89, 193-95.

73. Ibid., pp. 195-97, 213-14, 226-27, 230-31.

74. J. A. H. Guibert, *Défense du systême de guerre moderne ou réfutation complette du systême de M. de M. . .D. . ..*, 2 vols. (Neuchatel, 1779), 1:117, 169-71.

75. Ibid., pp. 230, 238, 245-46.

76. Ibid., pp. 249, 255-56.

77. Ibid., 2:99, 168-74, 209-10, 216-18, 256-59, 269, 271.

78. Colin, *L'Infanterie au XVIIIᵉ siècle*, pp. 180-81, 255-56.

79. Paret, *Yorck*, pp. 40-41; Bacquet, *L'Infanterie*, pp. 124, 171-72.

80. Paret, *Yorck*, pp. 34, 55, 57, 60; Gumtau, *Die Jäger und Schutzen*, 1:67-69, 78, 80.

81. R. F. Weigley, *Towards an American Army: Military Thought from Washington to Marshall* (New York, 1962), pp. 4-5; D. Higginbotham, *The War of American In-*

dependence: *Military Attitudes, Policies, and Practice, 1763-1789* (New York, 1971), p. 87; E. Upton, *The Military Policy of the United States* (Washington, D. C., 1917) pp. 15, 17, 27, 39-40, 54.

82. Ward, *War of the Revolution*, 2:553; J. R. Rilling, *Baron von Steuben and His Regulations* (Philadelphia, 1966).

83. Ward, *War of the Revolution*, 1:89-91, 261; 2:510, 524, 528-29, 742-61; Fortescue, *History of the British Army*, 2:159, 233; F.V. Greene, *The Revolutionary War and the Military Policy of the United States* (New York, 1911), pp. 9-10.

84. Ward, *War of the Revolution*, 1:223, 358; Greene, Revolutionary War, pp. 88, 158.

85. Ward, *War of the Revolution*, 2:582-84, 729; Higginbotham, *War of American Independence*, pp. 246-247.

86. Luvaas, *Frederick the Great*, pp. 21, 93; Lauerma, *L'Artillerie de campagne*, pp. 54-55.

87. Lauerma, *L'Artillerie de campagne*, pp. 10, 13; Picard and Jouan, *L'Artillerie française*, pp. 56, 62, 90, 122-123.

88. Lauerma, *L'Artillerie de campagne*, pp. 14-18; Picard and Jouan, *L'Artillerie française*, pp. 21-23, 32-33, 42.

89. *Histoire de l'Academie Royale des Sciences* (Paris, 1759, 1767, 1769, 1772); M. Diderot, ed., "Artillerie," in *Encyclopédie* (Bern, 1781); *Lettres d'un officier du corps royale d'artillerie* (Paris, 1774).

90. Lauerma, *L'Artillerie de campagne*, pp. 38, 114.

91. Jean du Teil, *De l'usage de l'artillerie nouvelle dans la guerre de campagne* (Paris, 1778); A. Chuquet, *La Jeunesse de Napoléon* 3 vols. (Paris, 1897-99), 2:250-53.

92. Bacquet, *L'Infanterie*, pp. 74-81, 86, 135; Wilkinson, *French Army Before Napoleon*, pp. 89-90; Belhomme, *Histoire de l'infanterie*, 3:333.

2

The Impact of Revolution

The Revolution's early years witnessed a continuation of the reformist trend in the army. Increasing political ferment and the advent of war upset the process of orderly change and introduced a host of new problems and opportunities. Against a background of foreign war and internal strife, French civil and military leaders tried to combine the innovations produced by the Royal Army with the organizational and tactical requirements of a mass conscript force.

Among the first reforms deriving from revolutionary ideals was the abolition of aristocratic control of the officer corps. A law passed by the assembly on 28 February 1790 and sanctioned by the king on 21 March ended venality in the army and declared that all citizens were eligible for commissions. Talent, not birth, became the main criterion for officer selection. On 23 September another law declared that henceforth individuals would obtain commissions by competitive examination and that promotion up to the rank of colonel would be based on seniority. Above regimental level, seniority and royal nomination furnished the means of advancement.[1] Other reforms replaced regimental names with numerical designations, established all regiments at a strength of two battalions, reduced the number of foreign troops, and cut the officer corps to

51

9,406 men. On 29 October 1790, the artillery became a com-
pletely independent service, and on 11 January 1792 the
assembly created the first two-horse artillery companies.[2]

The new regime also took the first steps toward the creation
of a citizen army by abolishing on 3 March 1791 the unpopular
militia and by authorizing the new National Guard to act as a
reserve by permitting its members to volunteer to join the
regulars in wartime. Because of growing international tension,
the assembly on 21 June called for 26,000 volunteers from the
guard and raised the figure to 97,000 on 22 July. On 17 August
the assembly again raised its demands, calling now for 101,000
volunteers. By the end of the year, 34,000 guardsmen were
ready for action, while the others were in varying stages of
preparation.[3]

As the volunteers gathered, they found that a special committee had devised field regulations for them and for those who
remained at home. Divided between partisans of line and column, the committee members tried to combine the virtues of
both. Issued on 1 January 1791, the regulations called for the
use of the column by division for maneuver and assault and for
a two-rank line for fire action.[4] Generally, the Military Committee tried to provide simple, flexible rules for the inexperienced volunteers.

The Military Committee also wrote a new set of drill regulations for the line infantry. The Regulations of 1 August 1791, a
product of the reformist tradition in the Royal Army,
represented the culmination of the years of debate about the
most effective infantry formations and tactics. As with the National Guard drill book, the new infantry manual tried to combine the best elements of the various schools of tactical doctrine.

The nine-company battalion remained the basic tactical
unit. The rules retained the three-rank line and provided a
variety of firing methods. The first was fire of three ranks with
the front rank kneeling. The second method called for the first

two ranks to fire from a standing position while the third rank loaded muskets for the troops in front. In two-rank fire, the first round was to be a rolling volley from the left. Afterward , the soldiers would load and fire at will. The regulations directed officers to give their men t rget practice to improve the effectiveness of individual firing. Moreover, the regulations stipulated that for combat two-rank fire at will was the preferred form of fire action.[5]

The *Règlement* went to great lengths to provide explicit instructions for maneuvering in column and for conversions from line to column and from column to line. The rules allowed columns at deployment or full distance, half distance, and closed. In addition to the battalion column with a single company front, the regulations provided for the double-company column, known as the column by division, which had a two-company front and a depth of four companies. All movements for all columns were subject to identical words of command.[6]

When marching, troops used a noncadence step. The same step was used for linear evolutions in rough terrain. The regulations also called for maneuvers in cadence but left it to commanders to decide according to circumstances which step to employ.[7]

Marching columns changed direction either by a turn on a fixed pivot or by a more rapid maneuver wherein the first three companies turned on a fixed pivot while the other six made a left or right face and moved off on a diagonal at a hundred steps per minute, as compared to the regular gait of seventy-six. When they were behind the first companies, the troops made a quarter turn to regain proper alignment. In a closed column all subdivisions turned simultaneously on a moving pivot.[8]

Columns could deploy into line from any form of column. To form a full-distance column into line by the left, the column simply executed a left turn on a fixed pivot, marched parallel to the projected line, performed a half-turn and marched forward to the line. To form a line in advance of the column's direction of march, the leading platoon halted on the desired line. The other platoons made a quarter turn and marched off on an oblique until the right of each platoon reached the left of the one in front. The troops then turned toward the line and moved forward. The regulations also instructed commanders to combine the two methods if necessary by sending some platoons forward onto line and others by the left or right onto line.[9]

A half-distance column deployed in the same manner as a full-distance formation except for the forward-onto-line maneuver, which resembled the evolutions of the closed column. To deploy a closed column, the regulations provided a variety of methods. A closed column could deploy on any of its divisions. To deploy on the second divison, for example, that division halted on the desired line. The first division turned right; the third and fourth divisions turned left. The soldiers marched until their flanks were clear of the formation in front. Finally, the troops faced front and moved onto line. Movements were carried out successively — one division might already be on line while another was still moving into position. In combat, troops were to commence firing as soon as they were in line, rather than waiting for the other divisions to deploy.[10]

The *Règlement* devoted much space to linear evolutions. It instructed officers to employ the Prussian system of using several points of view to maintain direction and alignment. To change an advancing line's direction, the regulations called for turns on a moving pivot and the use of a fixed pivot to alter a stationary line.[11]

For multibattalion evolutions, the regulations directed senior officers to use any single maneuver or a combination of maneuvers best suited to specific terrain and battle conditions.[12] On a line, battalions maintained a distance of eight paces, advanced at a rapid gait, and could fire while on the move. Odd-numbered battalions would halt, fire, reload, and resume their advance. When the odd-numbered battalions rejoined the even-numbered units, the even units would halt and fire. When the entire line fired, the odd battalions fired first, then the even battalions, and the line then maintained an alternating fire.[13]

To increase the flexibility of a line of deployed battalions, the *Règlement* provided a variety of methods to shift a line. To enable a commander to refuse a wing, battalions simply turned at an angle representing the projected direction of the new line and marched forward. To change fronts at a right angle to the original line, one battalion did a half-turn on a fixed pivot while the others formed columns, marched to the new line, and deployed. Movements were successive — individual battalions moved on their own without waiting for the others. Thus some battalions would be marching while others were deployed and firing. If two lines of deployed battalions performed the same evolutions, the second line simply followed the maneuvers of the first.[14]

The *Règlement*, in its concern for linear formations, proper alignments, and the use of points of view, reflected the concerns of those who favored Prussian tactics. Instructions dealing with columns — including the double-company battalion column, provisions for successive deployment of subunits within battalion and multibattalion formations, and the use of a moving pivot and diagonal marches for conversions — indicate the influence of Guibert and his followers. The regulations of 1791 successfully combined the two tactical schools by allowing field commanders to use and combine specific rules according to particular geographic and battlefield conditions.

The regulations offered commanders a wide range of tactical options and encouraged them to use a variety of formations and maneuvers. Moreover, the manual avoided hard and fast rules for combat. It described the various columns and lines and explained methods of deployment and conversions, but it did not prescribe specific formations for every conceivable case. Rather, the drill book imposed a minimum of tactical constraints. It said almost nothing about light infantry tactics and gave no specific rules for combat.[15] Officers could therefore use lines, columns, and combinations of both at their own discretion. The *Réglement* presented the necessary tactical forms for combat and left it to field commanders to find the particular forms best suited for particular circumstances.

The creation of clear, flexible tactics ultimately increased the army's striking power, but other developments for a time hindered the growth of military efficiency. During the Revolution's early years, aristocrats continued to dominate the officer corps, and many of them opposed the new regime. In ever-increasing numbers they resigned their commissions, and by the start of 1792, about 4,100 had left the army. Ultimately, some 5,500 men, constituting a third of the artillery and two thirds of the infantry and cavalry officers, quit their posts.[16] Nobles who supported the Revolution, noncommissioned officers, and civilians with previous military service replaced them. The new officers were, by and large, open-minded and willing to accept military innovations. They were, however, inexperienced in leading large units, and many lacked confidence in themselves and in their men. Nevertheless, the task of testing the new tactics in the crucible of combat fell to them.

In 1792 and 1793 the French army barely avoided catastrophe. The army was simply not ready for war in April 1792. Formidable on paper, the army had only 99,000 men ready for action.[17] The regular units had not fought a major war since 1763, and, because of officer resignations, the soldiers suffered from shaken discipline and morale and were suspicious of those commanders who remained. Although the volunteers of 1791 received several months of drill before April, they were not an effective force. Many volunteers had previous military experience with either the regular army or the militia, but the volunteers had never seen action together and were suspicious of the regulars' loyalty to the Revolution. Thus, it was a divided, fragile force that moved into Belgium and fled at the first contact with the enemy.[18]

The next few months were equally disastrous. The French added 50,000 new recruits to the line army and raised more volunteer battalions, increasing their paper strength to over 400,000. Morale and efficiency did not, however, increase as rapidly as the army's numbers, and the Duke of Brunswick easily ruptured French defenses in the Argonne.[19] On 20 September 1792, as the new National Convention held its first meeting in Paris, the duke ordered his Prussian regulars to attack the last organized French field army between the Allies and the capital.

The French victory at Valmy saved Paris and the revolution. Fortunately for France, Valmy was an artillery, not an infantry, clash. The infantry never fired a shot. Before 1789, the artillery contained a high percentage of middle-class officers, most of whom supported the Revolution. In 1792 the artillery corps's morale was good, and its efficiency was quite high. Of all the service arms, the artillery was the best prepared to meet the professional soldiers of the Old Regime on equal terms. French field guns drove back the advancing Prussian soldiers, and their rapid accurate fire convinced Brunswick to retreat.[20] Valmy also gave a decided lift to French morale. On 22 September the convention proclaimed the birth of the Republic, and the army, its confidence restored, prepared new offensive operations.

On 6 November 1792, 40,000 French struck 13,200 Austrians near the small Belgian town of Jemappes. As a hundred Republican field guns gave covering fire, the French advanced in a line of double company battalion columns. On the right, terrain prohibited the use of columns. The Republicans, therefore, advanced in skirmish order against Austrian positions near Quaregnon. On the left, assault columns carried Hapsburg redoubts. In the center, the French columns tried to deploy into line for fire action but suffered heavy losses from artillery fire and fell back. Their commander, the Duke of Chartres, rallied them, formed a single, massive column and swept into the Austrian positions around Jemappes. Each side lost about 4,000 men, and the Austrians withdrew from Belgium.[21]

Jemappes was by no means a perfect battle. The French artillery failed to concentrate fire on critical points. The infantry maneuvered well but did not use its firepower effectively, and the columns, attempting to deploy at close range, suffered heavy casualties. The battle did, however, demonstrate that well motivated regulars and volunteers could work together to push home their attacks and that light infantry could play a significant part in combat.

Before the army could ingest these lessons, it found itself faced with a series of new crises that once again threatened to produce complete defeat. Austria and Prussia sent reinforcements to the west; new powers—England, the Netherlands, Spain, the Holy Roman Empire, and the Italian states—joined the war against France, and counterrevolutions errupted within the Republic. Moreover, the army began to disintegrate. The volunteers had originally signed up for one year's service. In December 1792 their terms began to expire, and in a matter of months over 60,000 of them went home. Shortages of food, clothing, and pay led thousands of others to desert.[22] The Allies meanwhile opened an offensive, recovered Belgium and the Rhineland, and once again invaded France. By the summer of 1793, the Republic faced the bleak prospects of military defeat and political collapse. If France was to survive the First Coalition's onslaught and defeat domestic counterrevolution, the nation would have to undertake a massive mobilization of its human and material resources.

The convention's first priority was to expand the army. On 21 February 1793, the government declared that all single men and widowers between the ages of eighteen and forty were in a state of requisition until 300,000 men joined the colors. The convention allocated a quota to each department and ordered local authorities to implement the decree.[23]

The partial mobilization brought new troops to the depleted army, but it also sparked counterrevolutionary insurrections in several provinces. Furthermore, the new recruits were too few to combat the First Coalition's forces. Consequently, the deputies began to contemplate a far more extensive mobilization effort. Speaking to the convention on 12 August 1793, Bertrand Barère, spokesman for the Committee of Public Safety, called for an immediate levy en masse.[24] Another committee member also demanded a mass national rising to defeat the Republic's foreign and domestic foes.[25] Two days later Barère returned to the rostrum to assert that no person was worthy of liberty who would not fight to defend it. The convention, as representative of the popular will, should act through the committee to organize and direct the national struggle.[26]

The Parisian sansculottes also called for a levy. On 16 August delegates from the city's sectional clubs came to the convention, denounced the February mobilization as a weak half measure, and demanded universal conscription. On the 18th the Lombard section urged the convention to create a nationwide levy.[27] Parisian demands for a mass rising, together with the military situation, stimulated the convention to action. To avoid an unorganized jacquerie and to strengthen the army, the deputies decided that, as representatives of the people, they would attempt to direct popular efforts with order and regularity.[28]

On 23 August 1793 Barère discussed in detail the committee's approach to national conscription. In a free country, he argued, all citizens had to participate in the defense of freedom. He rejected the idea of voluntary enlistments as characteristic of the Old Regime and counterrevolutionary federalism. All Frenchmen, he argued, had an obligation to serve the war effort in a capacity decided by the convention. Some would fight, others would supply the fighters, and still others would care for the wounded. In a crisis, men and women, young and old had to serve, and the government, as representative of the people, had the task of directing popular efforts and assuring the most efficient use of people, money, and material.[29]

On the same day the convention passed the famous levy en masse decree. The law created a national draft and provided for the mobilization of the nation's entire resources. The decree stated that for the war's duration all Frenchmen were in a state of permanent requisition. Young single men were to join the army; married men were to work in arms factories and transport provisions; women were to fashion tents and clothing and serve in hospitals; children were to make old linen into lint; and old men were to repair to the village squares to preach hatred for kings and loyalty to the Republic. Representatives from the convention, armed with plenary powers, were to assist district authorities in organizing the mobilization. Nobody could hire a substitute and the Committee of Public Safety received authority to direct weapons production.[30]

The military draft worked quite well. There was some desertion and malingering, but most eligible young men willingly answered their government's call. For the first time in modern European history, a state created a mass citizen army. Loyalty to the nation, a desire to protect the political and economic achievements of the revolution, fear of punishment, and public pressure led thousands to join the colors. The Republic had won the loyalty of most of its citizens and could therefore confidently place arms in their hands.

Conscripts rapidly swelled the army's ranks from 361,679 in February 1793 to 670,934 by January 1794.[31] By April there were 842,325 men under arms; in June, 893,000, and in August, 1,075,644. By the early autumn of 1794, the Republican armies contained 1,108,318 men, of whom 850,770 served in the field, while the remainder garrisoned fortresses or underwent training in depots.[32]

The levy enabled the Republic to build an army about three times as large as Louis XIV's largest force and five times as large as Louis XVI's armed forces. Population growth was not large enough to explain this startling change. The basic factor enabling the Republic to create the huge army of 1794 was the radical change in the state's political and social structure. Citizens had a personal stake in their government and were willing to fight to protect the regime.

After 1793, the citizen soldier and conscription remained as the basis of France's military structure. Numbers declined after 1794, falling to 346,000 by 1798.[33] On 5 September 1798 the government, in an effort to rebuild the army's strength and regularize manpower procurement, passed a Conscription Act ordering males between the ages of twenty and twenty-five to report for medical exams and registration. The act provided an orderly, flexible recruitment system. By August 1799 the army had expanded to 415,000 men[34] The Conscription Act was the logical culmination of the levy. From an emergency measure designed for immediate mobilization in a crisis, the French had moved to a regularized system designed to cope with long-term manpower needs.

The Committee of Public Safety also undertook the task of arming their new soldiers. Reliance on private or semipublic contractors simply did not suffice. Consequently, the government had to resort to massive intervention in the national economy. The committee established price and wage controls, directed foreign trade, set up its own arms factories, gave grants to businessmen to expand their facilities, and confiscated buildings for use as factories and arsenals.[35] The committee also made contracts with private arms manufacturers, established agencies to investigate the quality of weapons purchased, drafted workers into arms plants, and ordered scientists to write pamphlets describing the most efficient production methods.[36] The system was of course not without flaws. There was some corruption and waste, but on the whole the centrally directed economy worked. By combining stocks left by the royal government with its own production, the revolutionary Republic managed to provide its fighters with weapons and munitions.

The army's huge numbers also meant that the government

could not rely on the traditional system of fixed magazines to feed and clothe the troops. Necessity compelled the French to revise their logistics. Instead of using magazines, Republican troops lived off the country, requisitioning required food and clothing from the populace. The French also abandoned the practice of carrying tents and personal baggage in the field. Troops slept where they could—in homes or, if necessary, in the open.[37] The new system, or nonsystem, imposed great hardships on the soldiers, but simplified logistics did help increase the army's mobility.

As a growing number of men joined the colors, the government sought to organize them into effective operational units and at the same time combine line and conscript units. On 21 February 1793 the convention abolished all distinctions between regular and conscript battalions and directed each line battalion to join two conscript battalions in a new formation—the half or demi-brigade. Half-brigades were to contain 2,437 men and six light guns.[38] The first battalion of the 96th Line, for example, joined with the 6th Vosges and 5th Moselle battalions to form the 173d Demi-Brigade, while the 14th Line's second battalion joined the 6th and 10th Manche battalions in the 28th Half-Brigade.[39]

The convention created 196 half-brigades in February and added two more in August. The same law created 14 light half-brigades designed for greater maneuverability because of their smaller size. Otherwise, they resembled line demi-brigades.[40] Some commanders established half-brigades in 1793. General Houchard, for example, organized his 65,000-man army into demi-brigades in August, but many other generals could not immediately implement the decree because of the pressure of combat operations. The government, therefore, delayed the amalgamation until the following year. On 8 January 1794 the committee ordered the complete execution of the February decree, and by May the formation of half-brigades and the merging of line and conscript battalions were virtually complete.[41]

The amalgam sought to combine the discipline and experience of the regulars with the élan and patriotism of the conscripts. May line battalions, however, had a high proportion of new recruits, and volunteer and conscript units contained many men with previous military experience. Some half-brigades, like the 11th, had no regular battalion.[42] The amalgamation, nevertheless, worked well. The merging of conscripts and regulars helped reduce provincialism and exclusive regimental loyalties and contributed to the development of a national sentiment among the soldiers.

The merging of line and conscript units also enhanced the army's administrative efficiency. No longer did the government have to cope with a dual system of pay, promotion, drill, and logistics. Instead, it possessed a single unified force, centrally organized and centrally directed.

The February decree also dealt with the cavalry and artillery. The cavalry was to consist of 66,000 troopers serving in twenty-nine regular, eighteen dragoon, twelve chasseur, and eight hussar regiments.[43] The artillery remained unchanged except for the number of horse batteries, which grew to forty by the end of 1793 and fifty-four by early 1794.[44]

A final step in the organization of the Republic's army was the development of the multiarm combat division. In 1792 some army commanders had placed two infantry brigades under a single officer, but these units had no artillery or cavalry contingents. Other generals continued to regard the brigade as the largest subunit of a field army.[45] The decree of 21 February created a two-brigade division, but artillery and cavalry units remained under army, rather than divisional, control.[46]

In the field, divisional strengths varied widely, and divisional generals began to obtain organic artillery and cavalry elements. In 1794, for example, the Army of the North had fifteen divisions and the Sambre Meuse Army fourteen. The divisions contained from two to four half-brigades, with troop strength ranging from 7,800 to 13,400 men. Some divisions had no artillery, while others possessed as many as twelve guns. Distribution was haphazard, based as it was on need and availability. Many divisions had two or more calibers of cannon and a mixture of foot and horse guns. One unit, for example, had 12,000 men, three horse batteries, and four field guns, while another division had twelve field guns.[47] Some divisions also obtained cavalry contingents of widely varying strengths.

Despite the absence of uniformity, the multiarm combat division strengthened the French army. The division could march and fight on its own or as part of a larger force. An army could, therefore, move by separate routes, thereby speeding movements, and concentrate for combat not only before a battle but also during an engagement. Consequently, Republican generals did not have to engage in the time-consuming process of aligning their entire force before engaging the enemy. Troops could go into action as they reached the field, and generals could shift the focus of fighting during an engagement and even seek encounter battles.

After 1794, the French army continued to use the half-brigade and divisional system. On 1 February 1796 the government reorganized the demi-brigades, many of which were under strength because of casualties and an erratic replacement flow. The directory reduced the number of brigades to 110 line and 38 light formations by combining weak units. The 75th and 208th merged to form a new 56th half-brigade while the 70th, 117th, and 152d combined into the 40th. A new 28th half-brigade emerged by gathering together the old 183d and six unassigned battalions.

Divisions gradually attained a more regular, but still flexible, form. Although some divisions continued to have as few as two and others as many as five demi-brigades, the post 1794 division usually contained three half-brigades. The number of field guns continued to vary. Bonaparte in 1796 and '97 gave his divisions four to twelve guns depending upon the specific situation, and Messéna in 1799 supplied his divisions with eight fieldpieces and one or two horse batteries. Cavalry tended to serve in separate divisions, but many infantry divisions continued to maintain organic cavalry formations.[49]

The Republic's leaders also found officers to command the growing number of new formations. The keys to promotion were loyalty, experience, and ability. In 1793 the convention established rules for advancement. From sergeant to lieutenant colonel, one-third of all vacancies were to be filled by seniority and the remaining two-thirds by elections wherein members of a battalion in the rank with a vacancy chose an individual for promotion. Colonels and generals received advancement by government selection and seniority.[50]

Representatives on mission drawn from the convention served with the field armies between 1792 and 1794. They acted as political watchdogs and could suspend and arrest suspect officers. They could also promote individuals for bravery. After 1794, the government replaced the representatives with less powerful civil commissioners, but the roving deputies had accomplished their mission by helping create a loyal, proficient officer corps.[51]

Republican officers were strikingly different in social origins from their royalist predecessors. In 1792 there were fifteen noble generals for every two commoners. By 1793 the ratio had shrunk to fifteen to seven, and by 1794 commoners outnumbered aristocratic generals by four and a half to one. After 1794, the ratio of nonnoble to noble general officers stabilized at about four to one.[52]

Most nonnoble officers came from cities or large towns, and they had commercial, civil service, or military family backgrounds. Few traced their origins to the artisan or peasant classes. Most Republican generals had prerevolutionary military service. Some, like Bonaparte, Macdonald, Desaix, Houchard, Hoche, and Kellermann, had served in the Royal Army. Others, including Brune, Lannes, Suchet, Mortier, and

Moreau, had served in the National Guard. A third group, with Jourdan, Masséna, Oudinot, Davout, Erlon, Kléber, and Augereau in their ranks, had served in both the Royal Army and the guard.[53]

Republican generals were younger than their Old Regime opponents. Not all were great commanders, for, under the pressure of war and domestic crisis, the government occasionally promoted incompetents and dismissed able men for fancied disloyalty. The Republic was, however, generally successful in its efforts to find reliable, energentic commanders. Junior and senior officers alike were young, aggressive, and able tacticians. A measure of their ability was their success in molding regulars, volunteers, and conscripts into fighters able to face the Coalition's professional armies.

Before joining their battalions, recruits received preliminary training in depots. They learned individual and platoon evolutions, and, if time permitted, they exercised in battalion and half-brigade strength.[54] At Farmars in April 1793, for example, demi-brigades maneuvered daily, and at Maubeuge several half-brigades drilled together.[55] The commander of the Army of the North established a camp at Cambrai in the spring of 1793. Selected men from various battalions came there, learned to drill, and returned to their units to teach others. About 1,000 men went through the Cambrai school. At the Caesar encampment, troops received daily musketry instruction as well as battalion drill. Throughout 1793 and 1794 commanders used any lull in the fighting to resume tactical drilling.[56]

The basic drill manual was the 1791 *Règlement*. The army used it throughout the Revolutionary and Napoleonic period, and it remained the official set of regulations until 1831. Because of its clarity, officers were able to use the *Règlement* to train raw troops, and because of its flexibility, commanders could emphasize those aspects of training regarded as most immediately vital.[57]

The 1792 campaigns demonstrated the growing value of light infantry. Since the '91 regulations said nothing about skirmishing tactics, a provisional regulation of 5 April 1792 sought to fill the gap and instructed light troops to assist the main body's advance by employing aimed fire to disrupt the enemy's line.[58]

Field commanders began to direct their subordinates to make more use of skirmishers. In the summer of 1792 Dumouriez began to train small groups of regulars in light infantry techniques. In August 1793 Houchard ordered his battalion commanders to train sixty-four men per battalion as *tirailleurs*. In October General Jourdan ordered his divisional generals to make extensive use of light infantry tactics, since they were well suited to the capabilities of relatively inexperienced conscripts.[59] Even the most inexperienced soldier, operating individually, seeking cover, and using aimed fire, could inflict casualties on enemy troops drawn up in linear order. By their example, the skirmishers encouraged others to join them. Their success in turn strengtheneed the determination of troops assigned to operate in close order formations.

By supplementing the 1791 regulations with light infantry techniques, the French combined close order and skirmishing tactics. *Tirailleurs* were no longer isolated specialists performing special tasks away from the main battle force. Skirmishing became an integral part of battlefield tactics, since close order and light tactics were executed either by the same men or by subordinate units of a single tactical command. Thus, while the Allies maintained large, well-trained light infantry contingents functionally separate from the line troops, the French evolved all-purpose infantrymen able to operate as skirmishers, participate in assault columns, or take their places on a firing line.

A nine-company battalion usually marched to action in an open column, in contrast to Allied soldiers, who moved in closed columns to prevent desertion. Upon reaching the battle zone, the French would close their ranks while an Allied battalion opened out to deploying distance. Republican troops usually formed closed columns by division, a formation two companies wide and four deep. The companies stood in three-rank lines, and the column therefore resembled a rectangle, with eighty men across and twelve men deep. The ninth company, usually grenadiers, remained in the rear as a reserve. The battalion commander then had numerous options available to him. Depending upon tactical circumstances, he could detach companies and send them forward as skirmishers. He then could reinforce his skirmish line using his entire battalion as light infantry, if necessary. He could, alternatively, direct the companies remaining in column to deploy into line for fire action, or he could order the column to deliver a charge against an enemy line shaken by the skirmisher's fire. The demi-brigade enjoyed similar flexibility. The commander could place all three of his battalions in line or establish a line of battalion columns — three parallel columns covered by skirmishers. He could also put some battalions in line and others in column and shift formations from one mode to another during combat.[60]

With sufficient training and experience, battalions and larger formations learned to use the various tactical techniques, shifting and combining them according to specific battlefield requirements. In Flanders, for example, a battalion in column seized a hill on 22 March 1793. After taking the hill, the troops deployed into a firing line to fend off possible counterattacks. On 6 September French columns assaulted and captured Bambecke. On 8 September 1793 Jourdan's division at the Battle of Hondschoote began its advance in a line of columns, came under fire, dispersed, and continued to move forward in skirmish order. General Houchard sent a half-brigade to reinforce Jourdan. Moving in column, the additional troops also dispersed and joined the advance as *tirailleurs*. Other units, however, advanced in column. One

battalion in column successfully stormed enemy entrenchments and, having broken through, formed into line for
possible fire action. As the British and Hanovarians retreated,
the French pursued in skirmish order. *Tirailleurs* seized
Vlamertingen, supported breaching batteries at Ypres, and at
Furnes on 22 October light troops traversed a canal backed by
two lines of deployed infantry.[61]

In the following month, Jourdan, now an army commander,
attacked the Austrians, who were entrenched in the broken
terrain around Wattignes. The battle lasted two days, 15 and
16 October, and on both days the French employed a variety of
tactical techniques. Ballard's division on the 15th used double-
company assault columns to storm a village. Driven back twice,
the division finally drove Bohemian grenadier units from the
hamlet. Other columns penetrated Austrian fieldworks, but,
because of lack of experience, the troops failed to deploy rapidly into line to resist counterattacks. The French fell back, and
one regiment, forming a line, held back the Austrian pursuit
with volley fire. On the 16th Jourdan advanced again. A full
half-brigade moved forward in open order, took heavy losses
from an Austrian cavalry attack, but reformed into columns
and continued to push on.[62]

On other fronts, the French also used combinations of line,
column, and skirmishing tactics. During operations around
Toulon, the French attacked Fort Mulgrave on 11 November
using light infantry and columns of grenadiers.[63] In Alsace and
the Palatinate, broken terrain produced an extended war of
posts involving light troops, columns, and small lines. At
Notweiler, 14 September 1793, whole battalions acted as light
infantry inflicting severe losses upon several Austrian
regiments. On 19 September several French battalions attacked in column. One battalion moved forward in column,
deployed, engaged in a firefight, reformed into column, advanced, and deployed again. On 18 November in the Brumat
woods, an entire battalion of the 75th Line fought as

tirailleurs. General Desaix on 1 December used light infantry to pin the Austrian right and assailed their center and left with six battalions in a line of assault columns. On 2 December skirmishers and battalion columns attacked entrenchments at Berstheim, and on the 24th General Hoche used an entire division as skirmishers.[64]

Throughout 1793 the French tried to combine the best elements of the old linear order with column and light tactics. They achieved notable victories but were still far from perfecting their new system by the year's end. The Republican armies had devised the optimum tactical formations to attain the advantages of shock, firepower, and flexibility, but the soldiers lacked the experience to implement them. Lack of training and experience in fact produced many defeats. At Arlon in June, several French half-brigades tried to deploy from column into line, lost cohesion, and collapsed when they came under fire.[65] Austrian cavalry frequently caught and scattered light troops in open terrain and often struck telling blows against troops in line before they could assemble into squares. Saint Cyr summed up the situation in 1793, noting that a Republican battalion or half-brigade could defeat an equal number of Austrians or Prussians, but larger formations were not the equal of their foes because of their inability to maneuver effectively.[66] Despite their lack of tactical precision on the large unit level, the Republican armies in 1793 halted the Coalition's invasion and defeated domestic counterrevolutionary forces. Numbers, morale, and growing tactical proficiency at the company, battalion, and half-brigade levels provided the margin of victory. Additional intensive training during the winter of 1793-94 instilled greater confidence and skill in all ranks. Thus, when the French launched a general offensive in the spring of 1794, the armies had increased their ability to execute the various combinations of line, column, and skirmish tactics.

The Committee of Public Safety directed its main blows against the Allied forces in Belgium. Pichegru struck into

Flanders and Jourdan advanced on Charleroi. In April Pichegru's troops attacked Menin. Operating in open order, infantrymen sniped at allied gunners and silenced several defending batteries. Constantly relieved and reinforced, the skirmishers maintained a heavy and accurate volume of fire on the Allied lines and rendered several entrenched works untenable.[67] The French also used close order methods effectively. On 26 April, at Boussu Pichegru's men advanced in line and drove back Austrian regulars. Three days later, deployed Republican battalions seized an enemy post. On 18 May 1794, at Tourcoing, several French battalions fought in line while *tirailleurs* again demonstrated their versatility by penetrating between two Allied marching columns. The light troops opened fire, inflicted severe losses, and compelled their enemies to retreat. On 21 May, near Landrecies, two lines of battalion assault columns delivered a successful attack.[68] Thus, in Flanders the French demonstrated a growing tactical proficiency, and a similar demonstration soon occurred near Charleroi, where Jourdan's army, after numerous repulses, finally succeeded in crossing the Sambre River. The French then invested Charleroi. The Austrians sent a relief force. On 26 June 1794, around the small village of Fleurs, 70,000 French awaited the 52,000-man Allied army.

The Austrians struck all parts of the French position. On the left, General Kléber deployed his division in two firing lines. After stopping the Austrian advance, Kléber sent three battalions in pursuit. The troops advanced in line with skirmishers covering their flanks.[69] Another half-brigade advanced in battalion columns covered by skirmishers. On the French right things were more difficult. A division collapsed. The troops fled back across the river, save for a few who fought on as skirmishers, using gardens and ditches as cover. The collapse of the right in turn exposed General Lefebvre's division, which was fighting in linear order. Lefebvre responded quickly and, in a perfect drill book maneuver, wheeled three battalions into a new line covering the exposed wing. A firefight ensued.

Lefebvre held the Austrians and then launched several battalions in a counterthrust. The 80th Line, advancing in columns, encountered Austrian cavalry. While skirmishers in a
nearby wood gave covering fire, the 80th formed battalion
squares, repulsed the cavalry, reformed into columns, and
resumed the advance. In the center, Championnet's division
successfully held a series of fortified posts. Upon receiving
word — false, as it turned out — of a general retreat, the division
withdrew in good order. General Jourdan, having held his
reserves in closed columns, rushed them forward. Along with
Championnet's division, they formed a line of battalion assault
columns. Preceded by a thick screen of light troops, the six columns counterattacked and regained their initial positions.[70]

The French demonstrated their improved tactical ability on
other fronts. In October the 132d Line crossed the Roer River
in a line of columns at deploying distance. Light troops
covered the columns' advance. On 10 November the 22d Line
used assault columns to seize a bridge near Wessel, and at
Montaigne Noire in the Pyrenees, the 28th Line sent assault
columns and skirmishers to attack Spanish posts on 20
November.[71]

French tactics, though still not perfect, nevertheless produced victory. Thousands of well-motivated, patriotic citizen
soldiers, using varied combinations of close order and skirmish
tactics, met their foes on better than even terms. Some
observers believed that French success stemmed from the
swarms of skirmishers employing cover and individually aimed
fire. Others assumed that columns, with their ability to smash
extended lines, were the key to victory. In battle, the
Republican infantry used *tirailleurs,* columns, and lines singly
or in combination, according to prevailing conditions. The
regulations of 1791, a product of the Old Regime military
reformers, provided Republican forces with flexible close order
tactics that combined the line's firepower with the column's
shock effects. Republican military leaders added the use of
large numbers of light troops that worked in close conjunction

with the close order formations. The Republican soldier could in fact fight either as a skirmisher or as a member of a column or line. The ability to fight in close order or light formations and the capacity to shift rapidly from one mode to another provided the French with the means to combat Old Regime armies with a good prospect for victory.

After 1794, the French infantry made few changes in its tactics. Rather, in the process of constant campaigning, officers and men refined and perfected the system of '93 and '94. On numerous battlefields French infantrymen learned to respond rapidly and effectively to almost any military and geographic conditions.

The French waged an extended series of campaigns in Italy, where varied terrain produced varied tactical responses. At Lonato the Republicans worked in battalion columns at deploying distance, covered by skirmishers. Two battalions of the 145th Line stormed fortified posts.[72] In 1796 Napoleon Bonaparte took command of the Army of Italy. Although an artillerist by training, he soon learned the fundamentals of infantry tactics. In battle, he employed the same techniques as other Republican generals, surpassing them primarily in aggressiveness and in his ability to handle decisively larger formations. In his first Italian campaign, he demonstrated what a small, well-led, tactically proficient force could accomplish.

On 11 April 1796, at Monte Legino, the 17th Light, 32d Line, and a battalion of the 51st Line fought a defensive engagement, holding entrenchments while skirmishers fought with Croat light infantry. At Dego on 14 April, the 75th and 51st half-brigades used assault columns to capture Austrian redoubts. The following day, elements of the 51st, 32d, and 14th demi-brigades attacked in column while the 18th Line and 4th Light advanced in open order. At Lodi a column supported by sharpshooters stormed the Austrian-held bridge.[73] Serrurier's division attacked in three columns covered by skirmishers at Mondovi. At Roveredo Bonaparte used a combination of columns and light infantry, and at Primbolano he deployed the entire 5th Light as *tirailleurs*, followed by the 9th Line in three battalion columns. At Bassano the 4th attacked in column, as did the 18th and 75th at Rivoli.[74] Napoleon also used linear formations, and at Arcola the 32d demi-brigade formed up in line, fired, and, while still in line, delivered a bayonet charge. At Castiglione Masséna's division had the center battalion of each half-brigade in line and the flanking battalions in double-company columns, a formation known as the *ordre mixte*. The *ordre mixte* provided fire power and flank protection for a demi-brigade. Moreover, a brigadier could shift quickly from the *ordre mixte* to any other forms required by battle conditions. At the Piave River the 21st Line crossed the river in columns and deployed on the opposite bank, while at the Tagliamento crossing one division used the *ordre mixte* and another had a half-brigade in skirmish order with its flanks covered by columns.[75]

A Demi-Brigade in the Ordre Mixte

A Demi-Brigade in a Line of Columns

During the 1799 Italian campaign, the outnumbered French suffered severe defeats, but nevertheless continued to display an impressive tactical versatility. At the Adda River the 17th Light launched a bayonet charge in column with skirmishers giving covering fire. At Pastrengo the 106th fought in line. At Cassina Grossa the same unit attacked with columns and at Novi formed a line for fire action, charged in line, and then shifted front to deal with a flank attack.[76]

Having returned from Egypt, where he used divisional squares six ranks deep against cavalry, Bonaparte launched another campaign in Italy.[77] At Montebello, 9 June 1800, the 6th Light and 28th Line fought in linear formations while battalions from the 40th and 22d launched attacks in double-company columns. The 43d Line advanced with its center battalion in column and the flanking battalions in skirmish order. The 96th Line took an Austrian fortified post with a column assault, and the demi-brigade then moved into skirmish order to pursue. At Marengo General Boudet ordered his division to advance, with each demi-brigade having two battalions in line supported by one in column. Light troops covered the entire divisional front. General Desaix placed two half-brigades in the *ordre mixte*, supported by a third demi-brigade in line.[78]

In Germany French soldiers also demonstrated a growing tactical versatility. In May 1796 near Altkirch, a division in Jourdan's army advanced in a line of battalion double-company columns, followed by a division deployed in line. In June the 83d and 96th half-brigades attacked a village in column, and on 2 July the 21st Light used columns to assault Austrian entrenchments. Two days later the 21st Light used columns to attack a village.[79] On 9 July units of Moreau's army fought as light infantry and cleared a wooded area near Rosensol. On 30 August a full half-brigade advanced in open order, drove back enemy troops, and then formed into columns to pursue. In October 1796 at Biberach, Desaix's division fought in line while St. Cyr's operated mainly in columns screened by light troops.[80]

On 20 April 1797 the Sambre-Meuse Army crossed the Rhine again. The first unit across, the 76th Line, moved out in a line of battalion columns. The Austrians stopped them and then advanced. The 76th in turn detached a hundred men as skirmishers to slow the Austrians, and seven hundred men from the 100th Line crossed the river to reinforce the 76th. The men of the 100th marched in column to within two hundred paces of the enemy, deployed into line under the covering fire of skirmishers, and engaged in a musketry duel. The Austrians then fell back, with skirmishers in pursuit. Meanwhile, the 100th formed assault columns to rush a nearby village. As the column was advancing, its commander spotted Austrian reinforcements moving up and switched his line of advance to attack them. The Austrians, however, retreated upon sighting the column. At the same time, the 16th Light attacked another portion of the Austrian position, using columns screened by light infantry. The Austrians counterattacked, and a musketry duel between French and Austrian light troops ensued. The 17th Line and 76th Line then advanced in column, deployed into line, and joined the action. The Austrians fell back, and battalions from the 109th, 17th, and 31st half-brigades moved forward in column and assaulted a fortified village. After bombardment by horse artillery guns, twelve battalions, drawn from the 17th, 31st, 100th, and 109th demi-brigades, plus six battalions of the 3d Light and 3d Line, moved forward in a line of double-company columns. Shaken by the artillery and skirmish fire, the Austrians finally relinquished the field.[81]

In 1799 at Ostrach, a division placed its leading troops in line, with skirmishers on the flanks. In the second line, troops stood in battalion columns. At the first battle of Zurich in June, a division fought in line with *tirailleurs* as support. Two half-brigades remained in reserve. The troops were in column, ready to move to any threatened part of the front. At the second battle of Zurich in September 1799, troops from the 10th Light and 37th Line crossed the Limmat River and assaulted Russian troops on the Fahr Plateau in open order. The 10th

Light, 37th, 57th, 2d, and 102d half-brigades then attacked the Zurichberg in columns with a light infantry screen.[82]

Throughout the revolutionary wars, the field artillery worked in close coordination with the infantry. Prior to the Revolution, the French artillery possessed the most modern guns in Europe. Many officers adopted du Teil's views concerning the role of field guns in battle, and many artillery commanders remained loyal to the revolutionary regimes. Thus, in 1792 the artillery was better prepared for war than the infantry or cavalry. Moreover, the introduction of horse artillery batteries materially strengthened the corps and improved its capacity to work closely with the other service arms in combat.

Valmy was of course an artillery duel, and at Jemappes a hundred field guns, including two horse batteries, covered the infantry assault. During the retreat from Neerwinden in March 1793, field guns effectively covered the French right wing's withdrawal. The Neerwinden catastrophe also revealed a perennial problem that Republican governments never fully solved. The army hired horses and drivers for fieldpieces (but not for horse batteries) from private contractors. In July 1793, for example, four firms suplied 142,000 horses. The government in 1794 took direct control of transport facilities but in the following year reverted to the contract system. Frequently, civilians, hired to move field guns into combat, refused to go into danger and deserted with their mounts at critical moments. At Neerwinden drivers fled in droves, and the French, consequently, had to abandon many guns.[83]

The French, however, usually found drivers willing to take the same risks as soldiers, and the artillery generally functioned efficiently. At Hondschoote sixteen field guns and four howitzers silenced Allied guns, thereby facilitating the infantry's advance. At Wattignes a twelve-gun battery shattered an Austrian cavalry charge, and at Fleurs another twelve-gun battery helped Lefebvre's division hold off the Austrians.[84]

Bonaparte began his military career in the artillery corps, serving in a regiment commanded by du Teil's elder brother.

The Corsican even sided with the conservatives during the debates over the adoption of the Gribeauval guns. He argued that the old guns had greater range and less recoil than the new ones. By 1793, however, Bonaparte had become a supporter of the Gribeauval reforms, arguing that the new cannons were superior because of their maneuverability, ease of repair, and accuracy.[85] By the time he took command of the Army of Italy, Napoleon was well versed in the theoretical and practical aspects of gunnery.

In 1796 Bonaparte, like other Republican generals, gave his divisions organic artillery and retained a reserve under his personal control. He used substantial concentrations of guns and employed them primarily against enemy infantry, a policy identical to du Teil's theory.

At Lodi thirty field guns supported the infantry attack, and at Castiglione Bonaparte used a twenty-gun battery. He also retained five horse batteries in reserve, committing them when he struck at the Austrian left. The horse artillery silenced the Austrian cannons and then supported the infantry. On 3 January 1800 Bonaparte militarized the artillery drivers, and at Marengo field guns gave close support to Boudet's infantry and Kellermann's cavalry.

Other generals also employed artillery boldly. During the Sambre-Meuse Army's 1796 campaign in Germany, horse batteries operating near Rastadt on 5 July raced forward to silence enemy guns. On 9 July horse batteries again advanced to the front, unlimbered, and broke up an Austrian cavalry attack. In 1797 horse batteries worked in close coordination with forward infantry elements and occasionally joined in the pursuit of the retreating enemy.[87]

Rather than remaining immobile after the opening salvos, Republican gunners worked closely with the infantry throughout entire engagements. Artillerymen sought to inflict casualties on the enemy's infantry and avoided counterbattery work except when the opposition's artillery was inflicting severe losses on French troops or preventing French guns from carrying out their main task. Artillery units served not only at army level but also with divisions and demi-brigades. In 1795 divisions and armies had 1,250 field guns available, and the half-brigades possessed 1,350 cannons.[88] The artillery and infantry learned to work together. If du Teil's vision of raising the field artillery to become the decisive arm did not achieve complete realization, field and horse batteries did become an integral part of Republican battle formations. Artillery played a significant combat role from a battle's opening shots to the final pursuit of a defeated enemy.

The cavalry was the only arm that did not witness a marked organizational and tactical improvement. General Jourdan noted the deficiency of the mounted arm in 1793. Officer emigration, lack of training, and difficulties in procuring mounts contributed to the cavalry's weakness. Throughout the revolutionary wars, English, Austrian, and Prussian cavalry were usually superior to the French.[89]

Despite its inferiority, the Republic's cavalry often performed useful services. At Fleurs horsemen participated in Jourdan's counterblow in the center. In 1795 cavalry units of the Army of the North achieved the unique distinction of being the only horsemen ever to capture a fleet. French mounted units charged over ice-covered water and seized Dutch men-of-war. At Marengo eight hundred cavalrymen participated in the attack that turned the battle's tide against the Austrians.[90]

The cavalry, however, never became as effective as the infantry or artillery. In his first Italian campaign, Bonaparte employed few cavalrymen. Hoche in Germany, Masséna in Switzerland, and Brune in Holland also relegated mounted formations to a secondary role. In most campaigns, cavalry units confined their activities to screening the main army's line of march and reconnaissance. Horsemen were a useful adjunct to the infantry and artillery but were never their equal.

The Republic's armies did not base their triumphs on technical innovations; the artillery used the Gribeauval pattern guns, adopted in 1774, and the infantry fought with muskets designed in 1777. Rather, the drastic changes in French society wrought by the Revolution and the pressures of war encouraged and compelled Republican leaders to create their own style of fighting. The Republicans adopted many ideas and methods devised during the Old Regime, but they were not afraid to modify them or to add their own new ideas.

Guibert advocated and then rejected the concept of a citizen army composed of a small number of patriotic volunteers. The convention created a truly national army by mobilizing the full range of the state's human and economic resources. Republican infantry trained according to the regulations of 1791, a product of the long debate over tactical methods begun in the aftermath of the Seven Years' War. In combat, however, Republican infantry used the battalion column by division for assaults far more often than either Guibert or the authors of the *Règlement* had envisioned. Guibert advocated the creation of an all-purpose soldier capable of fighting in close order or as a skirmisher. The 1791 drill book did not deal with light infantry tactics, but the Republic's armies commonly used large numbers of *tirailleurs*. Individual soldiers learned to fight in line, column, and open order. Entire battalions frequently fought in skirmish formations. Larger units, including divisions, occasionally went into action as *tirailleurs*. The combat division, used occasionally during the Old Regime, became a standard Republican formation. Since they did not have to fight as part of a single, rigid battle line, brigadiers and battalion commanders received a greater degree of tactical freedom than was enjoyed by officers of similar rank in the coalition's armies. Tactical flexibility and individual initiative became the hallmark of the Republic's armies. An Old Regime army, in which desertion remained a constant problem, continued to require rigid discipline at all levels. A citizen army, in which soldiers were motivated by patriotism and hope of reward, as well as fear of punishment, could permit and encourage boldness and flexibility. The Republican soldier was often ill-clothed, irregularly paid, and poorly fed. On the march a French force looked more like a band of armed peasants than an army. In combat, however, the soldiers performed willingly. Some, of course, broke under fire; others deserted, but, sustained by patriotism and conscription, field formations kept their ranks filled. A mass conscript force employing flexible tactics changed the nature and style of warfare.

Traditionally, generals and statesmen were usually reluctant to fight, fearing heavy casualties. Consequently, the occurrence of more than one or two major engagements in a single campaign was a rarity. By contrast, Republican commanders and civilian leaders constantly sought action. The French, of course, suffered heavy losses — over 200,000 men were killed or wounded between 1792 and 1795.[91] The levy and later the Conscription Act, however, enabled the French to replenish their ranks. The new tactics enabled the army to train recruits quickly and get them to the active units. Consequently, the Republic could absorb its losses, replace men and continue attacking without pause. In December 1793, for example, General Hoche in Alsace attacked the coalition forces on the 16th, 17th, and 18th. He attacked again on the 24th and yet again on the 26th.[92] In 1794 Jourdan attacked along the Sambre River six times before capturing a firm bridgehead on the Austrian side. Pichegru struck at Ypres several times before surrounding the city.[93]

The French had the requisite manpower to mount campaigns designed to wear down Allied strength in constant engagements and then to strike a final, decisive blow. In 1794 Carnot, in the name of the Committee of Public Safety, ordered the Republic's armies to act constantly on the offensive. Persistant assaults would wear down the Coalition's armies, absorb their reserves and enable the French to wage a battle of annihilation.[94]

The French also abandoned siege warfare for its own sake. Carnot specifically instructed generals to ignore geographical objectives. They would, he argued, fall by default once the

Republic crushed the Allied field armies.[95] The French therefore made a standard practice of the occasional pre-revolutionary method of threatening a city in order to force an enemy field army to offer battle. The destruction of enemy armies in a series of unrelenting attacks became a basic Republican technique.

Naturally, casualties were heavy. The French suffered 4,000 killed and wounded at Jemappes, 3,000 at Wattignes, 7,000 at Fleurs, 4,500 at Arcola, 5,000 at Rivoli, 5,000 at Zurich, and 7,000 at Marengo.[96] Republican armies were, however, larger than ever before. Consequently, the percentage of casualties compared to the total number of men engaged declined in comparison to prerevolutionary battles. Old Regime armies lost anywhere from 9 percent to 41 percent of their manpower in individual battles, while Republican casualties ranged from 1 percent to 25 percent.

The existence of mass armies using flexible aggressive tactics enabled the Republic's leaders to devise far-reaching strategic plans with a reasonable expectation of success. In 1793 the French turned back the Allied invasion and defeated internal counterrevolutionary forces. In 1794 the Republicans conquered Belgium and most of the Rhineland. In the years following, French armies campaigned in Holland, Germany, Switzerland, Italy, Ireland, and Egypt. Despite some defeats, by 1799 France had defeated two coalitions and made substantial territorial conquests. War was no longer a game; it now produced decisive results.

The French Revolution produced a mass national army. The influx of hundreds of thousands of raw conscripts forced Republican officers to create tactics to suit the needs and capabilities of the citizen soldiers. For basic drill, commanders used the regulations of 1791. Embodying many concepts of Old Regime reformers, the *Règlement* taught basic evolutions and placed a minimum of constraint upon battlefield leaders. Troops learned to maneuver in column and in line and to change rapidly from one configuration to another. The

Republicans then added an increased emphasis on light infantry tactics and made skirmishes an integral part of all battle formations. The Republic produced soldiers who could fight as part of a line or column or as a skirmisher, according to circumstances. In battle, the French could shift quickly from one formation to another and thus seize fleeting tactical opportunities. Republican battalions could operate in any weather and maneuver and fight over almost any type of terrain. The French tactical system did not, of course, guarantee victory in every encounter. It did, however, produce a high percentage of triumphs when employed against the old linear style of combat. Republican tactics enabled the French to transform their conscript army into Europe's most formidable fighting force.

NOTES

1. S. Wilkinson, *The French Army Before Napoleon* (London, 1915), pp. 108-12.

2. Lieutenant Colonel Belhomme, *Histoire de l'infanterie en France*, 5 vols. (Paris, n.d.), 4:437-38, 447-48, 483-84; Wilkinson, *French Army Before Napoleon*, p. 115; M. Lauerma, *L'Artillerie de campagne française pendant les guerres de la Révolution* (Helsinki, 1956), pp. 93, 99.

3. E. Depréz, *Les Volontaires nationaux (1791-1793) (Paris, 1908), pp. 15, 100-101, 104, 107-8, 119.*

4. J. Colin, *L'Infanterie au XVIII siècle la tactique* (Paris, 1907), pp. 259-63.

5. *Règlement concernant l'exercise et les manoeuvres de l'infanterie du 1er aout. 1791,* French Army document (Paris, 1808), pp. 3, 33, 53-54, 84-85, 136, 149.

6. Ibid., p. 165.

7. Ibid., pp. 171-72.

8. Ibid., pp. 61, 125, 174-76, 188-90, 198.

9. Ibid., pp. 210-24.

10. Ibid., pp. 226-33, 274-77.

11. Ibid., pp. 240-42, 248, 267.

12. Ibid., pp. 315, 319-22, 327-31, 335-40.

13. Ibid., pp. 289-90, 319, 361.

14. Ibid., pp. 356-57, 366, 374-78, 381-85, 389. For a general discussion on the *Réglement,* see Colin, *L'Infanterie au XVIII siècle,* pp. 265-73.

15. J. Colin, *La Tactique et la discipline dans les armées de la Révolution correspondance du général Schauenbourg du 4 avril au 2 aôut 1793* (Paris, 1902), pp. lxlix-cii. Colin argues that the 1791 drill book said little about light infantry because skirmishers, by the very nature of their tactics, were not subject to precise regulations. On the other hand, French drill books written after 1791, as well as American and

Prussian manuals, did discuss light infantry tactics at some length. Thus it is equally reasonable to assume that the absence of light infantry instruction in the 1791 manual was a result of the authors' belief that skirmishing techniques were not important to the main battle force and that light troops would continue to perform their traditional limited tasks.

16. Wilkinson, *French Army Before Napoleon*, p. 120; Lauerma, *L'Artillerie de campagne*, p. 105.

17. Ministère de la guerre État-major de l'armée archives historiques (hereafter cited as Min. de la guerre), Carton B-244.

18. J. P. Bertaud, *Valmy la démocratie en armes* (Paris, 1970), pp. 202-5; P. J. Foucart and J. Finot, *La Defénse nationale dans le nord 1792 à 1802*, 2 vols. (Lille, 1890), 1:22, 28-29, 42.

19. Déprez, *Les Volontaires*, pp. 21-24; C. Rousset, *Les Volontaires, 1791-1794* (Paris, 1870), p. 49.

20. Lauerma, *L'Artillerie de campagne*, pp. 161-65.

21. Foucart and Finot, *La Défense*, 1:274; F. Barrière, *Bibliothèque des mémoires relatifs à l'histoire de France pendant le 18e siècle, Dumouriez* (Paris, 1886), pp. 366-68, Colin, *La Tactique*, pp. lxiii-lxiv.

22. A Chuguet, *Jemappes et la conquete de la Belgigue* (Paris, 1890), pp. 130-33, 166, 173.

23. *National Archives*, France, AFII Carton 9; *Rémimpression de l'Ancien Moniteur*, 31 vols. (Paris, 1840), 15:549-50.

24. Réimpression, 17:387.

25. Ibid.

26. Ibid., pp. 405, 412.

27. Ibid., pp. 410-11, 432.

28. Ibid., p. 474.

29. Ibid., pp. 474-75.

30. Ibid., p. 478; J. H. Stewart, *A Documentary Survey of the French Revolution* (New York, 1951), pp. 479-81.

31. Min. de la guerre, Cartons B¹244, B¹245.

32. Min. de la guerre, Carton B¹244; AFII Carton 212. Belhomme, *Histoire de l'infanterie*, 4:66-67, gives an even higher figure for the fall of 1794 — 1,207, 761.

33. AFIII Carton 149.

34. AFIII Cartons 150A, 151A.

35. For information on French economic mobilization, see AFII Carton 27, 77, 214A.

36. AFII Carton 214ᵇ.

37. R. W. Phipps, *The Armies of the First French Republic*, 5 vols. (London, 1926-39), 1:41.

38. Min de la guerre, Carton, XS.

39. J. Bouvier, *Historique du 96ᵉ régiment d'infanterie* (Lyon, 1892), p. 27; J. G. E. Simond, *Le 28ᵉ de Ligne historique du régiment* (Rouen, 1889), p. 49.

40. Min de la guerre, Carton Xᵖ5; *Réimpression*, 15:548.

41. Min. de la guerre, Cartons Xᵖ81, Xˣ4, B¹110.

42. Simond, *Le 28ᵉ de Ligne*, p. 7; Rousset, *Les Volontaires*, p. 303.

43. *Réimpression*, 15:548; G. T. Denison, *A History of Cavalry from the Earliest Times with Lessons for the Future* (London, 1913), p. 284.

44. *Réimpression*, 15:549; Lauerma, *L'Artillerie de campagne*, pp. 121-22.

45. Foucart and Finot, *La Défense*, 1:101-2.

46. *Réimpression*, 15:549; Phipps, *Armies*, 1:31.

47. AFII Carton 212; Lauerma, *L'Artillerie de campagne*, pp. 149-50, 180, 196.

48. Belhomme, *Histoire de l'infanterie*, 4:124; Simond, *Le 28ᵉ de Ligne*, pp. 55-57; Rousset, *Les Volontaires*, p. 303; A. Clement, *Historique du 75ᵉ régiment d'infanterie* (Paris, 1891), pp. 41-42.

49. Lauerma, *L'Artillerie de campagne*, pp. 221, 226, 239; *Correspondance de Napoléon Iᵉʳ* 32 vols. (Paris, 1858-69), 2:1530.

50. A. Soboul, *Les Soldats de l'an II* (Paris, 1959), pp. 174-76.

51. For studies of the representatives on mission and the civil commissioners, see H. Wallon, *Les Représentants du peuple en mission et la justice révolutionnaire dans les départments*, 5 vols. (Paris, 1889), vol. 1; J. Godechot, *Les Commissaires aux armées sous le directoire* (Paris, 1938).

52. G. Six, *Les Généraux de la Révolution et de l'Empire* (Paris, 1947), pp. 24-27.

53. Ibid., pp. 20, 30 – 31, 38, 44-45, 50.

54. J. Colin, *Campagne de 1793 en Alsace et dans le Palatinat* (Paris, 1902), pp. 19-21.

55. Min. de la guerre, Carton B¹12.

56. Ibid., Carton B¹18.

57. Colin, *La Tactique*, pp. lxi-lxii, lxiv-lv.

58. P. Paret, *Yorck and the Era of Prussian Reform, 1807-1815* (Princeton, N.J., 1966), pp. 67-69.

59. Min. de la guerre, Carton B¹20; V. Dupuis, *La Campagne de 1793 à l'Armée du Nord et des Ardennes d'Hondschoote à Wattignes* (Paris, 1909), pp. 315-16.

60. G. Duroisel, *Historique du 93ᵉ régiment d'infanterie* (La Roche-sur-yon, 1893), p. 314; T. A. Dodge, *Napoleon*, 4 vols. (New York, 1904), 2:173-74; Colin, *La Tactique*, p. lxliv. Bayonet attacks could force a shaken foe to flee rather than engage in hand to hand combat. They were also useful when inclement weather prevented the troops from firing their muskets.

61. Min. de la guerre, Cartons B¹18, B¹30; A. Chuquet, *Hondschoote* (Paris, n.d.), pp. 211-13; V. Dupuis, *La Campagne de 1793 à l'Armée du Nord et des Ardennes de Valenciennes à Hondtschoote* (Paris, 1906), pp. 469, 473-77; J. L. C. Gay de Vernon, *Mémoire sur les opérations militaires des généraux-en-chef Custine et Houchard pendant les années 1792 et 1793* (Paris, 1844), pp. 253-55.

62. Dupuis, *La Campagne de 1793 d'Hondschoote à Wattignes*, pp. 166-67, 185-86; Foucart and Finot, *La Defénse*, 2:249-50.

63. Napoleon, *Commentaires de Napoléon Premier*, 6 vols. (Paris, 1867), 1:21; E. Simond, *Historique des nouveaux régiments créés par la loi du 25 juillet 1887* (Paris, 1889), pp. 5, 37, 42.

64. G. Saint-Cyr, *Mémoires sur les campagnes des Armées du Rhin et de Rhin-et-Moselle de 1792 jusqu'à la Paix de Campo Formio*, 4 vols. (Paris, 1829), 1:100-101, 163, Colin, *Campagne de 1793*, pp. 22, 375, 387-88, 408; A. Chuquet, *Wissembourg* (1793) (Paris, n.d.), pp. 165-67; A. Chuquet, *Hoche et la lutte pour Alsace (1793-1794)* (Paris, 1893), p. 86.

65. Chuquet, *Wissenbourg*, pp. 32-33.

66. Saint-Cyr, *Mémoires*, 1:lxv-lxvi, 38-39, 53.

67. F. von der Goltz, ed., *Militärische Schriften von Scharnhorst* (Berlin, 1881), pp. 32-36, 52-53, 193, 223.

68. Phipps, *Armies*, 1:303; Min. de la guerre, Carton B¹30.

69. Phipps, *Armies*, 2:160; V. Dupuis, *Opérations sur la Sambre en 1794 Bataille de Fleurs* (Paris, 1907), pp. 339-40.

70. Dupuis, *Opérations sur la Sambre*, pp. 356, 584; Rélations de la Bataille de fleurs livreé le 8 messidor an 2, Mémoires historiques *274*; Phipps, *Armies*, 2:162; N. Soult, *Mémoires du Maréchal-Géneral Soult Duc de Dalmatie publiés par son fils prèmiere partie histoire des guerres de la Révolution*, 3 vols. (Paris, 1854), 1:168, 192; A. Jomini, *Histoire critique et militaire des guerres de la Révolution*, 15 vols. (Paris, 1820), 5:145-50.

71. Simond, *Le 28ᵉ de Ligne*, p. 46; G. du Martray, *Le 132ᵉ Demi-Brigade deux ans à l'Armée de Sambre-et-Meuse 1794-1796* (Paris, 1887) p. 60; A. du Casse, ed., *Géneral Vandamme et sa correspondance*, 2 Vols. (Paris, 1870), 1:196, 204.

72. Simond, *Historique des nouveaux régiments*, pp. 16-17; Dodge, *Napoleon*, 1:272.

73. A. Clément, *Historique du 75ᵉ régiment d'infanterie* (Paris, 1891), p. 47; J. Colin, *Études sur la campagne de 1796-97 en Italie* (Paris, 1898), pp. 82-83; Napoleon, *Commentaires*, 1:168.

74. Napoleon, *Commentaires*, 1:232, 235-36, 238; Clément, *Historique du 75ᵉ régiment*, p. 60; Dodge, *Napoleon*, 1:294-95; F. Bouvier, *Bonaparte en Italie 1796* (Paris, 1899), pp. 309-12.

75. Napoleon, *Commentaires*, 1:262, 297, 385; Bouvier, *Bonaparte en Italie*, pp. 146-47; *Correspondance de Napoléon Iᵉʳ*, 2:1589.

76. P. Berthezène, *Souvenirs militaires*, 2 vols. (Paris, 1855), 1:36; A. Duchâtelet, *Historique du 106ᵉᵐᵉ régiment d'infanterie de ligne* (Chalons-sur-Marne, 1890), pp. 56, 63-66.

77. A. Berthier, *Rélation des campagnes du général Bonaparte en Égypte et en Syrie* (Paris, 1800), pp. 16-20.

78. Simond, *Le 28ᵉ de Ligne*, p. 87; Capitaine de Cugnac, *Campagne de l'Armée de Réserve en 1800 deumème partie Marengo* (Paris, 1901), pp. 251-55; Bouvier, *Historique du 96ᵉ régiment d'infanterie*, p. 152.

79. Soult, *Mémoires*, 1:293; Bouvier, *Historique du 96ᵉ Régiment d'infanterie*, pp. 33, 135-36.

80. Duchâtelet, *Historique du 106ᵉᵐᵉ régiment*, pp. 20-21, 35-36.

81. Casse, *Le Géneral Vandamme*, 1:361-64, 366-69, 374-78.

82. A. Masséna, *Rapport fait par le général Masséna au Directoire exécutif sur les opérations du 3 an 18 vendémiaire an 8* (Paris, 1799), pp. 6-8; Soult, *Mémoires*, 1:17-18, 38-39, 105.

83. Lauerma, *L'Artillerie de campagne*, pp. 40, 138, 173.

84. Ibid., pp. 175-76, 182, 196.

85. F. Masson and G. Biagi, *Napoléon inconnu papiers inédits (1786-1793)*, 2 vols. (Paris, 1895), 1:241-42, 2:482-85; S. Wilkinson, *The Rise of General Bonaparte* (Oxford, 1930), pp. 2-3, 18.

86. Lauerma, *L'Artillerie de campagne*, pp. 243, 246-74, 271, 273; Dodge, *Napoleon*, 1:281.

87. Lauerma, *L'Artillerie de campagne*, pp. 208-9, 214-15.

88. D. G. Chandler, *The Campaigns of Napoleon* (New York, 1966), p. 143.

89. Min. de la guerre, Carton B¹*19*; H. Coutanceau and C. de la Jonquièré, *La Campagne de 1794 à l'Armée du Nord*, 3 vols. (Paris, 1907), 1:421; Dupuis, *La Campagne de 1793 d'Hondschoote à Wattingnes*, p. 44; L. E. Nolan, *Cavalry: Its History and Tactics* (Columbia, S.C., 1864), p. 25; Denison, *A History of Cavalry*, pp. 287-88.

90. Denison, *A History of Cavalry*, p. 302.

91. Dodge, *Napoleon*, 1:4.

92. Chuquet, *Hoche*, p. 160.

93. Min. de la guerre, Carton B¹*33*, *Mémoires Militaires du Maréchal Jourdan, Memoires historiques 608*².

94. E. Charavany, *Correspondance générale de Carnot, 4 novembre 1793-mars 1795* (Paris, 1908), pp. 300-304, 318-19.

95. Ibid., pp. 382-83.

96. Chandler, *Campaigns of Napoleon*, pp. 1118-21.

3

Napoleonic Warfare

Napoleon Bonaparte did not introduce any fundamental changes in the French army's organization and tactics until 1808. He was not, as Marmont contended, ignorant of tactics.[1] He fully understood the system inherited from the Republic, and although he often permitted subordinates to have a good deal of tactical initiative, he could, and did on occasion, issue detailed tactical directives.[2] Bonaparte's lack of innovation, therefore, does not indicate a failure to perceive the need for change but rather suggests satisfaction with the existing system.

Napoleon retained the nine-company battalion and the three-battalion half-brigade as basic infantry units. In 1803 he changed the term *half-brigade* back to the older name — *regiment*. He also abolished regimental artillery in an effort to enhance the infantry's mobility and provide greater gun power at higher unit levels. In other respects, Napoleonic regiments, ninety line and twenty-six light in 1803, resembled their Republican predecessors.[3]

Napoleon also continued to use the division. As in Republican armies, divisions varied in size and composition. At Austerlitz, for example, Caffarelli's division contained five regiments, Suchet's four, Drouhet's three, and Rivaud's three.[4] Divisions usually had organic artillery, but Bonaparte abolished divisional cavalry, placing mounted troops in separate divisions. The corps then became the smallest unit containing all service arms.[5]

Utilized on an ad hoc basic by the Republicans, the corps became a permanent feature of all Napoleonic campaigns. Corps size varied in order to baffle enemy intelligence, fit the size of a specific mission, and suit the capability of a commander. A corps contained from two to four infantry divisions, a brigade or division of cavalry, and from thirty-six to forty field guns.[6] In August 1805, for example, Bernadotte's Ist Corps contained two infantry and one cavalry division, with a total strength of 17,000 men. The IId Corps under Marmont had three infantry and a cavalry division, a total of 20,000. Davout's IIId Corps, with 26,000 troops, comprised three infantry and a cavalry division, and Soult's IVth Corps had four infantry and a cavalry division, with 26,000 troops.[7] In 1806 Bernadotte's Ist Corps had 21,163 men, Davout's IIId Corps 28,756, Soult's IVth Corps 28,960, and Augereau's VIIth Corps 19,538.[8] A corps could march independently and fight on its own. It could begin a major engagement and sustain itself until the rest of the army arrived.

Napoleon also expanded and modified the artillery's organization. In 1803 his armies contained eight foot and six horse regiments, a total of 28,000 men, including pontoniers and supply troops. A regiment consisted of twenty-seven companies, each with six fieldpieces and two howitzers. By 1813 the artillery corps consisted of nine foot and six horse regiments, plus two guard foot and one guard horse regiment. Together with pontoon and logistic elements, the artillery arm comprised 80,000 first line troops and 23,000 coast and garrison gunners. After 1802, the number of guns increased rapidly, and by 1805 Napoleon had 8,320 howitzers, 1,746 mortars, 4,506 heavy guns, and 7,366 medium and light cannons.[9] Bonaparte wanted to establish a ratio of four guns per thousand men and at one point attained a ratio of three per thousand.[10] He also changed gun calibers in the direction of heavier weapons. He replaced the four-pound cannon with a six-pounder and substituted twelve-pounders for many of his eight-pound guns. He also introduced a twenty-four-inch howitzer.[11] These changes were, however, matters of detail, and Napoleon later commented that "these changes modified the system of M. de Gribeauval; they were made in his spirit; he would not have disavowed them."[12] Moreover, Bonapare always retained the artillery tactics preached by du Teil and put into practice by the Republican armies.

Napoleon devoted much effort to the expansion and improvement of the cavalry, long the weakest service arm. Under the Republic, various types of cavalry served together, but Bonaparte separated them and assigned each specific roles. The heavy cavalry—fourteen cuirassier and two carbinier regiments, plus a Dutch regiment—served, in autonomous cavalry divisions. Located in the reserve, the heavy cavalry usually acted as a shock force. Twenty to thirty dragoon regiments formed the line cavalry. Their tasks included guarding communication lines, acting as flank guards for marching armies, executing raids, and, if necessary, serving as a shock force. The light cavalry comprised ten to thirteen hussar regiments, thirty horse chasseur regiments, and, later, eight lancer regiments. Their missions included screening the movements of the main army, scouting, and harassing and pursuing defeated forces.[13]

Bonaparte assigned cavalry units to individual corps and also established large cavalry reserves under his immediate control. In 1805 he placed 22,000 mounted troops in reserve. In 1806 the emperor held 18,000 horsemen in reserve and in 1808 kept 17,000 cavalrymen under army control. In 1809 the Grand Army had a 29,000-man cavalry reserve, and in 1812 the army in Russia had four full cavalry corps. Even in 1815, Napoleon fielded four reserve cavalry corps. Though never fully satisfied with the cavalry's strength and performance, Napoleon always tried to enlarge and improve the mounted arm.[14]

To raise troops Napoleon continued to use the 1798 Conscription Act. After 1805, the emperor secured the authority to fix the proportion of each class called to the colors. Selection within a given year group was by lot, and, until 1813, a draftee

could hire a substitute, thereby enabling the wealthier classes
to avoid military service. In emergencies, Bonaparte called up
men from previous classes who had originally escaped the draft
by drawing good numbers and drafted individuals in advance
of their year group's eligibility. Between 1800 and 1812
4,340,000 men attained military age, and Napoleon drafted
1,437,000 of them. Desertion became a serious problem as the
public grew weary of constant war. By 1813 about 10 percent
of the conscripts failed to report, but the conscription law
generally kept the army supplied with sufficient manpower.[15]

Bonaparte also reverted to the Old Regime system of using
foreign troops. Foreign contingents grew steadily. By 1807
non-French troops constituted about a third of the Imperial
forces. In 1812 two-thirds of the army in the Russian campaign
were foreigners. Only in 1813, with the loss of foreign
recruiting grounds, did the percentage of non-French troops
begin to decline.[16]

Napoleon obtained officers by following the Republic's
policy of promoting men for bravery or for long and meritor-
ious service. In 1805 about half of the officer corps had served
in the ranks. The emperor also established special schools to
train junior officers. In contrast to the Republic, however, promotion to general officer rank under the Empire slowed con-
siderably. The Republic once created 170 generals in a single
year, while the largest number to attain this rank in one year
during the Imperial period was thirty-seven.[17] Since the higher
ranks were already filled by 1799, promotion to the higher
grades naturally slowed. The image of every private carrying a
marshal's baton in his knapsack was a myth. The men who
became marshals were all officers and the majority of them
generals before Napoleon seized power. In the lower ranks,
however, it was still possible for an individual to ascend the
promotion ladder, and, as in the days of the Republic, the
career open to talent remained a viable policy.

Imperial troops continued to employ the regulations of 1791
as their basic drill book. The Grand Army also learned light in-

fantry tactics in combination with close order methods. Napoleon always used peaceful intervals to drill his troops. Between 1801 and 1803 special inspectors visited regiments, checking on maneuvers and testing the sergeants on their knowledge of the drill regulations. Battalion officers and sergeants met twice a week with their regimental adjutants to study tactics. The junior officers and noncommissioned officers then taught what they had learned to their enlisted men.[18] At the Boulogne camp in 1804 and 1805, Napoleon ordered officers to devote two days a week to battalion drill and target practice, three days to divisional drill, and one day to corps maneuvers. Every fifteenth day, the emperor conducted a grand maneuver involving the use of several corps.[19]

Flexibility, a hallmark of Republican commanders, also characterized Imperial officers. Though thoroughly familiar with the '91 *Règlement,* Bonaparte's general never bound themselves rigidly to every detail. They modified them to suit conditions and their own tactical preferences. Ney, for example, altered the '91 manual to conform to his own ideas. He emphasized the closed column by division as the basis of all maneuvers, abolished kneeling fire, directed his men to learn to charge in line as well as in column, and in a charge in line ordered the third rank to operate as skirmishers or to act as a local reserve. In fire action, Ney directed the third rank to act as a tactical reserve, rather than attempting to load muskets for the first and second ranks. For general combat, he favored use of the *ordre mixte.*[20] Other marshals also had their favorite tactical forms. Some emphasized linear deployment, others preferred columns, and still others adhered to the *ordre mixte.* Alterations of the manual were, however, changes of detail. All of Napoleon's commanders adhered to the spirit, if not the absolute letter, of the '91 regulations. By using the Republican system of merging close order and skirmish tactics in the same tactical units and by stressing constant training, the Grand Army by the fall of 1805 was Europe's most powerful military machine.

The Ulm campaign provided a vivid demonstration of the army's capacity for rapid movement. Carrying no tents and possessing a drastically reduced supply train, the French covered from twelve to forty kilometers per day and averaged thirty. Sleeping where they could and foraging for food at the end of a day's march, the Grand Army marched from the Rhine to the Danube and from the Danube to Ulm in seventeen days.[21] And this feat was by no means exceptional. In 1806 one of Davout's divisions marched 140 kilometers in about fifty hours.[22]

In combat, Napoleon's troops demonstrated great versatility in adopting the tactical postures required by rapidly changing circumstances. Even while under fire, French soldiers could shift from one formation to another with alacrity and precision. At Austerlitz Napoleon ordered one of Soult's divisions and Davout's IIId Corps to draw the Allied reserves to the Goldbach area on the French right flank and hold them there. Davout's corps had not reached the battlefield in full strength by the night of 1 December. Consequently, when the battle opened on 2 December, the IIId Corps had to enter combat as it arrived in the battle zone.

At the start of the battle, the 3d Line held back three and a half regiments until forced to retreat because of the arrival of additional Allied troops. The 108th Line and part of the 15th arrived and seized the village of Sokolnitz. Driven back, the French took up positions to the left of the village, where they operated in open order and held back the Russians until reinforcements arrived. The 48th Line, advancing in battalion columns, retook part of Sokolnitz and then engaged in house-to-house fighting with the remaining defenders. The 111th Line arrived next, and the entire regiment advanced as skirmishers. The 15th and 33d followed, moving in linear order. Russian reinforcements counterattacked and forced the French to abandon the town. The 15th and 33d then reformed into battalion assault columns covered by *tirailleurs* and retook the village and the surrounding heights.[23] Soult's division and

Davout's corps pinned the allied left wing, and Napoleon then launched his decisive attack in the center.

Generals Vandamme and St. Hilaire from Soult's IV Corps led the assault on the Pratzen Plateau. Soult instructed his commanders to employ columns screened by shirmishers and to form firing lines only when absolutely necessary. Vandamme on the left advanced in two lines of battalion assault columns screened by light infantry. When his troops came to within a hundred paces of the enemy, Vandamme deployed the leading two regiments into a firing line, while retaining the second line in columns. St. Hilaire advanced with a full regiment in the lead in skirmish order. Behind them followed four regiments side by side. Each regiment moved in double-company battalion columns with one battalion behind the other. Upon reaching the Pratzen, the leading battalions deployed into line. The other battalions moved up to fill in the gaps, until practically the entire division was in line. Legrand's division followed as a reserve. Each regiment moved forward in the *ordre mixte*.[24] Allied units on the plateau collapsed. The Russians sent up reinforcements. Both sides traded volleys until Soult moved up six twelve-pounder guns from his corps reserve. Their deadly close-range fire turned the tide. A second Russian attack crumpled under infantry and artillery fire. Later in the day, infantry and cavalry regiments of the Russian Guard attacked Vandamme's flank and shattered two battalions, but French Guard cavalry, horse artillery, and reserve infantry moved in to halt the enemy attack.[25] Soult's corps combined and changed formations with speed and precision to meet rapidly shifting conditions. Field artillery and cavalry worked closely with the infantry, providing vital support at several critical moments.

Other corps performed with equal facility. Bernadotte's men entered combat on Soult's left and then withdrew from the fighting and reentered the battle further south. Lannes's corps contained a high proportion of raw recruits but, nevertheless, acquitted itself well. The 30th, 17th, and 61st Regiments opened gaps in their ranks to permit their own

AUSTERLITZ 2 DECEMBER 1805
SITUATION OF FRENCH ARMY AT ABOUT 10:00 AM

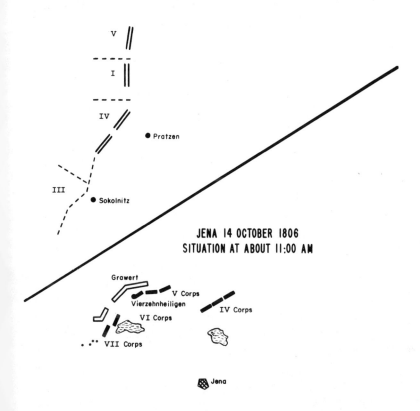

cavalry to pass through and then closed up and drove off, attacking Russian horsemen with musket fire. Fighting with a line of deployed battalions supported by a second line of battalion columns, Lannes pushed back the Allied left and prevented it from sending help to threatened positions in the center.[26]

At Austerlitz the Grand Army combined the various arms and tactical methods to achieve a stunning victory. Moreover, the army demonstrated its ability to wage an encounter battle and to shift positions during the course of an engagement. The IIId Corps entered combat directly from a route march; the 1st Corps shifted positions during the battle, and the IVth Corps used a division for defensive operations while employing two others in an offensive role. Artillery and cavalry joined the battle as circumstances required. A well-articulated machine, the Grand Army did not have to enter battle as a single body. It could maneuver and fight flexibly and respond rapidly and effectively to changing battlefield situations. Less than a year after the Austerlitz triumph, the Grand Army demonstrated its awesome capacities against the heirs of Frederick the Great.

The Prussian army in 1806, far from being a decrepit reflection of a dying order, was a well-drilled, well-organized force. The Prussians had fought well in the revolutionary campaigns, winning several engagements and suffering no major defeats. By eighteenth-century standards, Frederick's successors had brought the army to a high pitch of efficiency. Many high-ranking officers, it is true, were older than their French rivals. Brunswick was seventy-one; Hohenhole, sixty; Rüchel, fifty-two; and Massenbach, forty-eight. There were divisional officers in their late sixties and even some in their seventies. Advanced age does not necessarily imply senility or incapacity. The officers were in fact vigorous, experienced, and quite capable of leading troops in battle.[27] The rank and file were well-trained and disciplined. The Prussian army's only serious problem was that it was prepared to fight the wrong kind of war. The army had simply not changed with the times.

A number of officers realized the necessity for tactical reforms. In 1802 Scharnhorst founded a Military Society whose members debated and discussed reform projects. Scharnhorst himself, noting the effectiveness of French light infantry, called for more flexible Prussian tactics and called attention to the value of patriotism as a factor in troop morale.[28] Other members called for the introduction of light infantry tactics, the creation of a militia, the establishment of a reserve system, and even a levy en masse.[29] Prussia's leaders were satisfied, however, with the status quo. They did increase the number of riflemen in each battalion but regarded suggestions for more sweeping changes as unnecessary and socially dangerous.[30] The Prussians also introduced the divisional system, but in peacetime the regiment remained as the largest tactical unit. In 1806 the divisions had never trained or fought as operational units, and the commanders were unfamiliar with the untried formations.[31] Thus, with minor changes, Prussia went to war in 1806 with an army that resembled the force that had triumphed at Rossbach. It was to meet the victors of Ulm and Austerlitz in a dual battle matching the best of the Old Regime military against the best of the Revolutionary-Napoleonic armies.

Napoleon instructed his marshals that the general battle order for the forthcoming battle at Jena would be two deployed lines covered by light infantrymen. He also stipulated that his subordinates, once engaged, could modify the battle order according to prevailing conditions as long as they cleared the woods and villages around Jena and united their troops in the nearby plain.[32]

Lannes's Vth Corps opened the battle on 14 October 1806 by sending forward the 17th Light and a Grenadier battalion in line. Light infantry led the way, and two horse artillery guns marched with the first line. Behind them came the 34th Regiment in line and the 40th in column. A third element, the 88th and 64th, followed in column. The 17th Light engaged the Prussians in a firefight but ran short of ammunition; thus, the 34th moved up to take the 17th Light's place. The two regiments performed the complicated passage of lines with great precision, and the 34th advanced, continued the musketry action, and forced the Prussians to retreat.[33] The 88th and 64th then moved forward in column to seize a mill and a bridge.[34]

Meanwhile, the VIIth Corps moved up on the French left. The 16th Light sent a battalion into a woods in open order while the other two battalions marched around the woods, formed a firing line, and advanced while firing. Finally, they delivered a bayonet attack and drove back the shaken Prussians. The 14th Line supported the 16th Light by sending three companies into the woods. The 105th Regiment arrived on the field in column. It deployed into line but soon reformed into columns to pursue the retreating Prussians. The regiment then redeployed into line to beat off a counterattack. The Prussian infantry retreated, but a cavalry attack threatened the 105th's flank. A battalion quickly changed front, forming a new line obliquely to the rear, and successfully dealt with the Prussian horsemen.[35]

The Prussians, meanwhile, managed to push Lannes's Vth Corps from the village of Vierzehnheiligen, but Ney's VIth Corps moved up to fill the gap between the Vth and Augereau's VIIth Corps. The French retook the village, and Soult's IVth Corps arrived to strengthen Bonaparte's right flank. Two battalions of the 25th Light reinforced the 14th and 16th Light in the woods and directed aimed fire on the enemy infantry. The Prussians then sent General Grawert's 20,000-man division to retake Vierzehnheiligen. In perfect alignment, the Prussians marched up to the village's outskirts, halted, and began to deliver well-timed volleys while awaiting the arrival of additional troops before advancing further. It was a demonstration of linear warfare at its best. Lannes's response was to rush troops from the 100th, 103d, 40th, and 21st Light into the battle. Operating as *tirailleurs,* some of the new arrivals joined the men already in the woods, while others took cover in the town. For the next two hours the French directed aimed fire against Grawert's men, who continued to respond with measured volleys. The Prussians suffered enormous losses and inflicted almost none upon the French.[36] Despite its gallant stand, Grawert's division ultimately ceased to exist as a fighting force, and the whole Prussian line began to falter. The 84th, 88th, 44th, and 105th formed a line of columns screened by *tirailleurs* and moved forward. The Prussians retreated, under constant fire from French skirmishers.

General Rüchel, newly arrived on the field with 15,000 men, tried to stem the withdrawal, but upon sighting the advancing French, decided to join the retreat. Bonaparte's horse artillery guns, followed by skirmishers and finally by charging cavalry, soon turned Rüchel's orderly movement into a rout.[37] Rüchel's shattered force joined the decimated main Prussian force in headlong flight.

The Prussian force at Jena finally dissolved. It had fought bravely. Probably no other body of men in Europe could have withstood the punishment endured by Grawert's regiments without panicking. The Prussians, however, fought the wrong kind of war. They were outnumbered, moved too slowly, and lacked the flexibility necessary to counter French tactics. Napoleon won at Jena with superior numbers, but on the same day at Auerstadt Davout's IIId Corps met and defeated a much larger Prussian army, proof, if any more be needed, that the Grand Army's superiority was not simply a matter of numbers. Tactical superiority to Old Regime armies was a major source of Napoleon's victories.

At Auerstadt Gaudin's division made the initial contact with the Prussians. The 85th Line, flanked on the right by the 25th, advanced on the town of Hassenhausen, and cavalry scouts discovered the Prussian advance guard of 600 horsemen, an infantry battalion, and a field artillery battery. The 25th formed a square, but French guns drove off the enemy cavalry before it could charge. The 25th reformed into battalion columns and resumed its advance. Prussian cavalry, with artillery support, attacked a second time, and again the 25th formed a square. Prussian artillery threatened to decimate the tightly packed squares until the 25th detached four companies, which managed to capture the cannons. The regiment then fended off the cavalry and formed a firing line forward and slightly to the right of Hassenhausen while the 85th deployed into line in and around the village itself. The main Prussian force then arrived, and Gaudin sent the 21st and 12th Regiments to bolster his right. The 21st deployed into line directly behind the 25th,

AUERSTADT-GAUDIN'S DIVISION

1.

12 th

25 th   21 st

Hassenhausen

85 th

2.

12 th

25 th   21 st

85 th

3.

25 th   21 st

85 th

12 th

and the 12th formed double-company battalion columns on the far right and slightly to the rear so as to cover the flanks of the firing lines. Prussian infantry attacked but made no headway. Blücher then led a charge of twenty-five squadrons. The French met this attack by forming the 12th into a regimental square while the right battalions of the 25th and 21st formed battalion squares. The other battalions of both regiments remained in line. Gaudin's troops repulsed the Prussian cavalry after inflicting heavy losses.[38]

On the left, the 85th found itself outnumbered as more Prussian infantry reached the battlefield. The Prussians threatened to turn the regiment's left, but Davout pulled the 12th out of line and sent it to bolster the endangered flank. While the 21st Line extended its front, the 12th formed up in battalion columns, marched to the 85th's left, and reentered the battle. The regiment placed a battalion in line south of Hassenhausen and kept another in column to guard the uncovered left wing. The entire division continued its firefight with ever-increasing numbers of Prussians, who brought up sufficient troops to threaten both of Gaudin's flanks.[39]

Friant's division arrived in time to relieve the growing pressure on the French right. Entering the field in battalion columns, the 111th Line deployed into line and joined the firefight on Gaudin's immediate right. Prussian artillery inflicted heavy losses until the 108th Regiment sent its second battalion forward in an assault column to silence the guns. The 108th's first battalion, also in a column by division, simultaneously attacked and seized the village of Spielberg. The 33d Line deployed into line to the right of the village after sending four companies to secure a nearby woods. The 108th meanwhile continued to advance in columns screened by skirmishers. The regiment assailed and captured the village of Poppel. On Davout's right, Friant's 48th Regiment fought to contain the Prussian left and prevent it from launching a turning movement. One battalion advanced as skirmishers, supported by another in column formation. Friant's entire division then mounted a general attack. The 33d, 111th, and 108th advanced in a line of double-company columns screened by *tirailleurs*, and the 48th continued its pressure on the Prussian left with light troops and columns.[40]

Morand's division, the last to arrive, came into the battle on the French left. The division advanced in a mass of double-company columns covered by a thick screen of skirmishers. Just before he reached the fighting, Morand formed his men into a line of battalion columns at deploying intervals. Still covered by skirmishers, Morand's troops pushed up to the 12th Regiment's left, thereby relieving pressure on it and on the 85th, which was still grimly holding on in Hassenhausen. While keeping a battalion on his far left in column to guard his flank, Morand deployed the rest of his division into line and began a firefight. He halted the Prussian infantry, but the Prussians then launched a cavalry assault. The two battalions nearest Gaudin's men stayed in line, and the rest of the division formed battalion squares and repulsed the enemy horsemen. Morand then reformed his men into a line of columns covered by *tirailleurs* and advanced. The 61st attacked in column and broke through Prussian infantry units defending the head of a ravine. The 51st repulsed scattered infantry and cavalry attacks. A battalion of the 30th Line captured a Prussian battery and forced enemy infantry units south of Hassenhausen to fall back. The Prussians attempted to turn Morand's left, but the 30th, a battalion of the 17th and the division's artillery, which moved into the front line, broke up the attack. Morand resumed his advance beyond Hassenhausen and turned the Prussian flank. He then moved his guns to the front and opened a devastating fire on the Prussian infantry. Gaudin's division, though weakened by heavy losses, also advanced, and the Prussians began to fall back in disarray.[41]

The Prussians, as a last resort, committed their last reserve battalions in an effort to stem the retreat, or at least hamper and delay Davout's pursuit. Friant and Morand rushed their artillery to the front and unleashed a devastating barrage

AUERSTADT - MORAND'S DIVISION

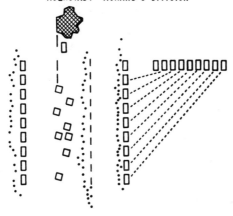

AUERSTADT - III RD CORPS - FINAL ADVANCE

Friant

Gaudin

Morand

☐ Column
— Line
☐ Square

against both Prussian flanks. The Prussians fell back, and
Davout ordered Gaudin to attack the enemy center while
Friant struck their left. Gaudin's 12th and 21st Regiments and
Friant's 111th, all in assault columns with a light infantry
screen, charged their shaken foes. The Prussians collapsed and
fled, and French skirmishers pursued to prevent them from
forming a new line of battle.[42]

The IIId Corps, with 27,000 men, defeated about 60,000
Prussians led by the Duke of Brunswick, one of Europe's most
prestigious commanders. As at Jena, the Prussians fought
bravely but were unable to respond effectively to French tactics. In 1805 and 1806, the Grand Army was so effective that
Napoleon was able to abandon the Republican system of
fighting a series of battles designed to wear down enemy
strength and pave the way for a final decisive thrust. Instead,
the Imperial forces achieved victory by winning one or two major engagements, followed by a vigorous pursuit. As in the days
of the Old Regime, Napoleon fought relatively few battles in a
single campaign, but, in contrast to the old way of war, the
emperor's engagements were tactically and strategically
decisive.

Not even the best armies are immune to defeat. At Eylau, a
battle fought in a raging snowstorm against a stubborn Russian
enemy and those few Prussian units that escaped the post-Jena
pursuit, the Grand Army sustained heavy losses and failed to
shatter its opponent.

On 8 February 1807 Napoleon ordered Augereau's VIIth
Corps and a division of the IVth Corps to advance against the
Russian left. Moving forward in a line of columns, the VIIth
Corps lost direction because of the blinding snow, strayed to its
left, and came up against the Russian center. There, a battery
of seventy-two fieldpieces opened fire at point-blank range.
The guns tore the VIIth Corps apart, and in half an hour the
French lost 5,000 men. The corps fell back in disorder, pur-
sued by cavalry. One regiment, the 14th Line, formed a square
and cut its way to safety but lost half of its effectives in the pro-

cess. The Russians then advanced against the French center, and Napoleon ordered Murat to attack them with four and one-half cavalry divisions, a total of 10,700 men.

Up to 7 February 1807, the cavalry had performed its limited functions with dash and efficiency. It had screened the Grand Army's march to Ulm, aided Soult's attack on the Pratzen, and, in the pursuit after Jena-Auerstadt, helped prevent the Prussians from rallying their scattered legions. At Eylau Napoleon for the first time called upon his mounted regiments to play a decisive battlefield role.

Murat's men swept aside the Russian cavalry, broke through two lines of deployed infantry, and shattered a third line of foot soldiers. The first two lines, reforming their ranks, threatened to trap the French cavalry, but the guard cavalry charged, broke the infantry again, and rescued Murat's command. The French cavalry took heavy losses but succeeded in halting the day's most dangerous Russian thrust. Later in the afternoon, Russian cavalrymen mounted another attack. French light cavalry squadrons, armed with carbines, rode forward, halted, and unleased a withering volley. Combined with the fire of infantry squares, the French staved off the enemy attack.[43]

Meanwhile, the French infantry began to put increasing pressure on the Russians. The IIId Corps struck the Russian left. The 33d, 48th, and 108th Regiments advanced in battalion columns and, under the cover of *tirailleurs,* formed into line to duel with Russian infantrymen. The Russians fell back, pursued by skirmishers. Friant's 33d and 48th and Morand's 51st then formed squares and repulsed a Russian cavalry charge. The 33d and 48th deployed into line to beat back another infantry assault. The 48th Line then formed assault columns and seized a village but fell back when Prussian reinforcements arrived on the field. Battalions from the 25th and 85th retook the town while elements of the 51st and 108th in open order penetrated and cleared a nearby woods. The 51st Line sent additional troops in skirmish order into another

EYLAU 8 FEBRUARY 1807

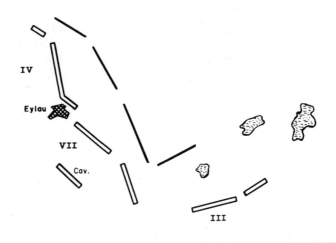

FRIEDLAND 14 JUNE 1807

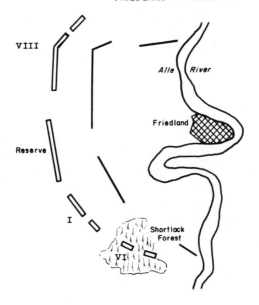

forest while the remainder of the regiment formed a square to meet another cavalry charge. After beating off the cavalry, the 51st formed into assault columns and, supported by four companies of the 108th acting as skirmishers, took another town. The arrival of more enemy reinforcements compelled the 51st to fall back. The 25th and 85th had to join the withdrawal. While the 51st took up positions in a wooded area, the 25th and 85th formed a firing line and, with support from the corps' artillery, drove back the Russian infantry. Morand then sent the 13th Light, 17th Line, and 30th Line into action. Forming a line of double-company columns with artillery in the intervals, the French moved forward. The Russians sent in an infantry attack, but the 61st Line added its weight to the French advance and forced the Russians to retreat.[44] With their flank endangered, the Russian commander finally ordered a general withdrawal.

Although the Grand Army gained possession of the battlefield, it had sustained heavy casualties. Moreover, the Russian army was by no means shattered. It withdrew in good order, and the French were too weakened to pursue. The Russians lost about 15,000 men, but the French left some 25,000 dead and wounded on the field. Napoleon himself was severely shaken by the battle's outcome. In letter after letter, he mentioned the grim fighting and heavy losses.[45] In a note to his wife, he even displayed an uncharacteristic distaste for the horrors of combat, noting: "The field is covered with dead and wounded. It is not the good part of war; one suffers and the soul is oppressed to see so many victims."[46] It seems that he came to the sudden realization that a single mistake or mischance could produce ruinous losses.

Friedland, 14 June 1807, was the last engagement where the Grand Army fought with its famous tactical precision. The battle began as a chance encounter when Lannes clashed with the main Russian army and sought to hold it in place until Napoleon arrived with reinforcements.

The Vth Corps's right flank encompassed the Shortlack Forest, and Lannes sent whole battalions and even an entire brigade into the woods, where they fought as skirmishers. Napoleon finally arrived with Ney's VIth Corps. Lannes shifted his troops to the left while Ney advanced on both sides of the forest. Marchand's division advanced in a column of double-company battalions, and Bisson sent his division forward in two lines of battalion columns. Russian artillery and cavalry, however, threw both divisions into temporary disarray. Dupont's division from the Ist Corps, supported by thirty field guns, stabilized the situation. As Dupont formed a firing line, Senarmont, the artillery commander, ordered his crews to move the guns ahead of the infantry. The crews manhandled the fieldpieces to within 120 paces of the Russian infantry and shattered them. The gunners then broke up a cavalry charge. Ney's infantry then resumed its advance and, along with Dupont's troops, broke the Russian left, thus assuring a French victory.[47]

After Friedland and the ensuing Peace of Tilsit, the emperor reorganized his army. In 1808 Napoleon stood victorious on the Continent, and he used the pause in hostilities to examine and reorganize his empire's administrative structure. Naturally, he included his army within his overall survey. He concluded that the army needed changes because of the casualties sustained between 1805 and 1807 and the consequent loss of veteran campaigners.

Napoleon's triumphs had not come without severe losses. He lost 9,000 men at Austerlitz; 7,000 at Jena; 7,000 at Auerstadt; 25,000 at Eylau, and 10,000 at Friedland.[48] In addition to those who fell in major battles, thousands more fell in lesser engagements. As veterans perished, Napoleon had to replace them with foreign troops and raw French recruits.

After 1805, the number of non-French troops serving the emperor grew rapidly. In 1806 Napoleon commanded 153,000 foreigners, and by 1808 of a total of 764,930 men, 227,749 were non-French.[49] Some foreign regiments served with distinction in numerous campaigns, but others were neither well trained nor well motivated. Though dedicated, the new French recruits lacked the experience that had made the

Grand Army of 1805-7 so formidable. Bonaparte, therefore, attempted to restructure his infantry formations in an effort to restore tactical flexibility.

Napoleon standardized his divisions, giving each two brigades with two regiments per brigade. On 18 February 1808 the emperor issued a decree dealing with the reorganization of the infantry regiments. Regiments were henceforth to consist of four operational and one depot battalion. Regimental strength was established at 108 officers and 3,862 men. The operational battalions were to contain one grenadier, one voltigeur, and four fusilier companies.[50] On paper, the 1808 formations were slightly larger than the ones they superseded, but, in fact, the new battalions were smaller than their predecessors, because commanders frequently removed the grenadier and voltigeur companies and placed them in specialist battalions. Thus, the new line battalions often contained just the fusilier units and numbered about 550 men.[51]

Battalions remained the basic tactical unit, and by reducing their size, Napoleon attempted to ease the task of commanders. By reducing the number of companies and making each remaining company stronger, the emperor similarly sought to ease the problems of battalion leadership by lessening the number of subordinate units. Some officers, however, felt that the 1808 reforms weakened the army's tactical efficiency. The new battalions, according to the critics, were too weak, the number of line infantry was too small, and the number of trained skirmishers was insufficient. Moreover, there was a growing tendency to assign light infantry tasks exclusively to the voltigeurs, a return to the old system of separating line from light troops, confining each to its separate role.[52]

After 1808, a growing military commitment in Spain and Portugal — a commitment ultimately involving over nine corps numbering over 350,000 — led to an ever-growing reliance on recruits and foreigners. Continual conflicts in eastern Europe placed additional manpower burdens upon the French Imperial system and increased the emperor's reliance upon new recruits and non-French soldiers.

As the army's tactical versatility declined, Napoleon began to rely more on mass and less on maneuver. Huge artillery concentrations and dense assault formations, which relied on the sheer weight of numbers to overwhelm an opponent, became characteristic of Napoleon's post-1808 battles. Bonaparte led 76,000 men at Austerlitz and 90,000 at Jena. Davout's 26,000 men fought and won their separate struggle at Auerstadt. About 75,000 Frenchmen fought at Eylau and 80,000 at Friedland. After 1808, Napoleon's field armies grew dramatically. At Wagram the emperor commanded about 170,000 troops; 133,000 men fought at Borodino; 115,000 at Bautzen; 120,000 at Dresden; and 195,000 at Leipzig.[53] The number of casualties also soared: 32,000 at Wagram, 30,000 at Borodino, 20,000 at Bautzen, 10,000 at Dresden, and 73,000 at Leipzig.[54] The results of these and other murderous encounters were disappointing. After 1808, Napoleon never won a battlefield victory that matched the triumphs of the 1805-7 period. His strategic ability was largely intact, but his army had lost much of its tactical finesse. Consequently, the emperor ceased to rely on maneuver and flexibility to destroy his enemies' armies in combat. Instead, he used masses of guns and men in efforts to overwhelm his opponents. Though he often succeeded in this aim, he never again destroyed an enemy army on the battlefield.

At Aspern-Essling on 21 and 22 May 1809, the reorganized French army fought its first major engagement. On the first day, voltigeurs and line troops fought in open order in and around the two villages. On the 22d Lannes attacked the Austrian center. Three divisions, composed largely of inexperienced troops, advanced in column. One division suffered such heavy losses from artillery fire that Napoleon sent a message suggesting that the commander deploy into line. Since the division had already closed with the Austrians by the time the messasge reached him, the commander ignored it. Later in the afternoon, five battalions of the Young Guard charged in column and recaptured Essling from the Austrians. At the end of the battle, voltigeurs tried to silence Austrian field guns with armed fire. They were partially successful.[55]

At Aspern the voltigeurs had functioned effectively, but the line units lacked the precision and flexibility of earlier campaigns. Once under fire, units rarely changed formation to respond to circumstances. Rather, they plunged ahead in whatever order they happened to have when they began to advance, relying upon artillery, shock, and numerical superiority.

Wagram witnessed the use of even greater concentrations of guns and men than Aspern-Essling. On 5 July 1809, 1,500 voltigeurs secured a bridgehead on the Austrian side of the Danube. A seventy-gun battery covered their crossing. During the fighting on 6 July, the French constantly employed massed formations. General Molitor attacked the village of Aderklaa with three regiments—the 2d, 16th, and 67th. All three regiments advanced in columns.[56] Gaudin's division advanced in two lines of columns. The first brigade formed regimental columns, and the second used a line of double-company battalion columns. Morand fought in two lines of battalion columns, Friant in a single line of columns, and Puthod in two large brigade columns. Oudinot's corps fought in three lines. Each line consisted of a division organized in a line of battalion columns.[57]

Macdonald's advance provides a striking example of the growing French reliance on infantry masses. The marshal organized his 8,000 men into a single column. In front, he placed two lines, each of four deployed battalions. Four battalions in column sustained the left, and nine battalion columns covered the right. A battery of a hundred guns supported his advance as he tried and failed to break the Austrian right. Macdonald lost 6,500 men, and, instead of threatening the Austrians, the emperor had to send reserves to save the column.[58] Macdonald claimed that his formation was accidental. He formed his corps to meet a cavalry attack and did not have the time to reorganize it before receiving the order to ad-

vance.[59] True as his explanation might have been, it is significant that Macdonald organized such a massive formation in
the first place and that, once in action, the corps did not attempt to adopt a more flexible posture. In 1806 French units
shifted formations while under fire. In 1809 the Imperial army
relied on the sheer weight of numbers alone.

Napoleon's army was not, of course, absolutely bound to
mass warfare. Broussier's division used a combination of line,
column, and light infantry, and Masséna's corps moved out of
the battle line, marched obliquely across the battlefield, and
formed a new front against the Austrians.[60] Such flexibility
was, however, becoming the exception rather than the rule.
Large batteries and massive troop concentrations were becoming the Imperial army's characteristic tactical method. After
Wagram, the Austrians withdrew in good order, and the
French had lost too many men to mount an immediate
vigorous pursuit. Napoleon remained Europe's outstanding
strategist, but his army had lost much of its tactical versatility.

The Austrians decided to fight in 1809 in part because of a
growing French troop commitment in the Iberian Peninsula.
After 1808, Napoleon sent ever-growing numbers of men south
of the Pyrenees. Many of these men were veterans, and their
absence from central Europe partially explains the tactical
decline of the armies operating in Austria, Russia, and Germany. Ironically, Napoleon's veterans and some of his most experienced marshals were unable to cope with the murderous
combination of rough terrain, guerrilla activity, and an improved British army. Thus, by the spring of 1808, the French
found their tactical capacity declining and their other problems compounded.

In Spain the Imperial forces employed the same tactics they
used elsewhere. Against the Spanish regular army, whose poorly organized regiments lacked even a common drill, the French
were usually successful.[61] At Rio Seco, 14 July 1808, the 22d
Chasseurs à Cheval crushed a line of Spanish infantry before
they could form squares. On 10 November at Gamoral, 5,000
French horse broke a Spanish force drawn up in line. At the

Somosierra defile on 30 November, the 96th Line advanced through the pass in double-company battalion columns, and the 9th Light and 24th Line moved in open order on the flanks.[62]

At Cardadeu, near Barcelona, St. Cyr on 16 December 1808 moved with virtually his entire force in assault columns with a light infantry screen. On 25 February 1809 at Valls, St. Cyr sent in four brigades, each in column with the individual battalions, aligned one behind the other. On 29 March 1809 at Madellin, the Spanish advanced in line with skirmishers in front. They made good progress until French cavalry struck their flank and scattered them.[63]

French tactics, however, were not effective against the British and Portuguese armies. At Vimero Junot relied primarily on assault columns and suffered a stunning defeat. At Corunna the French advanced in columns and halted to deploy. At Ocana Laval used entire battalions as *tirailleurs* to cover his assault columns, and at Talavera Ruffin, Lapisse, and Sebastiani advanced in a line of double-company battalions.[64] At Fuentes de Onoro Marchand advanced in assault columns covered by light troops, and at Albuera Gerard's division had four double-company battalion columns, one behind the other, with battalions deployed in line on both flanks, plus battalion columns protecting the flanks of the deployed units. At Salamanca General Ferey deployed seven battalions in line, and Foy used large numbers of skirmishers to cover his withdrawal.[65] All to no avail.

The French were unable to crush the Anglo-Portuguese army. Despite the presence of as many as 361,800 men in the peninsula and the employment of tactics that had hitherto produced victory, the Imperial army failed to defeat its enemies. Guerrillas pinned down thousands of men away from conventional battlefields and inflicted thousands of casualties. Logistical difficulties compounded French difficulties. Spain was a relatively poor country, and Napoleon's armies could not easily live off the land. The French had to scatter their troops to fight guerrillas and search for food. Consequently, they could never attain decisive numerical superiority over their English and Portuguese enemies. In 1810, for example, Masséna could concentrate only 60,000 men in Portugal, despite the presence of over 300,000 French soldiers in the peninsula.[66]

The failure to adjust to improved British tactics was another major factor in the ultimate defeat of Napoleon's forces in Spain. By 1810 Imperial officers were coming to realize that, on a man-for-man basis, the British were superior.[67] French tactics were never invincible. They were usually superior to the old linear order, which they were in large measure designed to counter. Over ten years of nearly constant warfare had convinced other powers of the need to reform and reconstitute their armies. By 1809, precisely the time when the French army's tactical capacities were declining, many states had completed, or at least begun, the process of revising their military systems. In central Europe Napoleon turned to vast numbers to attain victory. In Spain terrain and guerrillas deprived the French of this advantage. The marshals had to fight Wellington's army with equal and, at times, inferior numbers. They suffered defeat after defeat and finally had to withdraw from Spain. The tide also turned against Napoleon in central Europe, where the powers were finally able to place in the field armies that fought about as well as the French and that outnumbered them.

In 1812 Napoleon did have numerical superiority over the Russians, but the huge distances involved and the necessity to guard long lines of communication gradually eroded much of his initial superiority. On 7 September 1812 his army, 133,000 strong, clashed with 120,000 Russians at Borodino.[68] Both sides displayed fanatic heroism, and, tactically, they were evenly matched. Consequently, the emperor again resorted to the use of huge masses of men and guns and failed to win a decisive victory.

At Borodino over a quarter of a million men fought on a narrow front of four to five miles. There was little maneuvering on either side, save for sending in reserves to shore up threatened portions of the line or to try to pierce a wavering part of the

front. Essentially, the battle involved a head-on collision between two masses, with both sides employing large batteries of
over a hundred guns. Once in action, there was little
maneuvering. Morand's division, for example, advanced and
fought on a front of two deployed battalions with battalion columns on either flank. A second line of battalion double-
company columns sustained the front ranks. Both sides simply
fed in reserves, hoping to wear down their opponent. Napoleon
even used cavalry to capture the Grand Redoubt.[69] As at
Wagram, both sides suffered heavy losses. The Russians
withdrew in good order, and the French were too exhausted to
mount a vigorous pursuit.

During the disasterous retreat from Moscow, the French attempted to cover their withdrawal with blockhouses, garrisoned at times by entire battalions. Some units, despite appalling
losses, managed to retain their combat efficiency. On 13
November the 36th and 44th Regiments formed squares
against cavalry and then moved into double-company columns
to continue their retreat. Ney's rear guard constantly used
assault columns to slash through Russian units that tried to
halt and capture them.[70] Isolated instances of tactical
brilliance, however, did little to arrest the army's retreat and
collapse.

The Russian campaign destroyed the Grand Army, but
Napoleon soon raised another force, and by the summer of
1813, he deployed about 656,000 men in Germany.[71] The new
soldiers were, however, even less able than their predecessors,
because most of them lacked all but the most rudimentary
training. Moreover, the army of 1813 lacked regimental artillery, and because of the losses in Russia, the cavalry arm was
exceedingly weak. At Lutzen Napoleon had only 11,000
horsemen, and but 7,200 cavalry at Bautzen.[72] The cavalry
shortage limited French intelligence gathering efforts in 1813,
and the Imperial forces often had to move with inadequate
knowledge of enemy troop dispositions. Lack of mounted
troops also prevented the French from pursuing a defeated foe.
In 1813 Bonaparte won several battles, but his enemies escaped

to fight again because the emperor lacked the means of mounting a vigorous pursuit.[73]

If Napoleon's forces had declined in quality, the allies had continued to improve their armies' tactical capabilities. Furthermore, the Allies in 1813 were able to bring superior numbers to bear against the French. Between 1809 and 1812 Napoleon relied upon numerical superioroty to defeat enemies who were unit for unit as good as his own forces. In 1813, however, the emperor had to fight against forces that were equal to his own in quality and superior to his army in weight of numbers.[74]

In 1813 the French continued to use tactics resembling those of previous campaigns. At Lutzen the 23d Regiment fought in column, while the 151st, 153d, and 154th battled in line. A seventy-gun battery covered a charge by the Young Guard. Four columns, each containing four battalions, battered their way into the Allied positions. The IIId Corps fought in two lines of regimental columns. One division, the 8th, suffered severe losses and pulled out of the front line, the 10th Division taking its place. The 9th Light and 17th Provisional stormed a village in column, and the 9th and 11th Divisions formed brigade squares to resist cavalry assaults.[75]

At Bautzen a sixty-gun battery gave fire support to an infantry thrust. The 8th Division charged a hill in columns while the 9th in column and the 10th in line supported the attack. The 9th then moved forward to sustain the attack and the 11th Division deployed into line behind it.[76] The two battles cost the French about 40,000 men. In each case, Napoleon won control of the battlefield and inflicted heavy losses on his enemies, but he failed to destroy his rivals in battle. The Prussians and Russians bent but did not break. They retreated in good order, leaving few prisoners, guns, or standards in the emperor's hands. The French were too battered to pursue, and the Allies could reform and reinforce themselves and fight again.

The entrance of Austria into the war on the side of the Coalition shifted the balance decisively against Napoleon. Because of his strategic ability, the emperor could still defeat Allied commanders, but his subordinates could not. The Coalition inflicted sharp defeats on marshals and generals who led independent commands away from the emperor's direct supervision, thereby nullifying Napoleon's own victories. The days of the IIId Corps at Auerstadt were long past. Allied armies defeated Oudinot and Macdonald and managed to destroy Vandamme's corps and to capture Vandamme.

Recognizing the tactical deficiencies of his army, Napoleon sought to enhance its combat capacities. In July he ordered his generals to conduct extensive target practice for the infantry. Using live rounds, the troops were to learn aimed as well as volley fire.[77] In October he directed the infantry to use the two- rather than three- rank line for fire actions. He also reduced columns to six ranks. His object was to enable his units to cover a wider front, deceive the enemy as to the size of his formations, and make more efficient use of firepower.[78] Field commanders seem to have ignored these orders. Their unwillingness to change and the pressures of active operations combined to prevent the introduction of tactical reforms. Consequently, the Imperial forces continued to fight in their customary tactical style — a style that could no longer produce substantial victories.

Numbers finally told. Given troops and leaders of roughly equal merit, the side with the most men and material will probably win. After the Battle of Dresden, Napoleon never won another major victory. Inexorably, the Coalition's armies closed in upon him and finally brought him to battle on their own terms. At Leipzig the Allies amassed sufficient numbers to risk a decisive battle. During the engagement, both sides fought with skill and courage, but the Coalition's numbers proved to be decisive. Napoleon lost his hold upon Germany and had to fall back behind the Rhine.

Napoleon's 1814 campaign is reputed to be one of his greatest. Time and again, he lashed out successfully at the invading Allied armies. Skillfully using internal lines, he moved quickly from place to place and won clash after clash — all to no avail. Unlike his earlier campaigns, he was, in 1814, combating enemies who used tactics similar to his own, and, instead of leading experienced veterans, he was directing a force that consisted largely of hastily drafted conscripts. Many of his soldiers were in fact little more than boys called up to fill in the losses sustained in Germany. Napoleon had at his disposal only 250,000 men, including garrison and depot units. Many of his combat units were sadly depleted. The 136th Regiment had but 590 men and the 2d Light only 112 troops. At the Battle of Montmiral the VIth Corps numbered 2,917, and the entire field army had only 14,500 men.[79]

Strategically, the emperor sought to defeat the Allies in detail. Tactically, the French fought as they had for the past two decades. At La Rothière the 145th Line used columns covered by light infantry, and at Montmiral the guard attacked the Russians in column.[80] French cavalry shattered a Prussian infantry brigade at Vauchamps, and at Montereau field guns moved forward to cover a cavalry charge.[81] Napoleon used surprise and rapid marching to defeat Allied forces before they could concentrate. He won a series of resounding clashes, but his army lacked the ability to win decisively. As in 1813, the Allied armies were as tactically proficient as the French. The Coalition forces always escaped total defeat and finally brought overwhelming numbers to bear. Tactical equality and numerical inferiority spelled doom for the Empire.

In his final gamble to regain his crown, Napoleon and Wellington met in battle for the first and only time in their careers. The emperor led the 120,000-man Army of the North into Belgium in the spring of 1815 with the intention of defeating the Anglo-Prussian forces before the Austrians and Russians took the field. The Corsican's army in 1815 was a more effective force then the desperate men who fought so heroically the previous year. Most of the troops—including the 20,755 men of the guard—who marched into Belgium were veterans of several campaigns.[82] The army was filled with warlike aspirations, memories of past victories, and a thirst for revenge. On the other hand, there existed throughout the ranks a fear of betrayal. Many remembered the numerous defections of 1814.

The Army of the North was then an instrument liable to panic but capable of performing great feats of valor.

At Ligny the emperor's artillery performed with its customary excellence, doing great execution among Prussian reserve battalions on the forward slopes of the hills around the town. The Young Guard in assault columns stormed Saint Amand, and the Old Guard in double-company columns took Ligny, advanced beyond the town, formed battalion squares, and repulsed the Prussian cavalry.[83] Ligny, however, fell short of being a battle of annihilation. As in other battles after 1809, the enemy escaped destruction and prepared to fight again. Two days after Ligny, the Prussian army was ready to fight a major battle.

At Quatre Bras also the French fought well but unsuccessfully. Kellermann's cavalry caught the British 69th and 33d Regiments in line and scattered them. *Tirailleurs* cut down scores of British artillerymen and drove Dutch infantry from a woods. Wellington, however, sent up reinforcements and finally halted the French attack.[84]

On 18 June 1815 Napoleon, having sent Grouchy with 33,000 men to pursue the Prussians, led his remaining 72,000 men against Wellington's 67,000-man force. From the outset of the battle of Waterloo, both Ney and Napoleon mishandled their attacks. The IId Corps wasted valuable time and manpower in reducing Hougoumont, and at the same time the Ist Corps on the French right mounted a massive but poorly organized assault against the British center. Erlon drew up three divisions in a column of deployed battalions. Each division was 200-men wide and about twenty-four ranks deep. A fourth division advanced in a line of columns, and none of the divisions covered their advance with a light infantry screen. When the British opened fire, the Ist Corps was too tightly packed to return the fire effectively or to shift into different formations. Consequently, the corps suffered heavy casualties and had to retreat.[85]

French cavalry then drove off British horsemen, who were pursuing the retreating Ist Corps. Ney then launched a second unsuccessful infantry assault. After the infantry's second failure, Ney sent in a 5,000-man cavalry charge. The French forced the British infantry to form squares, and Wellington's gunners had to seek cover behind the infantry's bayonets. The French, however, had neglected to send up horse artillery batteries to blast the squares at close range. And Ney did not send in light troops to fire into the massed infantry, nor did he supply his cavalry with equipment to spike the guns or haul them away. Consequently, the emperor's cavalry achieved nothing. A second attack with about 10,000 horsemen also failed. A single horse battery accompanied this assault and inflicted heavy losses, but one battery was not sufficient to break Wellington's line. The infantry squares were able to withstand Ney's attack and repulse it.[86]

On the French right, the Prussian army began to reach the field. Blücher's men took Plancenoit. The Young Guard retook the town, but renewed Prussian attacks drove them out. Two Old Guard battalions, the 1st Battalion of the 2d Grenadier Regiment and 1st Battalion of the 2d Chasseur Regiment, formed assault columns and drove the Prussians out of the village. Meanwhile, Ney was attacking the British center with 6,000 men from the IId Corps. An attack in massed formation failed, but a second assault, with skirmishers, small columns, and horse artillery working together, succeeded in driving the British from La Haie Sainte. *Tirailleurs* then advanced and began to fire on the British center, killing gunners and inflicting severe losses upon the infantry.[87]

In a final bid for victory, Napoleon ordered his Old Guard to break the British Center before the Prussians overwhelmed his right. The first line, consisting of six battalions of the 3d Chasseur and 4th Chasseur Regiments, advanced in a line of columns. Each battalion had a frontage of seventy-five to eighty men and a depth of nine. A second line—composed of the 2d Battalion, 1st Chasseur Regiment; 2d Battalion, 2d Chasseur Regiment, and 1st Battalion, 2d Grenadiers—also in battalion double-company columns, followed but gradually in-

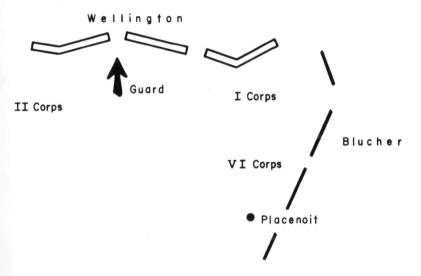

WATERLOO – LAST PHASES
JUNE 18, 1815

Wellington

Guard

II Corps

I Corps

Blucher

VI Corps

● Placenoit

clined its line of march to the left, until there were, in effect, two formations, each consisting of a line of double-company columns. Neither group of battalions put out a covering force of skirmishers, and the British shattered the guardsmen before they could deploy into line or charge home in column.[88]

After the guard's repulse, the entire Army of the North collapsed and fled the field. Some minor actions were fought after Waterloo, but the defeat of 18 June effectively marked the end of Napoleon's final bid for power.

Bonaparte began his career as a royalist artillery officer and received his first important command from the revolutionary Republic. His first Italian campaign resembled in many respects campaigns on other fronts. He waged a war of movement and fought numerous engagements. No single battle was in itself decisive, but all of them served to wear down Austrian

strength and will to resist. By blockading Mantua, he forced
the Hapsburgs to try and relieve it, and, like Jourdan at Fleurs,
Napoleon met and defeated the relief forces. Although he was
better at mobile war than most of his fellow generals,
Napoleon, nevertheless, followed the Republican doctrine of
waging a war of attrition.

Between 1805 and 1807 Bonaparte won his most spectacular
victories. With an experienced army drilled to near tactical
perfection, he annihilated his enemies on the battlefield. In action he took numerous risks, weakening the right at Austerlitz,
and moving his army into easily defended terrain at Jena. He
did so because he knew that his troops could overcome
obstacles insurmountable to an Old Regime army. Moreover,
Auerstadt proved that the Grand Army, even when outnumbered, could still score decisive victories.

After 1808, however, the army's tactical ability declined.
Never again did the Grand Army destroy an enemy force in
battle, and the emperor had to resort to bludgeoning tactics.
Superior numbers of men and guns, rather than superior tactics, became the key to victory. After 1808, Napoleonic battles
involved ever-growing numbers, produced higher casualties,
and lacked decisive results.

The emperor's rivals, meanwhile, instituted reforms to
counter French tactical methods. Thus, as the French army
lost its tactical edge, hostile forces were improving. Ultimately,
Napoleon had to face enemies whose armies were, tactically, as
good as his own. Superior French strategy could still produce
victories, but by 1813 the Allies had the numbers and the tactical ability to meet Napoleon on better than even terms, thus
paving the way for the emperor's final defeat.

NOTES

1. A. Marmont, *On Modern Armies*, trans. Captain Lendy (London, 1865), pp.
14-15.

2. *Correspondance de Napoléon Ier*, 32 vols. (Paris, 1858-69), 11: no.9535.

3. D. G. Chandler, *The Campaigns of Napoleon* (New York, 1966), p. 340.

4. S. C. Pratt, *A Précis of Modern Tactics, Originally Compiled in 1873 by Col. Robert Home* (London, 1892), p. 238.

5. Chandler, *Campaigns of Napoleon*, p. 340.

6. Ibid., p. 332.

7. Ibid., p. 1103.

8. H. Houssaye, *Iéna et la campagne de 1806* (Paris, 1912), p. 26.

9. Chandler, *Campaigns of Napleon*, p. 357.

10. Napoleon, *Commentaires de Napoléon Premier*, 6 vols. (Paris, 1867), 6:40, 101.

11. Chandler, *Campaigns of Napoleon*, p. 360.

12. Napoleon, *Commentaires*, 6:38.

13. Chandler, *Campaigns of Napoleon*, pp. 352-55; Min. de la guerre, Carton C2 736 indicates that in 1809 the French cavalry comprised fourteen cuirassier, two carbinier, thirty dragoon, twenty-eight chasseur, and ten hussar regiments.

14. Chandler, *Campaigns of Napoleon*, pp. 1105, 1117, 1163; Houssaye, *Iéna*, p. 26; Min. de la guerre, Carton C² 522.

15. Chandler, *Campaigns of Napoleon*, pp. 333-34, A. Meynier, "Levées et pertes d'hommes sous le Consulat et l'Empire," *Revue des études napoléoniennes, 30(1930): 30-35.*

16. Min. de la guerre, Carton C² 697.

17. Chandler, *Campaigns of Napoleon*, p. 335; J. Mistler, ed., *Les Cahiers du Capitaine Coignet* (Paris, 1968), p. XII.

18. J. G. E. Simond, *Le 28e de Ligne historique du Régiment* (Rouen, 1889), p. 103.

19. A. Marmont, *Mémoires du Maréchal Marmont Duc de Raguse de 1792 a 1832*, 9 vols. (Paris, 1857), 2:231. A. du Casse, *Le Général Vandamme et sa correspondance*, 2 vols. (Paris, 1870), 2:108.

20. J. Ney, *Memoirs of Marshal Ney*, 2 vols. (London, 1833), 2:325, 364, 367-68, 379, 381-82.

21. Chandler, *Campaigns of Napoleon*, p. 391.

22. Ibid., pp. 148-49.

23. Général Davout, ed., *Opérations du 3e corps 1806-1807, Rapport du Maréchal Davout Duc d'Auerstaedt (Paris, 1896), pp. 213-25.* Despite the date on the title, the report does include comments on Austerlitz.

24. Napoleon, *Correspondance de Napoléon Ier*, 11:9535; Min. de la guerre, Carton C2 29; Simond, *Le 28e de Ligne*, pp. 117-18; Pratt, *Précis of Modern Tactics*, p. 239; Casse, *Le Général Vandamme*, 2:154; A. Clement, *Historique du 75e régiment d'infanterie* (Paris, 1891), p. 96, C. Duffy, *Austerlitz 1805* (London, 1977), p. 16.

25. Chandler, *Campaigns of Napoleon*, p. 430; J. Chavanon and G. Saint-Yves, *Joachim Murat (1767-1815)* (Paris, 1905), p. 121-22. Duffy, *Austerlitz*, pp. 136-37.

26. Chandler, *Campaigns of Napoleon*, p. 428; E. Coste, *Historique du 40e régiment d'infanterie de ligne* (Paris, 1887), p. 62, Duffy, *Austerlitz*, p. 124.

27. C. von der Goltz, *Rossbach et Iéna*, trans. Commandant Chabert (Nancy, 1896), pp. 69-70.

28. F. von der Goltz, ed., *Militärische Schriften von Scharnhorst* (Berlin, 1881), pp. 224-26.

29. C. von der Goltz, *Rossbach et Iéna*, pp. 208-9, 213-17, 234-35, 262, 275-76.

30. P. Paret, *Yorck and the Era of Prussian Reform, 1807 1815* (Princeton, N.J., 1966), pp. 90, 102-3.

31. F. N. Maude, *The Jena Campaign, 1806* (London, 1909), p. 16; *Kriegsge-*

chichtliche Einzelschriften, vol. 10, *Nachrichten über Preussen in singer grossen Katastrophe*, Prussia, General Staff, Historical Section (Berlin, 1881), pp. 443-47, 498-99.

32. Napoleon, *Correspondance de Napoléon Ier* 13:1104; P. J. Foucart, *Campagne de Prusse (1806)* 2 vols. (Paris, 1887), 1:622-24.

33. Foucart, *Campagne de Prusse*, 1:625, 632-33; Houssaye, *Iéna*, p. 78.

34. Foucart, *Campagne de Prusse*, 1:634-35.

35. Ibid., pp. 657-59, 662.

36. Houssaye, *Iéna*, pp. 99, 109; Maude, *Jena Campaign*, p. 156; Chandler, *Campaigns of Napoleon*, p. 484.

37. Houssaye, *Iéna*, p. 111; Chandler, *Campaigns of Napoleon*, p. 488.

38. Davout, *Opérations du 3e corps*, pp. 34-36, 231.

39. Ibid., pp. 37-38, 231-32. For a Prussian account, see *Nachrichten über Preussen*, pp. 514-20.

40. Davout, *Opérations du 3e corps*, pp. 38, 222-24.

41. Ibid., pp. 39-45; Houssaye, *Iéna*, pp. 131-37; Foucart, *Campagne de Prusse*, 1:674, 679, 682, 687 – 90.

42. Chandler, *Campaigns of Napoleon*, pp. 543-44.

43. Chavanon and Saint-Yves, *Murat*, pp. 142-43, 153-54; G. T. Denison, *A History of Cavalry from the Earliest Times with Lessons for the Future* (London, 1913), pp. 305-9; Récit de la bataille de Preussich – Eylau, Mémoires historiques 647.

44. Davout, *Operations du 3e corps*, pp. 161-69, 283-84, 286.

45. *Correspondance de Napoleon Ier*, 14: no.11788, no.11789, no. 11798, no.11876.

46. Ibid., no.11813.

47. T. A. Dodge, *Napoleon*, 4 vols. (New York, 1907), 2:176-77; Campagnes de Prusse et de Pologne 1806-1807, Mémoires historiques 659.

48. Dodge, *Napoleon*, 4:750-51. These figures are approximate. Other authors give slightly different accountings of casualties in various battles.

49. Lieutenant Colonel Belhomme, *Histoire de l'infanterie en France* (Paris, n.d.), 4:314, 344-46, 400-401).

50. Min. de la guerre, Cartons Xs 4, Xs6; *Correspondance de Napoléon Ier* 16:no.13574.

51. Belhomme, *Histoire de l'infanterie*, 4:393-94.

52. P. Berthèzene, *Souvenirs militaires*, 2 Vols. (Paris, 1855), 1:164.

53. Chandler, *Campaigns of Napoleon*, pp. 1118-21.

54. Ibid.,

55. Dodge, *Napoleon*, 3:267-68, 270-71.

56. General Koch, ed., *Mémoires d'André Masséna Duc de Rivoli Prince d'Essling Maréchal d'Empire*, 7 vols. (Paris, 1966-67), 6:311, 420; Relation sur la bataille près Wagram, Mémoires historiques 672.

57. Pratt, *Précis of Modern Tactics*, p. 246.

58. Koch, *Mémoires d'André Masséna*, 6:318, 428.

59. A. Macdonald, *Souvenirs du Maréchal Macdonald Due de Tarente* (Paris, 1892), p. 156; Bataille de Wagram, Mémoires historique 9103.

60. Koch, *Mémoires d'André Masséna*, 66:415-19.

61. For a description of the Spanish army in 1808, see C. Oman, *A History of the Peninsular War*, 7 vols. (Oxford, 1902-30), 1:89-94.

62. Ibid., pp. 100, 170, 422, 457.

63. Ibid., 2:66-67, 87, 160-63.

64. J. W. Fortescue, *A History of the British Army*, 13 vols. (London, 1910-30), 6:226, 228, 383, 7:239-40, 248; W. F. P. Napier, *History of the War in the Peninsula and in the South of France from the Year 1807 to the Year 1814*, 6 vols. (Paris, 1839), 2:49.

65. Fortescue, *History of the British Army*, 7:194, 497, 499; Napier, *History of the War in the Peninsula*, 3:110, 111.

66. Napier, *History of the War in the Peninsula*, 2:643; Journal historique de la campagne de Portugal (5 septembre 1810- 12 mai 1811), Mémoires historiques 916.

67. Girod de l'Ain, *Vie militaire du général Foy* (Paris, 1900), pp. 98-99.

68. Chandler, *Campaigns of Napoleon*, p. 1119.

69. Dodge, *Napoleon*, 3:574-75, 583; Chavanon and Saint-Yves, *Joachim Murat*, p. 222; E. Henckens, *Mémoires* (The Hague, 1910), p. 128.

70. R. M. de Fezensac, *The Russian Campaign, 1812*, ed. and trans. L. B. Kennett, (Baton Rouge, La., 1970), pp. 65, 78; H. Beulay, *Mémoires d'un grenadier de la Grande Armée (18 avril 1808- 15 octobre 1815)* (Paris, 1907), pp. 56-57.

71. Belhomme, *Histoire de l'infanterie*, 4:621-22; F. N. Maude, *The Leipzig Campaign, 1813* (London, 1908), p. 149.

72. Lutzen et Bautzen mai 1813, Mémoires historiques 902².

73. Campagne de 1813, Mémoires historiques 690; Berthèzene, *Souvenirs militaires*, 236, 248; Macdonald, *Souvenirs*, p. 198.

74. Maude, *Leipzig Campaign*, p. 139; Campagne de 1813, Mémoires historiques 688.

75. Chandler, *Campaigns of Napoleon*, p. 886.

76. P. J. Foucart, *Bautzen une bataille de deux jours 20-21 mai 1813* (Nancy and Paris, 1897), pp. 305, 325.

77. *Correspondance de Napoléon Ier* 25:20295, 20296.

78. Ibid., 26:20791, 20792, 20793.

79. F. W. O. Maycock, *The Invasion of France, 1814* (London, 1914), pp. 37-38; J. Colin, "La bataille de Montmirail," *Revue des études napoléoniennes* 4 (1914): 338-39; Campagne de France 1814, Mémoires historiques 715.

80. Colin, "La Bataille de Montmirail," pp. 352-53; E. Simond, *Historique des nouveaux régiments crées par la loi de 25 juillet 1887* (Paris, 1889), pp. 26-27.

81. Chandler, *Campaigns of Napoleon*, pp. 974, 979.

82. Ibid., pp. 1115-17.

83. A. F. Becke, *Napoleon and Waterloo: The Emperor's Campaign with the Armée du Nord, 1815* (London 1939), p. 115; Campagne de 1815, Mémoires historiques 900 BIs2; H. Lachouque and A. Brown, *The Anatomy of Glory: Napoleon and His guard, A Study in Leadership* (Providence, R.I. 1961), p. 480.

84. Fortescue, *History of the British Army*, 10:303-4.

85. Becke, *Napoleon and Waterloo*, p. 194; Fortescue, *History of the British Army*, 10:360-62; J. Naylor, *Waterloo* (London, 1960), pp. 132-34; A. de Maricourt, ed., *Mémoires du général Nougès (1777-1853) sur les guerres de l'Empire* (Paris, 1922), p. 274; E. Martin, *Le 55e regiment d'infanterie* (Avignon, 1905), pp. 84-85.

86. Becke, *Napoleon and Waterloo*, p. 208.

87. Fortescue, *History of the British Army*, 10:383-85.

88. Ibid., pp. 388-89; Naylor, *Waterloo*, p. 170; Lachouque and Brown, *Anatomy of Glory*, pp. 487-88.

4

Napoleon's Enemies

The European powers possessed well-trained, well-led armies, but, nevertheless, they suffered constant defeat at the hands of French Republican and Imperial forces. Superior French manpower was not the sole cause of Allied failures, for in many campaigns numerical disparity was not particularly one-sided. In 1794, for example, the First Coalition placed 220,000 men in Belgium and the Rhineland. The Republic sent about 350,000 troops against them.[1] The balance of forces was not so great as to guarantee a French triumph. At the start of the War of the Second Coalition in March 1799, the Allies actually outnumbered the Republican armies.[2] The French also fought and won against superior numbers at Austerlitz and Auerstadt. Lack of cooperation among the Allied powers and mistakes in generalship contributed to the failure of several coalitions, but, gradually, military thinkers came to realize that the root causes of their defeats lay even deeper. A general, they concluded, could lose a battle or even a campaign because of bad luck, poor judgment, or insufficient numbers. Perpetual defeat, however, indicated that something was seriously wrong with the fundamentals of the military system's training, tactical doctrine, and recruitment.

The pressure of defeat, coupled with the hope of revenge, compelled leaders of states opposed to French hegemony to reform their armies. England refined the linear system of combat to increase its effectiveness. Austria and Russia tried to introduce French tactics, and Prussia engineered a revolution from above in order to reproduce the spirit as well as the forms of Napoleonic tactics.

When Britain entered the war in 1793, William Pitt had only 38,945 regulars available for action on the Continent. The various regiments were ill-prepared for war. Battalions lacked a common drill, officers neglected troop training, and each commander established his own drill regulations. Gen. David Dundas had issued a drill book in 1788. It was officially adopted by the army in 1792, but officers generally ignored its existence.[3] The British did create horse artillery batteries and established a driver corps for field guns, but during the campaigns of 1793, 1794, and 1795, the infantry remained wedded to its haphazard methods of tactics and training and suffered grave defeats despite the bravery of individual units.[4]

In the wake of the disastrous Continental campaigns, the British realized the need to create more effective tactics. In 1795, and again in 1798, the Duke of York directed that all battalions use the Dundas regulations.[5] The *Rules and Regulations* established the three-rank line as the fundamental battle order, but left room for commanders to introduce modifications, as required by circumstances. If necessary, battalions could turn on a moving instead of a fixed pivot and employ a two-rank firing line.[6] Dundas also devoted a few pages to light infantry. For the most part, light troops were to train and fight like line infantry, but they could occasionally use a two-rank line with open files and move at the run, although they still had to keep close enough together to be able to reform a standard line quickly.[7] The Dundas regulations established a standard drill for the entire army, and, although they emphasized traditional linear tactics, they did leave room for individual innovation.

Other officers devoted their attentions to improving Britain's light infantry. As early as 1794, a general stationed in the West Indies set up a camp for light infantry training, and in Corsica the British recruited three local battalions of light troops. In

1797 the Duke of York ordered generals to devote more attention to skirmishing techniques, and in 1798 General Howe
trained thirteen companies as light infantry at a camp in Essex.
The 90th Foot in Minorca learned skirmish tactics, and Col.
Francis de Rottenberg, an Austrian with light infantry experience, took command of the fifth batalion of the 60th Royal
Americans. The battalion received rifles capable of firing one
shot a minute. On 17 January 1800 the government ordered
fourteen regiments to detach men to an Experimental Corps of
Riflemen, where they would receive light infantry instruction.[8]
Officers began to translate works on light infantry from the
German, while others advocated enlarging the number of units
trained in open warfare techniques.[9]

By January 1801, 500 men had been trained as riflemen.
Early in 1803 the government decided to transform entire battalions into light infantry units and established a training camp
at Shorncliffe. Sir John Moore took command of the 52d, 43d,
and 95th Regiments.[10] He made Shorncliffe an active service
camp, and soldiers trained under realistic conditions. He did
not neglect close order drill, but his main concern was to create
skirmishers who could operate flexibly and independently.
Moore therefore emphasized initiative and aimed fire and introduced discipline based upon respect and hope of reward
rather than upon fear. He chose officers who could lead by
example and careful instruction, introduced milder
punishments, and gave promotions as rewards for superior performance.[11] Moore's methods were sufficiently impressive to
convince the army to expand the light infantry. After 1805, the
95th (Rifle) Regiment grew to three battalions, and the 68th,
85th, 71st, and 51st regiments received light infantry instruction.[12]

By 1809 the British regular army had grown to over 200,000
men. Including the light companies serving in line battalions,
about 20 percent of the soldiers could operate as skirmishers.
In the French army after 1808, only 17 percent of the troops
habitually fought in open order.[13] Many British light infan-

trymen, especially the riflemen, became expert shots. They could fire and reload from a prone position, and used rifle pits for cover while sniping at their foes.[14] British light troops were, in every respect, the equal of their French counterparts.

Meanwhile, line officers began to use the two-rank firing line on a regular basis. In Egypt in 1801 and in southern Italy in 1806, commanders found that the two-rank line enabled battalions to cover a longer front and increased the regular infantry's firepower. In Portugal and Spain Arthur Wellesley, the future Duke of Wellington, combined the two-rank line, the expanded and reformed light infantry, and the use of terrain for surprise and protection to demonstrate that the reformed British army could defeat Napoleon's legions.

At Vimero, 21 August 1808, Wellington placed nine battalions behind the crests of hills, where they were invisible to the French. On the forward slopes, he deployed riflemen and light infantry companies. As the French advanced, the British skirmishers slowly retreated, holding the *tirailleurs* in check and preventing them from discovering and firing upon the main line. When the French columns neared the crests, the British moved forward in line and delivered volleys at point-blank range. Taken by surprise, the French could neither charge in column nor deploy into line. They retreated in disorder. Still in line, the British pursued, halting periodically to deliver additional shattering volleys.[15]

At Corunna, 16 January 1809, the 42d and 50th Regiments shattered the columns of the French 31st Line. Light troops and riflemen also inflicted severe losses, halting a cavalry pursuit and killing a general in the process.[16] Upon returning to the peninsula in 1809, Wellington organized his army into permanent divisions and detached officers to train the Portuguese army in British tactics. The Portuguese army contained forty-eight line and seven light battalions in 1808, and five new light battalions were added in 1809. The Portuguese soon reached a high level of proficiency, and some battalions were ultimately integrated into the British divisions.[17]

On 27-28 July 1809 Wellington met the French at the battle of Talavera. Once again, the two-rank line, light infantry, and utilization of terrain for protection and surprise proved to be a superior combination. Victor's corps advanced in a line of columns covered by light infantry. Wellington pulled two of his brigades off the skyline of a hill and ordered the troops to lie down to avoid losses from artillery fire. When the French neared the top of the hill, the British rose and fired before Victor's men could react.[18] On another part of the front, the 40th, 53d, and 7th Regiments halted Laval's division with a volley and completed their discomforture with a bayonet charge, an indication that the two-rank line could also act offensively.[19] In the center, eight British battalions shattered French columns and then charged. The advance became disorganized. The French sent in fresh troops and pushed the British back in disorder. Three reserve battalions then moved forward; the retreating troops passed between the intervals of the fresh units, reformed, and halted the French.[20] The British ability to reform scattered battalions testifies to the efficiency and cohesion of Wellington's forces but also indicates that no tactical system, however proficient, is ever entirely safe from defeat.

Napoleon, meanwhile, decided to finish the Iberian Campaign. After defeating the Austrians in 1809, he sent several veteran corps to Spain, bringing his troop strength to 350,000. He placed Marshal Masséna in charge of the forthcoming offensive, designed to drive the British out of Portugal.[21] Bonaparte assumed that 33,000 British soldiers, no matter how good, could not withstand the crushing numerical superiority of his legions. He ignored the army's gradual decline in tactical proficiency, and he seriously underestimated the effectiveness of the Spanish guerrillas, who forced the French to disperse thousands of soldiers, leaving them with a reduced force to face the Anglo-Portuguese army.

Spanish guerrillas in 1808 and 1809 usually operated in small, poorly organized, indifferently equipped, and badly led bands. Their main activities were isolated ambushes of small units and assassinations. Competent leaders soon emerged and began to organize the guerrillas into large, effective formations. Operating in Navarre and upper Aragon, Mina led a three-battalion force in 1810, and by 1812 he commanded nine infantry battalions, two cavalry regiments, and an artillery park.[22] Villacampa, operating in Aragon and Valencia, led a force of 4,000 infantry and 300 cavalrymen; Empecinado wielded four infantry battalions and a cavalry regiment; and the Duran division had over 3,000 troops.[23]

Guerrilla formations sought engagements with Imperial units of equal size and were often successful. Mina, for example, trained his men to fight in a three-rank line with a screen of skirmishers. In battle, he ordered his men to deliver two volleys and then, because of ammunition shortages, execute a bayonet charge. When faced with superior numbers, his men would scatter and proceed to a predetermined rendezvous.[24]

Guerrilla bands, both large and small, ambushed convoys, attacked fortified posts, and disrupted French communications. Guerrillas also supplied vital intelligence to Wellington's command. The French soon found themselves in a nearly impossible situation. The Imperial Army in Spain was simply not large enough to control or supress the guerrillas. One officer noted: "We found ourselves in the middle of a population of ten or twelve million almost all of whom were in arms against us."[25] Though large enough for conventional operations, the Imperial forces in Spain were too few to wage effective partisan war.

Moreover, the French also had to combat the British and Portuguese armies. Faced with two nearly insoluable problems, the French dissipated their forces. They used large, yet insufficient, numbers against the guerrillas in an effort to guard the cities, vital posts, and main roads. Consequently, Masséna lacked the necessary numbers to overwhelm Wellington. When he invaded Portugal in September 1810, he had 64,947 men to employ against 54,274 Anglo-Portuguese troops.[26]

On 27 September 1810 Masséna struck at the Anglo-

Portuguese army in an effort to crush it before Wellington could withdraw to prepared defensive positions around Lisbon. The Battle of Bussaco offered still another demonstration of the superiority of British tactics. Reynier's corps advanced in two lines of columns covered by skirmishers. The British waited behind the crest of a hill. When the French neared the top, the 74th and 21st Portuguese regiments moved up and fired before the leading French regiment could react. The French tried to form a line, but Wellington's men moved forward until their line overlapped the French. The British and Portuguese moved their flank companies forward, thus forming a concave line around the French. Withering volleys then shattered Reynier's regiment. Meanwhile, the 45th, 88th, and 8th Portuguese advanced in line, halting to deliver volleys. Covered by skirmishers, who kept the French voltigeurs in check, the duke's men forced the French 36th Line and 2d Light to retreat. The British 9th struck a French brigade in the flank, and the 52d and 43d Regiments, screened by riflemen and Portuguese light infantry, used a sunken road for concealment and cover. When Ney's corps approached to within ten paces, the British rose, fired, and charged. The English then wheeled companies to strike the French flanks, taking them in a deadly semicircle of fire. The French fell back, having lost 4,480 men, and Wellington, with 1,252 casualties, resumed his planned withdrawal to Lisbon.[27]

At Lisbon Wellington demonstrated his mastery of terrain- and field-fortification techniques. The Torres Vedras works protecting Lisbon consisted of three lines of mutually supporting redoubts. The seizure of any single position would be a major and costly operation. The forts were held by second line troops, and Wellington's entire field army stood ready to fall on any French column that managed to break into his lines. The defensive line was so strong that Masséna never attempted to breach it, and in March 1811 he began to retreat to the Spanish frontier. Wellington followed and laid siege to a series of fortresses along the Portuguese-Spanish border. To Wellington, terrain was not simply an obstacle to cross or avoid; it was an integral part of his tactical system, used consciously to strengthen his hand in battle.

At Fuentes de Onoro, 3 May 1811, the French attempted to break the siege of Almeida. Wellington again had most of his line hidden, this time in a ravine. He handily repulsed a frontal assault. Two days later, Masséna attempted to turn the British flank. Wellington responded by moving his 1st and 3d Divisions, along with some Portuguese units, to a new line at right angles to his original position. The new line was also concealed and protected by the crests of hills. The British beat off French assaults, and light units defeated voltigeurs in bitter open order fighting in the village of Fuentes.[28]

On 16 May Marshal Soult, marching to relieve the garrison of Badajoz, met an Anglo-Spanish force under General Beresford's command near Albuera. Soult tried to turn Beresford's right with two divisions, but Beresford quickly established a new line to protect his flank. The British threw back the French infantry, who had tried to advance in line. The British then pursued, but French cavalry caught a deployed brigade in the flank and shattered it. Polish lancers did great execution. Soult resumed his attack, but Spanish units and two British brigades halted the French, although the voltigeurs inflicted heavy losses on the deployed Anglo-Spanish infantry. Another French division advanced in columns. British infantry drove it back. The French tried to deploy, but British volleys shattered them before they could complete their evolutions.[29]

Albuera offers still another example of British tactical effectiveness but also demonstrates that, unless it was carefully handled, the two-rank line was vulnerable. By advancing too rapidly, a brigade exposed itself to a cavalry riposte, and, lacking cover and a light infantry screen, the Anglo-Spanish line endured heavy punishment. Albuera was one of the bloodiest peninsular battles and one of the few in which French and Allied losses were about equal.

Up to 1812, most of Wellington's victories were defensive. Whether fighting to cover a retreat or to block a French relief force, the British tended to operate from defensive positions. At Salamanca, however, the duke demonstrated that the British tactical system was also effective in launching tactically offensive moves.

In the days prior to the battle, Wellington, with 51,000 men, maneuvered against Marmont's 48,000-man force. Marmont operated against the British right, hoping that, by threatening Wellington's flank, he could force the duke to abandon his thrust into Spain and compel him to withdraw into Portugal in order to protect his supply lines. On 12 July 1812, Marmont continued to advance his left against the British right. One of his divisions moved off too rapidly creating a gap between itself and the main army. Wellington then decided to seize this opportunity and attack.

The British 3d Division marched across the front of the leading French division, deployed under hostile artillery and skirmish fire, and fired upon the leading battalions. The French, still in column, collapsed and fell back in disorder. Wellington next committed his 4th and 5th Divisions against the French main force. Covered by light infantry, the British advanced in line toward the French, who were deployed in a line of columns. British volleys shattered the French, and Wellington's few cavalry units pursued. The French counterattacked with four battalion columns. The British 6th Division quickly formed a line overlapping the advancing columns. Again, British fire was effective, and in the space of a few minutes, the French lost 1,500 men and retreated.[30]

Salamanca demonstrated that British tactics were effective on the tactical offensive. On several occasions, Anglo-Portuguese troops wrested high ground from the French by use of superior firepower. The ability of his forces to bring more muskets to bear on a unit-for-unit basis provided Wellington with a constant measure of superiority.

Wellington also devised effective measures to counter

superior numbers of field guns and cavalry. The use of natural cover usually gave British infantrymen protection from French artillery fire. Against cavalry the British used squares quite effectively. At Fuentes de Onoro, for example, the Light Division, holding positions in front of the main line, came under cavalry attack. The troops formed into five separate squares and retreated for two miles, fending off Imperial horsemen during the entire withdrawal. At El Bodon the 5th and 77th Regiments retreated in squares for six miles in the face of constant cavalry attacks.[31] Thus, by 1812 Wellington's army had demonstrated that it could beat off attacks by superior numbers, offset weaknesses in artillery and cavalry strength, and, given a rough numerical equality, press home tactical offensives.

In 1813 and 1814 the Anglo-Portuguese army continued to defeat Imperial forces. At Vittoria Wellington attacked and shattered a smaller French force. During the engagement, riflemen forced French field guns to move back out of range, and the infantry continued to use terrain for protection: the 92d, for example, sat down to avoid French fire.[32] Again, the two-rank line with a light infantry screen demonstrated its effectiveness.

Marshal Soult led the furious resistance in the Pyrenees. In the mountain passes, French skirmishers proved very deadly, but British, Portuguese, and Spanish troops were their equals. At Ordal, 13 September 1813, skirmishers inflicted severe losses on the 27th Regiment but failed to halt the Allied advance. At Nivelle Clinton's division, in two lines covered by light infantry, proved more than a match for the French, and at Orthez in February 1814, despite the efforts of *tirailleurs,* the British were again triumphant.[33] The British tactical system had gained undisputed supremacy over French methods.

The Waterloo campaign was the first encounter between Wellington and Napoleon and the last great clash between British French tactics. If the Imperial Army of the North was a fragile mixture of recruits and veterans, Wellington's forces were not the same fine body of men who had fought in Spain. Many veterans had gone to fight against the Americans, and the Allied army in Belgium contained relatively few veterans, many inexperienced troops, and numerous Dutch and German units of uneven quality.[34] Thus, the emperor and the duke led armies of approximately equal capacities, and the ensuring Battle of Waterloo was to be a contest of command decisions and rival tactical systems. On both counts, the British proved superior.

Napoleon hurled massive, poorly coordinated assaults against Wellington's position, while the duke relied primarily on his standard method of combining the two-rank line, light troops, and terrain. British and French light troops battled in the woods around Hougoumont, and at La Haie Sainte riflemen picked off French artillerymen. When the Imperial Guard launched its final assault, the British 1st Foot Guards were hidden and protected by the banks of a sunken road. When the French approached to within fifty or sixty yards of their position, the guards rose. Their line overlapped the advancing French battalions, and they unleased a devastating volley before Napoleon's men could charge or deploy. The 52d, which had remained concealed on a nearby reverse slope, rose, advanced, deployed against the flank of the Guard Chasseurs, and delivered a volley at point-blank range. On the other flank, the 33d and 2d Battalion of the 69th Regiment carried out a similar maneuver.[35] Waterloo confirmed once again that linear formations, operating with light troops and using terrain properly, could defeat the French tactical system.

Unlike the British, Continental powers did not attempt to refine and improve the linear order in order to counter French tactics. Rather, the Austrians, Russians, and Prussians sought in varying degrees to adopt Imperial methods.

Up to 1805, the Hapsburg army used a drill book written in 1769. Modeled on Frederick the Great's methods, the regulations emphasized linear tactics. By the 1790s the Austrian light infantry, perhaps the best corps of light troops in all of Europe in the 1760s, began to train and operate as line infantry. When they did operate as light troops, they confined their activities to the traditional war of posts and did not support the line troops in combat.[36] Years of defeat, culminating in the dual catastrophies of Ulm and Austerlitz, convinced the more forward-looking members of the military establishment that changes in tactical doctrine were vitally needed.

Archduke Charles, the most successful Hapsburg general, was among the first to call for change. After studying previous campaigns, he noted that Austrian light troops covered the deployment of the battle line and pursued or screened retreats but took no part in the main battle. French skirmishers, by contrast, accompanied the main body into action, and during the battle they assisted the troops in line or column by using aimed fire against the enemy's line. Austria, he asserted, should imitate the French by increasing its number of light troops and improving its training. As much as one third of the army should be trained to act as light infantry. Moreover, the light units, after preparing the way for the main attack, should be prepared to sustain the attack with aimed fire or, if circumstances required, return to the line and fight as regular infantry.[37]

At first, Charles sought to improve coordination between line and light infantry, but he also began to appreciate the tactical value of battalion columns. The basic battle order, he asserted, would be the three-rank firing line, but the army should use battalion columns for maneuver during an engagement. Reserves in combat should form up in columns, and columns and light infantry should pursue defeated foes. Columns should also be used against salients, entrenchments, and fortified posts. Finally, Charles concluded that all infantry should learn to fight both as skirmishers and as part of close order formations.[38] Experience had demonstrated to Charles and his followers the need for more flexible tactics and the necessity to coordinate closely the actions of light and line infantry in battle.

After 1805, with Charles playing a leading role, the

Austrians began to compile a new drill manual. Completed in 1807, the *Auszug aus dem Exercier Reglement für die K. K. Infanterie* retained the three-rank line for fire actions and introduced a double-company battalion column for battlefield maneuvers and assaults on fortified posts and entrenchments.[39] The Austrians also created nine chasseur battalions and trained fourteen men in each line company as skirmishers.[40]

The Austrians also created permanent combat divisions and corps. In 1808 Austrian battalions contained six companies. Brigades of two regiments had a light artillery battery, and divisions had a medium battery.[41] Austrian corps, like their French counterparts, varied in size and composition according to the mission and the commander's abilities.

Although Austrian officers continued to show a preference for the linear order of battle, they did begin to make greater use of columns and light infantry. At Essling, 21 May 1809, General Hohenzollern's twenty-two battalion corps advanced in two lines of battalion columns at deploying intervals. On 6 July at Wagram, the Austrians employed double-company columns at deploying distance, covered by a thick light infantry screen.[42]

After Wagram, the Austrians had to reduce their army to 150,000 men. Vienna also abandoned its hesitant efforts to create a statewide militia. The emperor, always suspicious of the revolutionary implications inherent in a militia system, never wholeheartedly supported the concept. Although revived later, militia battalions served primarily as garrison and training units, and the Hapsburgs never seriously tried to create a levy en masse or a citizen army.

In order to restore their military strength, the Hapsburgs sought to strengthen their financial resources and avoid war until a favorable opportunity arose. The French catastrophe in Russia gave Austria the chance to devote its resources to the strengthening of the regular standing army. By January 1813 Francis had 184,000 men under arms, and by March the Austrian army numbered 311,000 active troops, plus 133,000 men in depots and garrisons. By the year's end, the Hapsburgs had a force of 568,000 men, with 389,000 of them serving in the field.[43]

During the 1813 and 1814 campaigns, the Austrians continued to rely primarily on the three-rank firing line. They did, however, demonstrate a growing appreciation of the value of light infantry. On 16 October 1813, for example, skirmishers from Klenau's corps fought in open order for two hours against French *tirailleurs*.[44] The Austrians also created special light divisions. Each brigade in each of the two light divisions contained two or three chasseur battalions, a horse artillery battery, and from six to twelve light horse squadrons.[45] Although conservative and hostile to change, the Austrian army by 1815 had familiarized itself with columns and had begun to employ light troops in conjunction with close order formations.

The Russians maintained an army that trained and fought in the traditional linear order. In 1799 Czar Paul sent an army to fight beside the Austrians in Italy. The commander, Alexander Suvorov, was one of the few Russian generals who had thought deeply about tactical questions, and he was prepared to meet French tactics with a system of his own. In his youth, Suvorov had fought Prussians, Turks, and Poles, and in 1794 he wrote a book, *Science of Victory*, proposing a tactical system based upon his years of combat experience. Suvorov argued that speed and shock were more effective battlefield methods than the Prussian style of fighting currently used by the Russian army. To achieve speed and shock, he advocated that units enter action as soon as they got within range of the enemy instead of waiting for the entire army to deploy into perfect lines. The key to victory was to get into action quickly and attack immediately. Suvorov believed that linear formations and firepower were important, but he wanted to make linear combat more flexible and aggressive.[46]

During the 1799 campaigns, Suvorov characteristically covered his advancing lines with skirmishers, delivered bayonet attacks in line, and fought encounter battles, feeding troops into action as they arrived on the field. He also sought to provide close artillery cooperation. His infantry regiments had four light guns; cavalry regiments received horse batteries, and he kept a horse artillery reserve under his personal direction.[47] Despite his success, Suvorov remained a unique figure in the Russian army, and his reforms died with him. His contemporaries and successors ignored his innovations and remained wedded to the linear tactical system.

The crushing defeat at Austerlitz reawakened Russian interest in tactical reforms. The czar and his military advisors, some of whom had served with Suvorov, concluded that the Russian army needed greater flexibility in maneuver and combat. They decided to provide the needed changes by adopting elements of Napoleon's tactics. After 1805, therefore, the Russians introduced battalion double-company columns, increased the number of light infantrymen, and sought to integrate light and close order tactics.

At Eylau, the Russians employed four divisions in battalion columns with a screen of skirmishers covering the advance. During the battle, the 24th Chasseur Regiment attacked a village in column while light infantry provided covering fire. Russian columns attacked Morand's division while light troops fought in several small towns. Other regiments deployed into line and engaged the French in firefights.[48] At Friedland the Russians again used battalion columns for maneuvers and assaults.[49]

After 1807, the Russian army concentrated upon refining and perfecting their new tactics. One observer noted that officers spent much time teaching their men how to form columns and squares and how to maneuver in column.[50] The Russians also increased the number of specialist light infantrymen, making extensive use of Siberians for this role. In addition, the Russians gave line troopers a measure of light infantry training.[51]

Alexander also expanded his armed forces and organized them into combat divisions. By June 1812 the Russian army contained 116 line and 50 light regiments backed by 102 foot and 22 horse batteries. Including 66 cavalry regiments, the czar had a total of about 409,000 men under arms.[52]

During the 1812 campaign, the Russians demonstrated increased proficiency in the use of French tactics. On 18 July, for example, French voltigeurs from Legrand's division clashed with Russian line infantry from the Kalouga and Sewsk regiments near Jakoubovo. The Russians fought in open order and delayed the French advance. The next day the Russians counterattacked, using assault columns and skirmishers. The French withdrew across a river, and, in an action reminiscent of Lodi, Russian grenadiers in column stormed the bridge while skirmishers provided covering fire.[53]

On 20 July Russian units near Golovchitska attacked in battalion columns. Skirmishers and horse artillery guns supported the columns. The Russians finally had to retreat, and light troops covered the withdrawal. A grenadier battalion joined the light units and fought in open order.[54] On 5 August three regiments launched a counterattack, using a line of battalion double-company columns preceded by a skirmish line.[55]

At Borodino the Russians, like the French, used a deep battle order. On a front of approximately two and one-half miles, Kutusov had five corps drawn up in two lines sustained by two lines of cavalry, with still more cavalry in reserve. Each infantry division drew up in two lines of battalion columns with a screen of *tirailleurs* in front.[56]

During the battle, both sides used massive infantry attacks backed by massive artillery concentrations. Bagration, for example, massed three hundred guns against French columns attacking the Grand Redoubt. He counterattacked, using a line of battalion assault columns and skirmishers. Other Russian regiments fought in line and formed squares against cavalry charges.[57] When the Russians withdrew, chasseur regiments in open order covered the retreat and checked French efforts to pursue.[58]

During the French retreat, Russian infantry continued to

employ French tactics. Cossack light cavalry harassed their fleeing foes, using sled-drawn light artillery effectively. At Stakow near the Beressina, the 12th and 22d Chasseurs fought French voltigeurs. Several Russian line units joined the chasseurs. Lacking experience, they suffered heavy losses in the open order fighting, but the chasseurs in turn inflicted severe casualties on the French.[59]

Throughout 1813 and 1814 the Russian army improved its combat flexibility. At Konigswarta, May 1813, the 18th Division marched into action in a single closed column with one battalion column behind the other. Upon sighting an Italian formation, the Russians deployed into line and attacked. The Italians retreated, and the Russians formed into a line of columns covered by skirmishers and pursued.[60]

At Bautzen the Russian right wing held a wooded area with light infantry, sustained by line troops drawn up in columns. Light troops also held several villages. The French assaulted the villages, and the Russians sent line infantry to support the chasseurs. A French corps then moved forward in a line of columns, but a forty-eight-gun battery held them back. The French advanced again, with their leading battalions in line, and the Russians, outnumbered, had to retreat. Chasseurs covered the retreat, delaying the French pursuit until the line units could escape in good order. On another portion of the field, three grenadier battalions from the Pavlofsky Regiment advanced into a woods, where they fought as skirmishers throughout the day.[61]

The Russians managed with fair success to imitate French tactics without making any basic changes in their political and social structure. The army remained a force of conscripted serfs led by aristocratic officers. The Russians, nevertheless, adopted the double-company battalion column for battlefield maneuver and assault. They also expanded the number of specialist light infantry units and occasionally used line infantry in skirmishing roles. Moreover, the Russians began to use light troops in close coordination with line and column formations.

The Russians introduced their reforms at about the time that the Grand Army's quality was declining. Consequently, the czar's forces were able to face Napoleon's armies with a reasonable prospect of victory. Although the Russians continued to show a marked preference for mass formations and attacks, the army's tactics by 1815 had become markedly more flexible.

In Prussia after the disasters of 1806 and 1807, there was little popular resentment over the state's humiliation and no evidence of a desire for revenge. A small group of dedicated reformers composed of army officers and bureaucrats realized that Prussian recovery required sweeping military and political changes. The army would have to adopt French tactical methods, but the reformers believed that military innovations were predicated upon prior political reforms. An army composed of serfs and mercenaries, they felt, lacked the ability and the will to adopt a new tactical doctrine. The first task was, therefore, to close the gap between the people and the state. The reformers wanted first to transform subjects into citizens who had a personal stake in Prussia's future. Then they wished to create a citizen army and provide the new army with flexible effective tactics. Thus, military and political reform were mutually interdependent.

Prior to 1806, the reformers had been a distinct minority. They remained so until the October catastrophe convinced the king and many of his advisers that, if Prussia was to survive, change was necessary. The reformers gained a large measure of influence at court after 1807. Despite spirited opposition from those who had a vested interest in the old order, and vacillating support from the monarch, the reformers were able to institute the beginnings of a revolution from above.[62]

On 9 October 1807 the government granted serfs personal freedom. They could henceforth marry, migrate, and learn a trade without their manorial overlord's approval. Serf freedom was hedged with many restrictions — a freed serf who remained on the land still owed all the former services, including obligatory labor on the lord's lands. Those who owned small farms continued to owe manorial dues until 1810, when the crown established a system of converting manorial tenure into private ownership. Despite continuing restrictions, the serf had become a free man, able to make his own way without legal subjugation to an overlord.[63]

The reformers also abolished the caste system. Property became interchangeable among classes, and by a decree of 6 August 1808, individuals, regardless of class, became eligible for army commissions on the basis of talent. Education and bravery, rather than noble status, became the basis of officer selection, a clear case of adoption by the Prussians of the French system of promotions based on ability. In November 1808 the crown introduced municipal self-government. City governments were to be elective and responsible — a policy that reflected the efforts to enable the middle classes to participate in the life of the state.[64]

After 1808, some reformers wished to go even further and transform Prussia into a constitutional monarchy. They encountered mounting resistance, but their initial efforts created serious breaches in the old absolutist system. They also laid the foundations for a government based on popular acceptance, thereby paving the way for the creation of a citizen army.

Efforts to create a citizen army, however, met with violent opposition from conservatives, vacillating support from Frederick William III, and hostility and harassment from the French. The reformers were, nevertheless, able to establish the framework for a popular conscript force.

On 15 July 1807 Frederick William established a Military Reorganization Commission to transform the army into an effective fighting machine. Dominated by Scharnhorst, a leader in the movement for civil and military reform, the commission began to prepare the way for the creation of a citizen army. On 31 August the commission recommended that the state's armed forces consist of a regular army backed by a popular militia. On 15 March 1808 the commission called for the application of the principle of universal military service, and in December it proposed the institution of conscription for males between the ages of twenty and thirty-five. There were to be no exemptions. Selection for the active army would be by lot, and those not selected would be placed in the militia.[65]

The king agreed to open the officer corps to all subjects and to humanize the army's discipline. He refused, however, to sanction the creation of a citizen army. In September the French insisted that Prussia reduce its army to 42,000 and forbade the creation of a militia. Afraid of the French and suspicious of the revolutionary ideas inherent in the concept of universal service, the monarch continued to oppose all efforts to establish a citizen armed force. Consequently, the old recruiting system remained in force until 1813, and the reformers had to abandon their efforts to create a popular conscript army.[66]

The reformers resorted to the famous *Krümper* system first suggested by Scharnhorst in July 1807. The system involved the training and release of soldiers into a ready reserve, but, far from creating a huge secret army, the system did little more than train a body of replacements for the regular units. By 1813 the *Krümper* system had produced only 33,600 men.[67]

The king, meanwhile, remained reluctant to challenge France. He removed Scharnhorst and Stein from office under French pressure. He remained neutral during war between France and Austria in 1809 and even supplied a corps to assist the Grand Army's invasion of Russia. As the remnants of the Imperial Army limped back to Poland and Germany, the Prussian monarch still refused to sanction any action against the French. Only the actions of General Yorck forced his hand and led him to declare war on Napoleon and to establish a citizen army.

Commander of the corps that had joined the Grand Army in Russia, Yorck had withdrawn during the retreat to East Prussia. There, on 30 December 1812, he signed the Convention of Tauroggen with the Russians. According to the convention's terms, Yorck was to cease fighting the Russians and adopt a neutral posture. Before Berlin could react to what was technically an act of treason, Stein and other reformers swarmed into East Prussia and began to implement many of their long-desired reforms. Stein and Yorck arranged for a meeting of the East Prussian *Landtag,* which on 9 February 1813 created and mobilized a *Landwehr* consisting of all able-bodied men between the ages of eighteen and forty-five.[68]

Faced with the possibility that the reformers would create a national army without his consent, the monarch decided to join the reformers before he lost control of the national movement. Frederick William therefore transferred his headquarters to Breslau, out of the reach of French forces. He then mobilized the regular army and gave authorization for the formation of volunteer *jaeger* battalions. On 9 February the crown abolished all exemptions from military service, and on 17 March a royal order established a statewide *Landwehr* based on the East Prussian model. All men aged seventeen to forty not serving with the regulars or volunteers were to enter the *Landwehr.* A month later the government created a *Landstrum* consisting of all men aged eighteen to sixty not currently enrolled in the *Landwehr.*[69]

Although there was some resistance, the overwhelming majority of the Prussian populace accepted national conscription. In the spring of 1813, Prussia had 42,000 regulars, 33,600 *Krümper* troops, 8,000 volunteers, and 115,000 *Landwehr* men under arms. Despite the losses suffered at Lutzen and Bautzen, the Prussians by August had 72,000 regular and 156,000 *Landwehr* infantrymen and 12,600 regular and 18,500 *Landwehr* cavalry. The Prussian army ultimately reached a peak strength of some 280,000, or 6 percent of the kingdom's total population. In September 1814 the government issued a revised draft law in order to give the conscription system a permanent long-term structure. Draftees were to serve three years in the regular army, two years in the reserve, six years in the first line *Landwehr,* seven in the second line *Landwehr,* and ten years in the *Landstrum.* Those not called to the colors also had to serve in the *Landstrum.*[70] Prussia could not have created or supported such a force by using the old methods of recruiting or organization. Only by adopting the revolutionary concept of a national conscription act was the monarchy able to field a force of sufficient size to fight the French and gain recognition from other powers of Prussia's restored great-power status.

While producing their own version of the levy en mass, the Prussians, like the French in 1793, had to organize their army into effective combat units and create a viable tactical system.

The Prussians adopted the army corps. A Prussian corps numbered about 30,000 to 32,000 men. It contained four or more large brigades. Each brigade in turn was composed of from six to nine infantry battalions. (The Prussians did not use divisions.) The corps also contained cavalry and artillery elements. The Prussian army integrated regular and *Landwehr* units on the brigade level. The *Landwehr* maintained its own uniforms and officers, but *Landwehr* regiments served side by side with regular formations. A brigade usually contained a mixture of regular, reserve, and *Landwehr* regiments. Yorck's corps in 1814, for example, contained a brigade — the 2d — that included the 1st and 2d East Prussian regiments and the 6th Silesian *Landwehr* Regiment. The 8th Brigade consisted of the Brandenburg Regiment, the 12th Reserve Regiment and the 14th *Landwehr* Regiment.[71] In 1815 the IIId Corps had nine line and twenty-one conscript battalions.[72]

The common brigading of conscript and regular regiments served roughly the same function as the amalgam of '93. The *Landwehr* and line units encouraged one another, while combining discipline and esprit in the same formation. The Prussian version of the amalgam thus paved the way for the establishment of a truly national army.

While striving to create a citizen army, the reformers also sought to produce an effective tactical system. Even before the catastrophe of 1806, Scharnhorst and others had vehemently critized the rigidity of the linear battle order. Scharnhorst noted that during the 1790s the Allies lacked a body of light infantry able to support the main force in combat. He advocated the introduction of double-company battalion columns for maneuver and assault and called for the establishment of a light infantry corps trained to operate in close cooperation with the columns.[73] The Military Reform Society, founded in 1802, acted as a vehicle for reformers. Many members noted that the linear order made it difficult, if not impossible, for commanders to seize sudden opportunities during an action. The necessity of adhering to a precise deployment scheme prevented alterations of a prearranged battle array. Consequently, tactical opportunities were usually sacrificed in the interest of proper alignment. Scharnhorst in 1800 and von Boyen in 1804 advocated training the third rank as light infantry, but before 1806, the army undertook only the most minor and inconsequential modifications of the linear system. The introduction of company sharpshooters and fusilier battalions in 1787 had almost no impact on tactics. The sharpshooters soon became noncommmissioned-officer replacement pool, and the fusilier units soon took on the characteristics of line battalions.[74] Up to 1806, Prussian tactics differed little from the tactics of Frederick the Great.

After Jena, however, even the most obdurate recognized the necessity of changing Prussian tactics. Among the tasks of the Military Reorganization Commission were the creation of new drill regulations, the introduction of battalion columns, and the creation of a body of light troops able to operate as part of the main battle force.[75]

Even before the committee completed its deliberations, field officers accepted the need for tactical change. At Eylau the Prussian contingent, led by General Lestocq, demonstrated that it could quickly learn and use some elements of the French system. In fighting Ney's corps, the Prussians at one point used five companies of line infantry as skirmishers. In another instance, a battalion column covered by skirmishers assaulted a town and then deployed into a firing line on the far side of the village.[76]

On 20 November 1807 a cabinet order based on the committee's recommendations reorganized the structure of infantry
regiments. Henceforth, line regiments contained two grenadier
companies, two musketeer battalions, and a light battalion.
The entire third rank of each line unit was to receive light infantry instruction, thus raising the percentage of troops that
could operate in open order to one-third of the total.[77]
On 3 June 1808 Frederick William issued a Provisional Instruction for the Training of Troops. The instruction called for
the teaching of aimed fire and stated that when the third rank
operated in skirmish order, firing was to be left to the judgment of junior officers and noncommissioned officers. Enlisted
men were also encouraged to use their initiative in selecting
targets. In November the government disbanded its *jaeger*
regiment and created in its place two *jaegers* and a sharp-
shooter battalion stationed in different parts of the country.
The new formations helped acquaint line infantrymen with
tirailleur tactics.[78]

Between March and July 1809 the government issued additional drill manuals. Gneisenau wrote a set of regulations for
light troops. Skirmishers, he said, were to cover the maneuvers
and deployments of lines and columns. They were also to fight
in broken terrain, mask troop movements, and fill gaps in a
battle line when necessary. A provisional infantry drill book,
issued in July, retained Greisenau's instructions for light
troops, provided details on methods of forming closed columns, and emphasized the elimination of purely ceremonial
evolutions. Henceforth, drill was to be as practical as possible.
The government also issued in July an instruction on the operation of brigades in combat. Skirmishers were to lead the advance, followed by infantry in line, in turn supported by troops
in columns. Commanders were permitted to vary this arrange-
ment according to actual combat conditions.[79]

The 1809 manuals paved the way for a more flexible tactical
system, but the various regulations lacked specific detail, and
the troops lacked the experience to use effectively the new
rules. To rectify this situation, Scharnhorst proposed, and

Frederick William accepted, the suggestion that one officer supervise all light infantry training. In February 1810 General Yorck became inspector of all light troops. He had orders to conduct maneuvers and to write instructions designed to prepare soldiers to cope with war's reality.[80]

Yorck issued his first set of light infantry drill regulations on 17 March 1810. In them he emphasized the need for uniform, realistic training that established general procedures while at the same time encouraging individual initiative. Yorck desired that, in battle, individuals apply the general rules flexibly and with due regard for specific circumstances. Yorck directed that light troops learn aimed fire and also that they learn to load their weapons in all positions, including prone. In battle, light troops were to exercise initiative, while at the same time taking care to integrate their activities with the actions of the line infantry. Light troops were to support the advance of columns and harass enemy formations with aimed fire. Skirmishers were also to be able to fight in close order formations.[81]

After extensive maneuvers, Yorck on 16 May 1811 issued a revised light infantry manual in which he again emphasized the need for light infantry to be equally proficient in regular and skirmishing tactics. In effect, he sought to end the distinction between line and light troops and sought to produce an all-purpose soldier able to employ all of the various tactical forms as required by specific conditions.[82]

Other reformers, including Clausewitz, also advocated the creation of all-purpose soldiers.[83] In January 1811 the king appointed commissions to write drill books for the infantry and cavalry. Scharnhorst chaired the infantry commission, and Yorck was an active member. The results of their labors appeared at the start of 1812.

The regulations of 1812 sought to provide a guide for action, leaving implementation to the common sense of individual commanders.[84] The drill book called for the employment of a three-rank firing line. Troops were to employ volleys or aimed fire. The regulation established an attack column of forty files by twelve ranks. The firing line's third rank was to operate either as part of the line or as skirmishers. The front ranks of every battalion were also to learn *tirailleur* tactics for use in emergency situations. In combat, skirmishers were to screen close order formations and prepare the way for assaults by use of aimed fire. In providing rules for the fusilier battalions, the regulation established the company, rather than the battalion, as the basic tactical unit. Company commanders were to organize their men in line, column, or skirmish order, depending on actual conditions. Battalion commanders were to retain general direction of the individual companies.[85]

The Prussians had thus gone even further than the French in extending tactical initiative to subordinate elements. Republican and Imperial armies relied upon the battalion as the basic tactical unit in combat. Like the French, the Prussians sought to train infantrymen to fight in either skirmish or close order formations. The Prussians then went beyond a mere copying of French tactics and encouraged even the most junior officers to display individual initiative in combat.

The 1812 regulations also established guides for action for leaders of large units. The manual suggested that a brigade move into battle with two fusilier battalions deployed as skirmishers, followed by three musketeer battalions in separate columns. A fourth battalion, the brigade's grenadiers, artillery batteries, and cavalry squadrons were to act as reserves. Commanders then enjoyed a wide range of options. The regular infantry battalions could deploy into line for a firefight or launch a column assault. Moreover, a brigade, because it was organized in depth, could shift units during combat and mount successive efforts against a foe, instead of relying on a single attack. Although somewhat imprecise in dealing with artillery and cavalry, the 1812 regulation effectively codified previous efforts to improve infantry tactics.[86]

During the campaigns of 1813, 1814, and 1815, the Prussian army was far from perfect. Many troops lacked sufficient training to be thoroughly familiar with the new tactics. Other troops were poorly armed and equipped, and the various arms often failed to coordinate their actions. On the other hand, the reformed Prussian army was more highly motivated and tactically more versatile than its Frederickan predecessor. Mechanical control and discipline had become relatively less important than the ability to respond flexibly and to exploit favorable circumstances in action.

At Lutzen Blücher successfully attacked Souham's division with two lines of columns screened by light troops.[87] At Montmirail, Yorck sent four battalions to attack the French. The two regular and two *Landwehr* battalions advanced in double-company columns behind a skirmish line.[88] At Laon two Prussian brigades in lines of columns launched a night attack.[89] During the Waterloo campaign, the Prussians lost at Ligny in part because Blücher insisted on keeping his columns on the forward slopes of a hill, thus exposing them to French artillery fire. After the battle, however, the Prussians retreated in reasonably good order. They outmarched the French to the Wavre River. There the bulk of the army pushed on to the Waterloo battlefield while the IIId Corps successfully held off Grouchy's attacks. In fighting at the Wavre, Prussian infantry, operating in open order, held the village against repeated French assaults.[90]

By 1815 the Prussians had greatly improved their tactics and overall military capacity. The soldiers were well motivated, and the officers generally adopted a flexible approach to tactical problems. By accepting the need for reform and placing the study of war on a systematic basis, the Prussians managed to create an army that could meet Napoleon's forces on an equal footing.

Ironically, European battles and military changes had little impact upon the new American nation. After 1783, the regular American army declined. In 1792 it contained only 5,000 men and declined to 3,800 men by the early 1800s. The government decided to rely primarily on the militia for national defense, but in 1792 Congress rejected proposals for a federally trained militia and left questions relating to the organization and training of the militia to the individual states. The result was a proliferation of units, training manuals, and even weapons. The militia had little combat value, but the absence of any serious threat from a major power enabled the new nation to do without a large standing force.[91]

The War of 1812, however, revealed the glaring weaknesses of the American armed forces. Using varieties of Prussian-style drill (the regulars in fact trained according to Steuben's original manual), the Americans, militia and line units alike, were rarely a match for the reformed British regiments. Even in open order combat, a style in which the Americans might have excelled, given their frontier experience, the British were superior. At Bladensburg and Buffalo, for example, British light troops easily defeated American skirmishers. Gen. W. S. Scott trained his men according to the French 1791 regulations and was able to meet the British on roughly even terms, although his light troops remained inferior to British skirmishers. Scott, moreover, was exceptional. Other commanders continued to rely on linear formations and performed poorly. Save for the Battle of New Orleans, where peninsular veterans sought to launch a frontal attack against an entrenched enemy, the British were generally dominant in field engagements.[92] The American army had not kept pace with European developments and, by 1815, was just beginning to adopt French-style tactics that the British had already surpassed.

Years of defeat ultimately convinced the European powers that tactical reforms were a basic necessity for countering French dominance. Superior diplomacy and strategy might well have been nullified had the Allied armies been unable to defeat Napoleon's forces in battle. All of the powers adopted some aspects of the French tactical system. The British, while retaining the linear battle order, created a body of light infantry to cooperate closely with the line troops. Austria and Russia adopted the battalion column and increased their number of light troops. The Prussian reformers not only copied French tactical forms but also sought to create the same spirit that motivated France's citizen soldiers.

The French had imposed a tactical revolution upon Europe's armies. Reluctantly, perhaps—but inevitably—rulers, statesmen, and generals felt compelled to begin creating a national army that used flexible tactics. Initiative replaced rigid discipline as the key to victory. After 1815, many tried to ignore the lessons of the revolutionary and Napoleonic wars. Others tried to reduce the lessons to a series of simple formulas. Flexible tactics emphasizing individual initiative were, however, the basis of future wars, and powers ignoring this fact did so at their peril.

NOTES

1. Min. de la guerre, Cartons XP3, XP81, and B1244.

2. Min. de la guerre, cartons B1237, B3381; AFIII Carton 151A.

3. R. Glover, *Peninsular Preparation: The Reform of the British Army, 1795-1809* (Cambridge, 1963), pp. 6, 117-19; J. F. C. Fuller, *British Light Infantry in the Eighteenth Century* (London, 1925), pp. 191-92.

4. Glover, *Peninsular Preparation,* pp. 86-87.

5. Ibid., p. 121; *Rules and Regulations for the Formations, Field-Exercise, and Movements of His Majesty's Forces,* British Army (London, 1798), pp. iii-iv.

6. Ibid., pp. 7, 19, 23, 81-82, 135-39.

7. Ibid., pp. 72, 77, 280; Fuller, *British Light Infantry,* pp. 173, 195-97.

8. Glover, *Peninsular Preparation,* pp. 125-26, 128-29; Fuller, *British Light Infantry,* pp. 216, 229-30; W. H. Cope, *The History of the Rifle Brigade* (London, 1877), pp. 1-2; J. F. C. Fuller, *Sir John Moore's System of Training* (London, 1925), pp. 36-38.

9. Fuller, *British Light Infantry,* p. 186.

10. Fuller, *Sir John Moore's System,* pp. 40-41, 215.

11. J. F. Maurice, ed., *The Diary of Sir John Moore,* 2 vols. (London, 1904), 2:83; W. Surtees; *Twenty-five Years in the Rifle Brigade* (London, 1833), pp. 41–42; Edward Costello, *The Peninsular and Waterloo Campaigns,* ed. A. Brett James; (London, 1967), pp. 7-8.

12. Glover, *Peninsular Preparation,* p. 29.

13. C. W. C. Oman, *Wellington's Army, 1809-1814* (1912; reprint ed., London, 1968), p. 85.

14. Cope, *History of the Rifle Brigade,* pp. 93, 103; J. Kincaid, *Adventures in the Rifle Brigade* (London, 1830), p. 103.

15. C. Oman, *A History of the Peninsular War*, 7 vols. (Oxford, 1902-30), 1:243-59; M. S. Foy, *Histoire de la guerre de la péninsule sous Napoléon*, 4 vols. (Paris, 1824), 4:333-34.

16. Oman, *History of the Peninsular War*, 1:584-91; Cope, *History of the Rifle Brigade*, pp. 34-35; J. W. Fortescue, *A History of the British Army*, 13 vols. (London, 1910-30), 6:383.

17. Oman, *History of the Peninsular War*, 2:212, 444-45.

18. Ibid., pp. 523-25.

19. Ibid., pp. 534.

20. Ibid., pp. 538-40; Fortescue, *History of the British Army*, 7:248-49.

21. E. Longford, *Wellington: The Years of the Sword* (New York, 1969), p. 216.

22. F. Espoz y Mina, *Memorias del General don Francisco Espoz y Mina: Biblioteca de autores españoles* (Madrid, 1962), 146:200-208.

23. D. Gascon, *La Provincia de Teruel en la Guerra de la Independencia* (Madrid, 1908), p. 222; *The Military Exploits etc., etc. of Don Juan Martin Diez, The Empecinado* . . . trans a general officer (London, 1823), pp. 128, 136.

24. Espoz y Mina, *Memorias*, pp. 41-42, 57, 105, 153, 200-201; J. M. Iribarren, *Espoz y Mina: el Guerrillero* (Madrid, 1965), p. 193.

25. Retraite des armées françaises d'Espagne et bataille de Vitoria, Mémoires his toriques 774.

26. D. Horward, *The Battle of Bussaco: Masséna vs. Wellington* (Tallahassee, Fla., 1965), pp. 83, 90.

27. Horward, *Battle of Bussaco*, pp. 97-128; Fortescue, *History of the British Ar my*, 7:513, 529; Oman, *History of the Peninsular War*, 3:367-81, M. Girod de l'Ain, *Vie militaire du général Foy* (Paris, 1900), pp. 102-3; M. Glover, *Wellington's Penin sular Victories* (London, 1963), p. 36.

28. Oman, *History of the Peninsular War*, 4:320-40; Fortescue, *History of the British Army*, 8:161 69.

29. Oman, *History of the Peninsular War*, 4:374-95; Fortescue, *History of the British Army*, 8:194-205; W. F. P. Napier, *History of the War in the Peninsula and in the South of France from the Year 1807 to the Year 1814*, 6 vols. (Paris, 1839), 2:330-42; J. Bouvier, *Historique du 96e régiment d'infanterie* (Lyon, 1892), p. 221.

30. Glover, *Wellington's Peninsular Victories*, pp. 72, 76-78; Napier, *History of the War in the Peninsula*, 3:106-7; Fortescue, *History of the British Army*, 8:491-96.

31. Oman, *Wellington's Army*, p. 100.

32. Fortescue, *History of the British Army*, 9:174-76.

33. Ibid., pp. 378, 437, 508.

34. M. Glover, *Wellington as Military Commander* (London, 1968), p. 189.

35. Fortescue, *History of the British Army*, 10:358, 383; J. Naylor, *Waterloo* (Lon don, 1960), pp. 169-70.

36. G. Rothenberg, "The Hapsburg Army in the Napleonic Wars," *Military Affairs* 37, no. 1 (Feburary 1973): 1.

37. Albrecht and Wilhelm, Archdukes, eds., *Ausgewählte Schriften des Erzherzogs Carl von Oesterreich*, 5 vols. (Vienna, 1893-94), 1:107-29.

38. Ibid., 5:111-14.

39. *Auszug aus dem Exercier Reglement fur die k.k. Infanterie von Jahr 1807,* Austrian Army document (Vienna, 1807), pp. 36-40, 121-23.

40. Rothenberg, "The Hapsburg Army," p. 2; Général Koch, ed., *Mémories d'André Masséna Duc de Rivoli Prince d'Essling Maréchal d'Empire,* 7 vols. (Paris, 1966-67), 6:31-32.

41. Koch, *Mémoires d'André Masséna,* 6:31.

42. E. Gachot, *1809, Napoléon en Allemagne* (Paris, 1913), p. 175; R. Home, *A Précis of Modern Tactics* (London, 1882), pp. 53-56; E. Buat, *Étude critique d'histoire militaire 1809 de Ratisbonne à Znaim,* 2 vols. (Paris, 1909), 2:253.

43. Rothenberg, "The Hapsburg Army," p. 4; O. Regele, *Feldmarschall Radetzky* (Vienna, 1957), p. 118.

44. G. Bertin, *La campagne de 1813 d'aprés des témoins oculaires* (Paris, 1895), pp. 198-99.

45. M. H. Weil, *La campagne de 1814,* 4 vols. (Paris, 1891), 1:9.

45. P. Longworth, *The Art of Victory: The Life and Achievements of Field-Marshal Suvorov* (New York 1965), pp. 214-18, 313.

47. General Grouchy, *Précis des opérations de l'Armée d'Italie depuis l'affaire de l'Adda jusqu à la bataille de Novi, Mémoires historiques* 443.

48. R. Wilson, *Brief Remarks on the Character and Composition of the Russian Army and a Sketch of the Campaigns in Poland in the Years 1806 and 1807* (London, 1810), pp. 98-101, 105, 240.

49. Ibid., p. 157.

50. Ibid., p. 9.

51. Ibid., pp. 9, 12-13.

52. D. G. Chandler, *The Campaigns of Napoleon* (New York, 1966), pp. 749-50.

53. G. Fabry, *Campagne de Russie,* 5 vols. (Paris, n.d.), 4:30-33.

54. Ibid., pp. 35-36.

55. Ibid., p. 53.

56. K. von Clausewitz, *La campagne de 1812 en Russie,* trans. M. Bégouën, (Paris, 1900), pp. 122, 127; G. Bertin, *La Campagne de 1812 d'après des témoins oculaires* (Paris, 1805), p. 99.

57. Bertin, *La campagne de 1812,* p. 112.

58. A. Duchâtelet, *Historique du 106eme régiment d'infanterie de ligne* (Chalons-sur-Marne, 1890), p. 110.

59. R. M. de Fezensac, *The Russian Compaign, 1812,* ed. and trans. L. B. Kennett, (Baton Rouge, La., 1970), p. 64; P. Berthezène, *Souvenirs militaires,* 2 vols. (Paris, 1855), 2:121-22; A. L. A. Langeron, *Mémoires de Langeron général d'infanterie dans l'armée russe campagnes de 1812, 1813, 1814* (Paris, 1902), pp. 74-75.

60. Ibid., pp. 172-76.

61. Ibid., p. 180; G. Cathcart, *Commentaries on the War in Russian and Germany in 1812 and 1813* (London, 1850), pp. 156-57, 162.

62. For general background on the reform movement, see G. A. Craig, *The Politics of the Prussian Army, 1640-1945* (Oxford, 1956), chap. 2 passim.

63. Ibid.

64. Ibid., see also G. S. Ford, *Stein and the Era of Reform in Prussia, 1807-1815* (Princeton, N.J. 1922).

65. Craig, *Politics of the Prussian Army,* p. 47.

66. Ibid., pp. 48-49.

67. Chandler, *Campaigns of Napoleon*, p. 872; W. O. Shanahan, *Prussian Military Reforms, 1786-1813* (New York, 1945), p. 178.

68. Shanahan, *Prussian Military Reforms*, pp. 173-96; E. Carrias, *L'Armée allemande son histoire, son organization, sa tactique* (Paris, 1938), p. 29.

69. Craig, *Politics of the Prussian Army*, pp. 59-60; F. N. Maude, *The Leipzig Campaign, 1813* (London, 1908), p. 58.

70. J. B. A. Charras, *Histoire de la guerre de 1813 en Allemagne* (Leipzig, 1866), pp. 226-27; Carrias, *L'Armée allemande*, pp. 30-32: Maude, *Leipzig Campaign*, pp. 151-52; F. L. Petre, *Napoleon's Last Campaign in Germany, 1813* (London, 1912), pp. 21-25.

71. J. Colin, "La Bataille de Montmirail," *Revue des études napoléoniennes* 4 (1914): 342.

72. W. H. Kelly, *The Battle of the Wavre and Grouchy's Retreat* (London, 1905), pp. 52-53.

73. F. von der Goltz, ed., *Militärische Schriften von Scharnhorst* (Berlin, 1881), pp. 226, 304-5, 309.

74. P. Paret, *Yorck and the Era of Prussian Reform 1807-1815* (Princeton, N.J., 1966), pp. 56-60.

75. Paret, *Yorck*, pp. 122-23.

76. Wilson, *Brief Remarks*, pp. 257-59.

77. Paret, *Yorck*, pp. 139-40. For training purposes, each regiment also had a depot company.

78. Ibid., pp. 141, 147-48; C. F. Gumtau, *Die Jäger und Schutzen des Preussischen Heers*, 3 vols. (Berlin, 1834), 1:216-221.

79. Paret, *Yorck*, pp. 149-52.

80. Ibid., p. 153.

81. Gumtau, *Die Jäger und Schutzen*, 3:80-100.

82. Parkinson, *Clausewitz: A Biography* (New York, 1971), pp. 124-25.

83. Ibid., p. 168.

84. Paret, *Yorck*, pp. 179-80, 182.

85. Ibid., 180-86.

86. Ibid., 187-88.

87. R. Tournes, *Lützen étude d'une manoeuvre napoléonienne* (Paris, 1931), p. 329.

88. Colin, "La Bataille de Montmirail," p. 355.

89. *Kriegsgeschichtliche Einzelschriften, vol. 12, Das Nachtgefecht bei Laon am 9 März 1814*, Prussia, General Staff, Historical Section, (Berlin, 1889), p. 777.

90. Kelly, *Battle of the Wavre*, pp. 86-87.

91. R. F. Weigley, *Towards an American Army: Military Thought from Washington to Marshall* (New York, 1962), pp. 5, 11-13, 18, 20.

92. J. Kimball, "The Battle of Chippawa: Infantry Tactics in the War of 1812," *Military Affairs* 21(19678-68): 172-74, 186; G. Tucker, *Poltroons and Patriots*, 2 vols. (New York, 1954), 2:540, 546; S. Carter, *Blaze of Glory: The Fight for New Orlenas, 1814-1815* (New York, 1971), pp. 253-61; G. R. Gleig, *The Campaigns of the British Army at Wshington and New Orlands, 1814-1815* (London, 1879), pp. 63-66, 170; W.

5

Tactical Innovation after 1815

After 1815, military leaders faced two problems: the need to absorb the experience of the Napoleonic wars and later in the century the necessity to repond to major new developments in the efficiency of weapons. These two problems produced a dichotomy in tactical thinking and practice. Concentration on Napoleonic methods created a new status quo. As Frederick's system dominated the late eighteenth century, Napoleon's became the norm for early nineteenth-century tactics. Officers studied, modified, and refined Imperial doctrine but saw no need to introduce fundamental changes. Improved weapons, on the other hand, compelled changes. Firearms attained greater range, accuracy, and rate of fire. Increased firepower ultimately spelled the end of close order combat formations and made light infantry tactics the sole effective battle order. Thus, the tactics developed in the decades after Waterloo were a product of diverse attitudes: the desire to adapt previous experience to present circumstances and the necessity to respond to conditions created by the introduction of new and improved weapons.

Despite Napoleon's ultimate defeat, the French army after 1815 continued to employ Imperial tactics, which had, after all, contributed to many spectacular victories. Moreover, there was a tendency on the part of the army to ignore Wellington's methods and attribute French failures to factors extraneous to the army's structure and doctrine. Many of the emperor's marshals decided to serve the restored Bourbon regime. They lent their prestige and experience to the Royal Army. Naturally, they used the drill and tactics they had learned during the days of the Republic and Empire. Some former Napoleonic officers wrote memoirs or military tracts wherein they too voiced their support of their former mentor's tactical doctrines.

Marmont, for example, maintained that the Napoleonic *ordre mixte* coupled with *tirailleurs* was the most effective combat formation, since it combined shock, firepower, and flexibility. He agreed with Napoleon in replacing the three-rank line with a two-rank firing line but otherwise recommended no basic changes in infantry tactics.[1] General Morand called for increased emphasis on light infantry training, but, like Marmont, he believed that columns and skirmishers working in close conjunction provided the best battle order.[2]

From Saint Helena, Bonaparte, reflecting upon his experience and upon warfare's future, added his weight to those who were satisfied with the present state of tactical arts. Infantry, Napoleon asserted, should be able to operate in both close order and skirmish formations, and training should enable individual soldiers to shift rapidly from one formation to another.[3] Since firepower was critical in combat, Napoleon noted that the linear order, with its emphasis on fire rather than on shock effect, should be the habitual combat mode, but he also asserted that columns were still useful for both assault and maneuver. An effective army, therefore, had to be prepared to employ both lines and columns, according to specific tactical conditions.[4] Napoleon recognized the value of field fortifications and advocated the introduction of a two-rank firing line, but in other repects, he remained satisfied with Republican-Imperial tactical doctrine.[5]

Baron de Jomini, the best-known military commentator of the nineteenth century, was interested primarily in devising rules for war's strategic conduct, but he also evinced an interest in tactics. In his own experience, he wrote, he had seen both linear and column formations used in battle. When employed properly, lines and assault columns were sufficient tools for an efficient commander. Textbooks used at military academies also adhered to this view. The texts sought to distill the Napoleonic experience and describe precisely when to employ specific formations, but otherwise offered nothing new.[6]

Thus, in the aftermath of the Napoleonic wars, informed Continental military opinion saw no reason to alter current tactical systems. Familiarity with Napoleonic tactics and the lack of any significant improvement in weapons' effectiveness in the years immediately following Waterloo meant that there was no challenge to the current tactical methods. Peaceful conditions, together with a general desire to stabilize a continent shaken by decades of war and revolution, created an intellectual climate of opinion opposed to major innovations. The continuing mystique of the deposed emperor sanctified his system not only for Frenchmen but also for those who had imitated him in order to defeat him.

After the second restoration, Louis XVIII reorganized his army's structure but retained Napoleonic drill and tactics. In an effort to obliterate the army's close association with the Imperial tradition, the government abolished the regimental organizations and replaced them with departmental legions. Each legion, on paper, contained two line and one light battalion, and each line battalion had a voltigeur company. The new formations never reached their full strength, and in 1820 the royal government reestablished the regimental system, creating sixty line and twenty light regiments.[7] The monarchy in 1818 also issued a drill book. The manual was, however, simply the regulations of 1791 with a Bourbon seal of approval. There were no changes.[8] When the French army entered Spain in 1823, it employed typical Napleonic tactics. The 13th Line, for example, attacked Carthagène using double-company battalion columns with a light infantry screen.[9]

In 1831 the July Monarchy revised the 1791 drill book. Issued on 4 March, the new regulations retained the three-rank firing line but allowed the employment of a two-rank line in exceptional circumstances. The new manual provided instructions for shifting from three to two ranks and back to a three-deep line. The 1831 regulation retained the double-company battalion column for maneuver and assaults, reduced the number of evolutions, and simplified the maneuvers of both lines and columns. The regulation also contained a special section on light infantry techniques. The specialist voltigeur companies were to perform light infantry functions in most circumstances, but line troops were to receive light infantry training, and in emergencies, line troops were expected to be able to operate as *tirailleurs*.[10] Thus, the first official revision of infantry tactics in forty years kept most of the 1791 system, recognizing only the value of the two-rank line in emergencies and giving formal recognition to the importance of light infantry techniques.

Improvements in infantry weapons, combined with their combat experience in Algeria, led the French in the years after 1831 to undertake further tactical reforms. Gradually, the French came to a greater appreciation of the value of firepower and skirmishing techniques.

The gradual industrialization of western Europe witnessed a marked growth in the number of inventors and a change in their status. Inventors ceased to be regarded as isolated eccentrics and became highly prized community members. New designs for producing items of mass consumption abounded, and as more and more individuals turned their attentions to devising new and better machinery, some of them, inevitably, began to examine the possibilities of designing better weapons.

As early as 1807, an English minister developed a percussion system for sporting arms by producing a lock for striking fulminate primers. Paper percussion caps also came into use during the first decade of the nineteenth century. In 1818 a Frenchman devised a percussion nipple and two years later developed a copper percussion cap. After 1820, others developed improved caps, and by the mid-1820s, metal caps were widely used by sportsmen.[11] Since the cap produced fewer misfires than the flintlock, the military began to take an interest in the new system. In 1831 the British army, for experimental purposes, adapted two hundred flintlocks to percussion firing. The newly modified weapons appeared efficient, and in 1836 the army issued percussion muskets to the guards battalions. After additional trials, a commission recommended in March 1838 that the entire army switch to percussion weapons. In May 1839 the government directed the army to convert its entire stock of flintlocks to percussion arms. The French also began to convert their weapons to the percussion system in the early 1840s and, in addition, began a limited introduction of rifled muskets. In 1837 special units in Algeria received rifled carbines firing cylindrical bullets to facilitate rapid loading.[12]

The improved weapons possessed greater accuracy and longer range than the flintlocks. They also suffered fewer misfires. Better weapons encouraged officers to reexamine their tactical systems. Campaigns in Algeria, commencing in 1830, gave the French additional impetus to improve their combat techniques. The Algerian compaigns were long and grueling. They involved long marches over rough terrain, numerous skirmishes, and occasional large engagements. The French sent both specialist light units and line regiments to Algeria.[13] Consequently, officers from all infantry branches obtained combat experience, and many of them called for tactical changes in order to respond effectively to the changed battle conditions.

Military men quickly saw a need for additional light infantry formations. In 1830 the French raised two Zouave battalions. The battalions, recruited in Algeria, contained natives, French volunteers, and other European volunteers. The Zouaves had great mobility, could operate in all sorts to terrain, and fight either as light or line infantry. In 1837 the French created a third Zouave battalion and in the following decades continued to expand the number of Zouave units. By 1852 the army contained three full regiments of Zouaves. By this time, the Zouaves were almost all native Frenchmen and operated almost exclusively as light infantrymen.[14]

In addition to the Zouaves, the French created other specialist light units. In 1840 the government created the first chasseur battalions. The Second Empire continued to expand the number of light infantry formations, and by 1854 the number of chasseur battalions had grown to twenty. The army also raised by 1854 three African light battalions and fourteen foreign legion battalions.[15]

In addition to expanding the size and role of the army's light infantry component, officers began to suggest alterations of the infantry's tactics. Marshal Bugeaud, one of France's most successful nineteenth-century commanders, summed up the tactical lessons he had learned in Algeria between 1830 and 1832. He asserted that infantry was most effective when it used aimed fire at close range. Columns were useful for marching and for battlefield maneuvers but were rarely useful in combat. Bugeaud favored the two-rank line for most fire actions. Against cavalry, he recommended a three-rank line rather than a square.[16] In 1846 the government directed that Bugeaud's book, written originally for officers in the general's own command, be distributed throughout the army. The introduction of Bugeaud's work to a wider audience reemphasized the army's increased appreciation of the value of the deployed order and the two-rank line.[17]

The army, meanwhile, demonstrated a growing interest in fire action and light infantry techniques. In July 1845 the chasseurs received a special set of drill regulations. The chasseur manual called for the use of a two-rank line and aimed fire.[18] Soldiers were to learn to deliver aimed fire from all positions, including prone.[19] Close order evolutions for the chasseurs continued to resemble the line infantry's methods as proscribed in the 1831 manual. Officers, for example, were directed to pay particular attention to training their men in these of the double-company column.[20] On the other hand, the 1845 regulations placed much emphasis on light infantry techniques, noting that companies and entire battalions could be deployed as light infantry. In such circumstances, troops were to use individual initiative in seeking cover and directing individual aimed fire against their opponents.[21] Although the 1845 regulations retained much of the Napoleonic tactical system, they did give official recognition to the growing importance of firepower and open order tactics.

Continued fighting in Algeria, plus further improvements in weapons' technology, convinced many officers of the necessity of further tactical reforms. Algerian fighting continued to follow the pattern of numerous skirmishes punctuated by occasional large clashes. Meanwhile, inventors produced a muzzle-loading percussion rifle with a rate of fire equal to that of smoothbores. In the early 1850s the French army equipped its chasseur and Zouave battalions with the new weapons and then began to supply the line units with rifles. By 1857 the entire army had received rifled muskets.[22]

The increased accuracy and range of the new weapons convinced a number of officers that still greater emphasis on open order tactics was necessary. In 1851 an infantry colonel argued that light infantry techniques had become so important that 40 percent of the infantry should be constituted as light troops.[23] Others also demanded increased tactical flexibility. Although the army did not fully comply with their demands, it did take cognizance of the calls for tactical changes. On 7 April 1852 the government directed that line infantry regiments adopt the 1845 chasseur regulations.[24]

In combat, however, the new regulations were not markedly different from Napoleonic tactics. The Second Empire introduced no major changes in the army's drill or tactical doctrine. Despite their employment of a two rank firing line and their growing recognition of the importance of aimed fire and skirmishing techniques, the armies of Napoleon III, serving in the Crimean and Italian campaigns, used tactics that would have been quite familiar to the first Napoleon.

At the Alma, 20 September 1854, the 3d Zouaves covered the 2d Division's advance. The Zouaves moved forward in a thick skirmish line supported by reserves in small columns. The reserves relieved and reinforced the skirmishers. The 2d Division advanced in a line of battalion columns while the 1st and 3d Divisions moved with a deployed line that was followed by a second line of columns.[25]

During the Italian campaign, the Austrians had better rifles. To counter this superiority, the French, by use of columns and skirmishers, sought to close quickly with their foes. Moreover, the terrain, hilly country dotted with numerous villages, further encouraged the employment of columns of assault and light infantry.[26]

On 20 May 1859 at Montebello, the 17th Chasseur Battalion, the 84th Line Regiment, and the 74th Line Regiment advanced to the village in skirmish order.[27] On 31 May a Zouave regiment attacking Palestro sent four companies forward as light infantry, followed by a battalion in a double-company column. Two Sardinian battalions supported the Zouaves and advanced in open order. The French and Sardinians engaged Austrian *jaegers* in and around the town. Both sides used individual aimed fire combined with short rushes from cover to cover throughout the engagement.[28]

On 3 June the French IId Corps stormed Robecchetto. An Algerian light infantry regiment sent in two battalions. Both battalions sent forward half their men in open order and kept the remainder in columns to act as relief and reinforcement.[29] The following day, the French and Austrian main forces clashed at Magenta. In assaulting the town of Magenta, the French fed troops into the village in column, whereupon they dispersed and fought individually or in small groups. On other parts of the field, commanders employed tactics as dictated by specific battlefield conditions. Guard Grenadiers and Zouave battalions at one point deployed into line and engaged in fire action. The 8th Chasseur Battalion and 23d Line Regiment fought in skirmish order while the 71st Line sent in a battalion assault column covered by two other battalions in linear order. The 52d Line and 45th Line attacked with columns screened by light infantry. Entire divisions during the engagement advanced in line; others moved in a line of double-company columns at deploying distance.[30] As in a Napleonic battle, commanders employed standard tactical forms and adapted them to battlefield conditions.

At Melegnano on 9 June, a chasseur and a Zouave battalion entered the village in column and then dispersed and fought in small groups.[31] Similar tactics prevailed at the Battle of Solferino, fought on 24 June. The 45th Line, covered by skirmishers, rushed a small town in column. The 1st Guard Division advanced behind a *tirailleur* screen in a line of columns, as did several line divisions. The 2d Guard Division advanced in two deployed firing lines. A battalion of the 76th Line and the 6th Chasseur Battalion took cover in a woods and directed aimed fire against Austrian positions while battalions from the 52d Line and 85th Line sent in battalion assault columns. Frequently, specialist and regular battalions advanced by short rushes, taking advantage of the cover offered by terrain features. Once near the Austrians, the French would deliver a final bayonet assault. Shaken by the effects of aimed fire, the Austrians often retreated when they saw the French storming toward them.[32]

Throughout the Italian campaign, the French employed tactics that closely resembled the techniques used by Napoleon I. Napoleon III's army was a long-service professional force that used conscription to fill the gaps left by volunteering. The wealthy could purchase exemption from the draft, and the emperor used the proceeds to offer reenlistment bounties. Officers believed in their professional army and practical experience. They mistrusted military theory, an attitude that reinforced the tendency to adhere to known traditional tactics. Despite improved weapons, the introduction of a two-rank firing line, and an increase in the number of troops performing light infantry tasks, Second Empire tactics were not very different from those of the First Empire. The battalion remained the basic combat element. The firing line, the column by division for maneuver and assault, and skirmishers, operating in support of close order formations, continued to characterize French battlefield techniques.

The victories in Africa, the Crimea, and Italy convinced most officers that French tactics were basically sound and in need of no fundamental changes. Drill books issued in 1860 and 1862 offered no departures from the regulations of 1845.[33] In 1867 regulations for battalion operations stated that, generally, an eight-company battalion would advance with two companies in front as skirmishers and six in column. Upon coming into range, the six companies would deploy for fire action while the skirmishers protected the flanks. After shaking the enemy with volley and aimed fire, the battalion would reform into a column and, covered by the skirmishers, charge.[34]

The decisive Prussian victory at Königgrätz, however, led some French officers to doubt the efficacy of their tactics. General Trochu, a former aide-de-camp to Marshal Bugeaud, asserted in 1867 that French drill regulations were too mechanical. The 1791 regulations were, he said, copied from Prussian methods and were never applied in combat. Working from the drill manual rather than from experience, the authors of the 1831 regulations produced a set of instructions that, save for minor details, was as rigid and formal as the '91 rules. Except for minor details, the regulations of 1845 and 1862 were in turn mechanical copies of earlier manuals.[35]

Although he did not recognize that the 1791 regulations were quite flexible for their time, Trochu did realize that advances in weapons technology imposed the necessity for sweeping changes in tactical doctrine. Weapons were rapidly becoming efficient; rifles had improved their range, rate of fire, and accuracy, and aimed fire was ever more deadly and more critical in battle. French tactics had to adjust to these new conditions, they had to evolve in the direction of greater individual initiative and greater emphasis on firepower. Thus, mechanical evolutions had to give way to a more flexible tactical system.[36]

Armand du Picq, another of Bugeaud's protegees, wrote, but did not publish, a searching study of tactical doctrine. His own experience, historical studies, and probing questions directed to his brother officers formed the basis of his concepts.[37]

Armies, du Picq argued, must have unity and confidence or they are mobs, and mobs do not win battles. Discipline and drill are the means of obtaining unity and confidence. Discipline and drill also prepare the soldier for combat. Success in battle, according to du Picq, is in large measure a matter of morale, which in turn is a matter of reliability, unity, and confidence. Drill must, therefore, enhance these qualities in individual soldiers.[38]

In ancient battles, drill and combat were virtually identical, thus easing the commander's problems of instilling his troops with good morale. There existed, du Picq argued, no such resemblance in modern battle.[39] Modern battles involved open order tactics and fire action. Consequently, soldiers must have confidence in their comrades and in their officers, and only realistic training could instill such unity and confidence throughout the organization.[40]

French training, de Picq went on to assert, was inadequate because close order methods had almost no value in modern combat. Columns charging with the bayonet simply could not produce a shock effect. There was in a column no physical impulse and no force of mass. Column charges succeeded only if the enemy was already demoralized and fled before crossing bayonets with the attackers. Thus, a column could produce only a moral impulse, and, against a steady force, the column would not only fail but also sustain heavy losses.[41]

Du Picq's solution was to rely heavily upon open order tactics. "The whole science of combat lies . . . in the happy proper combination of the open order, scattered to secure destructive effect, and a good disposition of troops in formation as supports and reserves so as to finish by moral effect the action of the advanced troops."[42] The thick line of skirmishers was essential in combat, especially as weapons became more deadly. A solid front was no longer necessary, and commanders should send out small groups of skirmishers and, when necessary, throw reinforcements into the intervals. Training should reflect this reality in order to prepare soldiers for real war and give them confidence in themselves and in their comrades.[43]

Both Trochu and de Picq recognized that fire action and open order tactics were becoming increasingly more decisive, but they were prophets without honor. Although they introduced a breech-loading rifle and a hand-cranked, multibarrel machine gun in the late 1860s, Napoleon III and his advisers refused to contemplate fundamental changes in the army's tactical doctrine. The new machine guns were, for example, placed with artillery rather than with infantry units. The French made minor adjustments in response to improvements in weaponry, but most officers felt that their tactical doctrine had proven effective in battle and needed no major overhaul.

The British, having emerged victorious in 1815, believed that their tactics were superior to those of any continental rival. The Duke of Wellington, active in the House of Lords, gave his blessing to the doctrines he had used so effectively, and historians like Napier glorified the Duke's methods. Napier, for example, noted that the two-rank line was invariably superior to the assault column. In 1824 revised field regulations called for the employment of the two-rank line in all fire actions.[44] Like the French, the British were willing to respond to technological change but felt no need to contemplate drastic changes in their tactics.

During the five decades after Waterloo, the British army fought numerous campaigns. Despite varying climates, terrain, and enemies, the English remained devoted to Wellingtonian tactics. Victory in most of their campaigns reinforced their general opinion that the two-rank line sustained by light infantrymen was sufficient to bring victory in almost all circumstances.

While remaining committed to their traditional tactics, military leaders recognized the importance of new weapons. In

1839 the army adopted the percussion musket, and in the 1840s noncommissioned received rifled muskets. In 1853 riflemen received the Miné rifle, which fired a cylindro-conoidal bullet, and in 1854 the entire army adopted the Enfield Patent 1853 rifled musket, which had an effective range of about eight hundred yards.[45]

In numerous campaigns in India, British tactics were effective. In Nepal the British relied heavily upon skirmishing tactics. In Burma the British defeated tribesmen who employed foxholes, and in Afghanistan the British, after losing an entire expeditionary force to guerrilla-style warriors, finally emerged triumphant.[46] In the two Sikh wars of the 1840s, the British faced opponents organized and trained along Continental lines, and the engagements bore an eerie resemblance to the peninsular battles.

Alarmed by the growth of British power in India, Sikh rulers turned to former Napoleonic officers to train their armies. After 1815, Jean Ventura, a former Imperial infantry officer, organized a model brigade. The brigade resembled a French brigade in both structure and tactics. Words of command were given in French, and Ventura used French drill books to train the Sikhs. By 1831 the Sikhs had twenty-one battalions trained according to French tactics, and by 1839 Sikh infantry strength had grown to thirty-one battalions, containing about 30,000 men. Claude Auguste Court, a former French officer, and Paolo Avitable, a Neapolitan, who had served with Murat, remodeled Sikh artillery. By the early 1840s the Sikhs had cast over five hundred field guns of the Gribeauval pattern, and horse batteries accompanied each infantry brigade.[47]

At the Battle of Mudki, 18 December 1845, Sikh gunners inflicted heavy losses, and their infantry fought doggedly. British and native infantry, advancing in a two-rank line, gradually pushed them back. At Ferozeshur, 21 and 22 December 1845, British and East Indian Company infantry again moved forward in a two-rank firing line, stormed the Sikh entrenchments, and beat back enemy counterattacks. Their disciplined volleys decided the engagements.[48] The British used similar tactics at Aliwal in January 1846. The Sikhs used skirmishers and field fortifications and pushed guns up to the first line, but they were often divided among themselves and failed to cooperate even on the battlefield. In these circumstances, superior British discipline was decisive.[49]

During the second Sikh war, both sides fought according to their own doctrine. At the siege of Muttan, September 1848, the British advanced in line with a skirmish screen. At Chillianwalla, 13 January 1849, part of the British force broke into small groups and fought in open order because of the terrain, but other regiments advanced and fought in line. At Gujerat, 21 February 1849, the British again advanced in line. The Sikhs attempted to penetrate a gap between two British divisions, but British field guns halted the enemy columns.[50]

During the Crimean war, the first major British clash with a European power since Waterloo, tactics again resembled the methods employed during the Peninsular Campaign. The Russians used double-company battalion columns with a skirmish screen, and the British relied upon the two-rank line supported by light infantrymen. The fact that Lord Raglan had fought at Waterloo served only to strengthen Britain's reliance on her traditional tactical doctrine.

At the Battle of the Alma, 20 September 1854, the British drew up in a line several miles long and tried to advance across very rough terrain. The skirmishers preceding the main force had little trouble traversing the broken ground. They then dueled successfully with Russian light troops. The line infantry, however, soon lost cohesion. Some regiments did manage to maintain their formations, but others became fragmented and had to move forward in small bands.[51]

Fortunately for the British, the Russians persisted in employing battalion columns, and the Russian infantry carried smoothbore muskets that were inferior in range and accuracy to the British rifled weapons. Consequently, when the Russians sought in a series of poorly coordinated attacks to hit the fragmented British line, their assaults withered away in the face of superior firepower.

The Kazan Regiment advanced in a massive column, but the 7th Regiment in line halted it before the Russians ever got within range. The Vladmir Regiment also advanced in a deep column. It too fell victim to the Miné rifles of the grenadiers. The Highland Brigade, in a line a mile long, then advanced and forced the Russians facing them to retreat.[52]

The British won at the Alma not because of superior generalship or better tactics but because of superior weapons. Had the British and Russian infantry employed equivalent weapons, Raglan's army might well have suffered a severe mauling. Unlike Wellington, who was a master of terrain, Raglan sent his troops over terrain that made it almost impossible for units to maintain a coherent line. The Miné rifle's superirority to the Russian musket, however, prevented the Russians from taking advantage of the British line's fragmentation. Uncoordinated Russian columns failed to defeat the fragmented British line because the English were able to attain fire superiority.

Inkermann, fought on 16 November 1854, was also a soldier's battle. Fog and rough terrain allowed even less command control than Raglan exercised at Alma. Again, the line bolstered by superior firepower withstood the assault column. The 47th, for example, resisted in line, and the 41st and 77th fired and charged in linear order. Many units of the 2d Division fought in open order because of the terrain, while other units fought in the standard manner.[53]

Victory in the Crimea and the successful supression of the Indian mutiny reinforced the conviction that the two-rank line sustained by skirmishers was sufficient in almost all circumstances. One officer insisted that rifled weapons were not a particularly important innovation. Skirmishers with rifles, he argued, could not win battles. A line that fired and charged with the bayonet was the only decisive key to victory. The rifle did permit the line to open fire at longer ranges, but the existence of rifled weapons brought no fundamental tactical changes.[54] Another officer complained that the army had become so self-satisfied that no reform proposal could ever receive a fair hearing.[55] Prior to 1866, the British saw no compelling reason to alter their tactical doctrine. Its success on battlefields stretching around the globe convinced most military figures that the tactics developed in the early part of the century were still viable. Improvements in weapons technology, far from compelling change, merely made conventional tactics more effective.

The Russians were also basically satisfied with the tactical system they had created during the Napoleonic wars. After 1815, the czars maintained a large standing army and used it in numerous campaigns against the Persians, Turks, Poles, Hungarians, French, and English. In 1826 the active army comprised 610,000 men, of whom 497,700 were infantry.[56] The conservatism of the Russian ruling class, along with the army's success in campaigns up to 1856, served to enshrine Napoleonic tactics and to convince the military that change was unnecessary.

The infantry employed the *ordre mixte* and the three-rank firing line. Training emphasized the battalion assault column and the bayonet attack, and an 1837 textbook used in officer training courses emphasized the continuing value of the tactics used at Eylau and Borodino.[57] In the 1840s the Russian army began to use percussion muskets, but since firing was done by battalion volleys, the army neglected to place much emphasis on aimed fire. Nor did military men pay careful attention to open order techniques. The number of units designated as light infantry was large: every division had a light regiment, and forty-eight men in each line company were supposed to be able to function as skirmishers. The light infantry units, however, trained and functioned like the line battalions. Their light infantry characteristics became a historical memory rather than a functional reality. Each army corps had a rifle battalion equipped with muzzle-loading weapons, but the Russian riflemen, although they did actually operate in open order, constituted a very small percentage of the army's strength.[58]

In battle, the Russians clung to their traditional methods. In the Caucassus and in some of the Turkish campaigns, individual commanders directed their men to use aimed fire and open order tactics. These leaders were, however, exceptions. In most engagements, the czar's men used the *ordre mixte*.[59] In the Crimea, the Russians habitually used assault columns that usually failed in the face of superior firepower and tactics. During the siege of Sebastopol, Russian infantrymen used small rifle pits with sandbags for protection. Rows of pits were eventually connected by trenches, thus enabling the defenders to prolong their resistance. Russia's field armies, however, failed to drive off the Allied siege force, and the city ultimately fell. The severe defeat in the Crimea, coupled with the death of Nicholas I, created conditions that caused military leaders to reexamine their tactical system. Even then progress was slow, and the Russian army continued to emphasize volley firing and bayonet assaults long after other powers changed their tactical doctrines to place increased emphasis on aimed fire and initiative.[60]

The Hapsburg armies also remained tied to their old tactics, which emphasized linear combat. Marshal Radetsky tried to devise more flexible tactics, and in 1834 he completed a new drill book. He trained the regiments stationed in Italy according to the new regulations and defeated the Italian efforts to throw off Austrian domination and to attain statehood in 1848-49. In 1853 the government adopted Radetsky's drill book for the entire army.[61] Radetsky's manual retained most of the 1807 regulations. He did call for greater use of columns for maneuver while troops were engaged in battle and sought to provide greater coordination among the infantry, cavalry, and field artillery. He also emphasized that commanders in battle should exercise the option of modifying the formal rules if circumstances so required.[62] The 1853 manual retained the three-rank line. Some of the troops in the third rank were equipped with rifles and acted as skirmishers. In addition, thirty-two rifle battalions were available for light infantry operations. The 1853 manual allowed bayonet attacks either in line or column but placed its major emphasis on linear combat. A regiment was supposed to advance with its first line deployed and the second line in battalion columns ready to act as support.

During the Italian war, the Austrians, despite the introduction of muzzle-loading rifles, continued to employ the linear order of battle. At Magenta, for example, an Austrian brigade moved forward with a light infantry battalion as a screen. Behind the light troops marched four deployed battalions, and behind them came three more deployed battalions.[64] At Solferino some Austrian regiments entrenched themselves. A Hungarian regiment formed a square to resist cavalry while the 35th Regiment charged in line. Even a number of frontier regiments fought in linear order.[65]

After their defeats, the Austrians revised their drill regulations. The Hapsburgs decided to imitate the French, and a new drill manual, issued in 1862, emphasized shock action and the extensive use of battalion assault columns.[66] Thus, the Hapsburgs began to emphasize shock tactics and close order methods at precisely the time that their next major foe—Prussia—was perfecting a tactical system based heavily on firepower, individual initiative, and open order tactics.

After 1815, the Prussians continued to study past wars and tried to derive from them lessons applicable to future conflicts. The army soon became interested in improved infantry weapons, and Prussia became the first power to adopt rifled breech-loading weapons. Johann Dreyse invented a rifle that loaded at the breech in 1839. This was the first bolt-action rifle to chamber a complete cartridge. The Dreyse needle gun had an effective range of about a thousand paces and could fire five to seven rounds per minute. The range was less than that of the rifled musket, but the rate of fire was much faster. Officers realized that there were risks involved in adopting a breechloader. Troops might fire off their ammunition too quickly, and the ease of firing from a prone position might encourage soldiers to seek cover at the expense of a unit's cohesion. The advantages of a breechloader — simplicity of loading, rapid rate of fire, and the ability to fire from a variety of positions — seemed to outweigh the drawbacks. In December 1840 the army adopted the needle gun and began to issue it to selected formations in 1841. By 1849 there were 268,000 Dreyse rifles available, and by the late 1850s guard regiments and at least one battalion in each line regiment possessed breechloaders. By 1865 the entire army was equipped with Dreyse rifles.[67]

The Prussians also realized that their new infantry weapons required major modifications in tactical doctrine. After Waterloo, the Prussians continued to use the 1812 regulations, which called for a combination of skirmish and close order tactics. Light troops began attacks, and the main body maneuvered in battalion columns. According to battlefield circumstances, the columns would deploy into line or charge.[68]

The introduction of the breech-loading rifle convinced the military of the need to place greater emphasis on firepower. In 1847 new regulations allowed the use of smaller company columns for maneuver and assaults. Skirmishers preceded the main body in action, and commanders could direct the company columns to form a firing line, launch a bayonet attack, or reinforce the skirmishers. The 1847 manual allowed entire companies, rather than just the third rank, to operate as *tirailleurs*. A battalion could send forward two companies as skirmishers and retain two as a reserve. The commander could, if necessary, send forward his remaining companies to bolster the skirmish line. Although senior officers continued to show a preference for the battalion column, the 1847 rules made it theoretically possible for all infantry to operate as skirmishers. Moreover, junior officers did experiment with the company column, gained experience in independent command, and learned to understand the potentialities of open order methods.[69]

The 1847 regulations were to serve the Prussians well in 1866, when for the first time an entire army used breech-loading rifles. Intelligently applied, the regulations demonstrated the growing importance of firepower and open order tactics on modern battlefields.

The opening engagements of the Austro-Prussian war clearly demonstrated Prussia's technical and tactical superiority. At Podol on 25 June, the Austrians employed battalion assault columns, while the Prussians relied on individual aimed fire. The Austrians retreated after losing 1,048 men. The Prussians suffered only 130 casualties. On 27 June the Austrians attacked Nachod in columns. They lost 5,700 men. The Prussians fought in an irregular skirmish line. They relied on fire rather than on shock and sustained only 1,122 casualties. On the same day, the Austrians at Trautenau defeated a smaller Prussian force and again suffered disproportionate losses.[70]

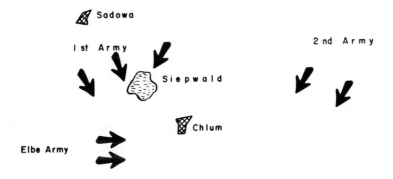

BATTLE OF KONIGGRATZ
3 JULY ~~1886~~
1866

Sadowa

1st Army

Siepwald

2nd Army

Chlum

Elbe Army

On 3 July 1866 the main armies met at Königgrätz. Despite inferior artillery and the staggered arrival of reinforcements, Prussian superiority of infantry fire provided the margin of victory. Throughout the engagement, the Prussians maneuvered in company columns and fought in skirmish lines. Generally, companies advanced with skirmishers in front. Upon making contact with the enemy, the skirmishers delivered aimed fire, and the remainder of the company relieved or reinforced the skirmishers.[71]

During the battle, Prussian infantry fought in the Swiepwald. They fought in open order and inflicted huge casualties on the Austrians before retreating. On other parts of the front, the Austrians attacked with battalion columns screened by skirmishers, and in every instance took heavy losses. At Chulm the Austrians lost 5,800 men in a single attack. In the entire engagement, the Prussians lost 9,153 men, while the Austrians sustained 43,000 casualties, a vivid testimony of the impact of rifled, breech-loading weapons combined with open, flexible tactics.[72]

The tactics employed by the great powers, especially French methods, had a significant influence not only on the smaller European states but also on non-European nations.

After gaining independence from Holland the Belgians proceeded to adopt French drill books, and employed French officers to train and inspect their regiments.[73] The Sardinians also copied French drill regulations. During the Italian war, the Sardinian 5th Division at Solferino attacked in a line of columns. The 11th and 12th Sardinian regiments also launched bayonet attacks.[74]

States far removed from Europe also copied European tactics. Egypt had numerous contacts with France. After 1815, the de facto Egyptian ruler, Mehemet Ali, who had fought Napoleon in 1799, organized his forces along French lines. His infantry tried to operate like Imperial soldiers, and Mehemet Ali even created horse artillery batteries to provide close artillery support to the footsoldiers. In June 1839 his army went into action against the sultan's forces. The Egyptian army drew up in two lines of double-company battalion columns. Light infantry covered the columns, and horse artillery batteries accompanied the infantry. The Egyptians attacked in column. Columns in the second line passed through the intervals in the first and launched bayonet attacks.[75]

In Asia the Sikhs copied French weapons and tactics, while in South America the revolutionary armies tended to imitate British methods. During the wars of independence, Bolivar employed thousands of British veterans. In 1819, for example, his army contained about 800 British and 200 German soldiers. In addition, he raised a British rifle battalion.[76] At the Battle of Boyaca, 7 August 1819, Bolivar's army advanced in columns screened by skirmishers and then deployed into line for combat. His army's drill was based primarily on British regulations.[77] Between 1817 and 1824 about 6,000 foreigners, most of whom were veterans of the British army, served the South American revolutions. Bolivar employed the volunteers as both fighters and instructors. After the victory over Spain, seven British volunteers became generals in the South American republics and perpetuated British tactics in the New World.[78]

The United States, despite its frontier experience and its open, adventurous environment, persisted in imitating European tactical doctrine. At West Point both staff and students carefully studied Napoleon's strategy and tactics. In 1815 Sylvanus Thayer went to Europe and bought about a thousand military texts, mostly French, and French was the only modern language taught at the academy. D. H. Mahan, after studying at the Metz artillery school, joined the faculty. For the remainder of his teaching career, he proclaimed to class after class that the modern soldier, to be a capable leader, had to study Napoleonic tactics.[79] Mahan's textbook on tactics called for a two-rank firing line and for the employment of battalion columns for maneuver and assault. In action, light troops, preceding the columns, would seek to disrupt the enemy line by use of aimed fire. The columns would then form a firing line or deliver a bayonet charge, according to circumstances.[80] Instructors and cadets formed a Napoleon Club where they discussed the emperor's methods, and Jomini was standard reading for cadets throughout most of the nineteenth century.[81]

Graduates of West Point entered an army that was organized along French lines. General Scott during the War of 1812 drilled his men according to the French 1791 regulations. In 1815 the government appointed Scott to head a board charged with reviving the army's drill. In February 1815 the board adopted French drill regulations for all infantry regiments.[82]

During the first half of the century, American drill books called for a three-rank line, with the third rank loading weapons for the front ranks. The drill books permitted the occasional use of a two-rank line, a rule similar to that of the French 1831 regulations. American manuals also gave directions for the formation of double-company columns.[83] Many militia manuals followed the regulations used by the Federal infantry. Militia regulations sought to instruct troops in methods of shifting rapidly from column to line and back to column. Some militia manuals provided instructions for skirmishers.[84]

During the Mexican War, American forces, a mixture of regulars and volunteers, fought in a manner that would have been thoroughly familiar to European professionals. At Palo Alto, for example, the Americans deployed from column into line while flanking units formed squares to counter Mexican cavalry. American artillery accompanied the advance and helped repulse mounted and infantry assaults. At Resaca de la Palma the rough terrain forced the American infantry to go into action in open order. At Monterrey assault columns, covered by light infantry, rushed the city's defenses. At Buena Vista the Mexicans had three light regiments. They skirmished with American regulars and Texas volunteers. The Mexicans then moved their main force forward in column and deployed it into line. The Americans also fought in line with horse artillery batteries in close support.[85]

During the Civil War, French influence on both Union and Confederate tactics remained strong. Since both sides equipped their soldiers with rifled weapons, they found themselves compelled to modify the accepted tactical system to respond to the impact of increased firepower.

At the start of hostilities, both sides trained their armies according to French drill manuals. The Confederates used Hardee's *Rifle and Light Infantry Tactics*. Hardee's work was based on the French regulations of 1845.[86] The American army had adopted it in 1855. Hardee joined the southern cause in 1861, and, perhaps because of this, the Federal forces issued their own drill book in 1862. Casey's *Infantry Tactics* differed little from Hardee's manual. Like Hardee, Casey based his tactics on the French regulations of 1831 and 1845.[87] Both sets of regulations recognized the importance of light infantry, noting that whole companies and even entire battalions could, if necessary, operate as skirmishers.[88] American tactics, however, continued to rely primarily on columns for maneuver and deployed lines for fire action. The two-rank firing line was still the basic combat formation.[89]

Throughout the war, many commanders continued to employ official doctrine. At Shiloh the Confederate army formed a thick skirmish line across its front. Behind it, Bragg's troops moved in a line of columns, and Polk's men formed a column of deployed brigades.[90] At Antietam Doubleday's division moved forward in two deployed lines. Williams, Green, Sedgwick, and French formed their divisions in a similar manner. During the battle, two regiments, the 51st New York and 51st Pennsylvania, charged a bridge in column. Light infantry covered the column and, after taking the bridge, the regiments then deployed into line.[91] At Fredericksburg a Federal division advanced in a column of deployed brigades covered by skirmishers.[92] Pickett's famous assault column at Gettysburg consisted of a line of skirmishers followed by successive lines of deployed battalions.[93] At Kenesaw Mountain Newton's division advanced in a column of deployed regiments.[94]

Since both armies carried weapons that could kill or wound

at a thousand yards, attacks by successive lines of deployed infantry were always costly and usually failed.[95] Gradually, officers and men began to devise new tactical techniques for both attack and defense. Attackers began to use more open, flexible assault formations. Defenders resorted to field entrenchments.

At Fort Donelson the 8th Missouri and 11th Indiana advanced by short rushes, halting periodically behind convenient cover to suppress enemy fire, and then resumed their advance.[96] At Antietam the 9th New York moved in a similar manner. Individuals advanced in short rushes. The troops then crawled into a rough line and made a short dash forward. At Spottsylvania Upton's brigade advanced under cover to within a short distance from the enemy lines. The brigade then launched its attack in close order. Other regiments, including the 5th Maine, 121st New York, and 96th Pennsylvania, also went into the attack using short rushes from cover to cover.[97]

Troops also began to make extensive use of field entrenchments. During the Peninsular Campaign, both sides constructed rifle pits and redoubts and used natural cover whenever possible. At Beaver Dam and Gaines Mill, Union infantry took cover behind fences and in ditches and dry streambeds. They also cut down trees to create obstacles and cover.[98] At Fredericksburg part of Lee's army established itself behind a stone wall, and at Gettysburg the 14th Connecticut, 71st Pennsylvania, 39th New York, 111th New York, 1st Delaware, and 12th New Jersey used walls and fences for protection. The 59th New York, 7th Michigan, and 20th Massachusetts dug shallow trenches or packed dirt around piled fence rails.[99]

During the Wilderness battles, both sides entrenched whenever possible. Confederate trenches at Spottsylvania had head logs, rifle slits, and traverses, and at Petersburg Lee's army held a trench system thirty-five miles long. Even small units in minor actions constantly entrenched themselves. On 13 February 1865, for example, the 11th Massachusetts advanced in line, and the troops dug in as soon as they made contact with the enemy. In March the 7th New Jersey and 40th New York made small probes of the enemy lines. They advanced and dug rifle pits as soon as the enemy opened fire.[100] During the Atlanta Campaign, Sherman noted: "I rarely saw a dozen of the enemy at any one time, and these were always skirmishers . . . who occasionally showed their heads above hastily constructed but remarkably strong rifle trenches."[101] Sherman also noted that even atacking armies invariably went for cover when the enemy opened fire. He concluded that the impact of increased firepower meant that field entrenchments had to become a critical tactical element in all combats. He also felt that, in the future, infantry would have to operate in thin, dispersed attack formations that relied heavily upon individual initiative.[102] General Schofield also noted that modern weapons rendered useless close order assault formations.[103] Light infantry was no longer to pave the way for close order formations. Skirmishing was to be the sole form of combat.

After 1815, military men tried to absorb the lessons of the Napoleonic Wars. Armies retained the tactical systems developed during the conflict-filled decades and afterward sought only modificatons of specific details. Improvements of infantry weapons — the percussion system, muzzle-loading rifles, and breech-loading rifles — forced additional change. Weapons enjoyed increased range, greater accuracy, and a more rapid rate of fire. Firepower became ever more decisive on European, African, Asiatic, and American battlefields. Many military men did not rapidly conclude that firepower had become the decisive tactical element. Few realized that the Enfield rifle, not the two-rank line, was the key to victory at the Alma and at Inkermann. The Austrians after 1859 even concluded that the key to success in battle was shock, not fire. Experience taught the Americans that the rifle and field entrenchment were dominant and made massed attacks almost impossible. The Prussians also realized the value of firepower. They early adopted a breech-loading rifle and revised their drill to place greater initiative in the hands of junior officers.

The Battle of Königgrätz demonstrated to Europeans, as the Civil War had shown Americans, that henceforth effective tactics had to emphasize firepower, open order tactics, and individual initiative.

NOTES

1. A. Marmont, *On Modern Armies*, trans. Captain Lendy (London, 1865), pp. 18-19, 25; idem, *The Spirit of Military Institutions*, trans. F. Schaller (Columbia, S. C., 1864), pp. 45, 49, 61.

2. Commandant Thiry, *Histoire de la tactique de l'infanterie française de 1791 à 1905* (Paris, 1905), p. 2; Général Thoumas, *Les Transformations de l'armée française*, 2 vols. (Paris, 1887), 2:447-48.

3. Napoleon, *Commentaires de Napoléon Premier,* 6 vols. (Paris, 1867), 6:7-8, 15-17.

4. Ibid., pp. 172, 174, 500.

5. Ibid., pp. 174, 280.

6. A. de Jomini, *The Art of War* (Philadelphia, 1862), p. 302.

7. Lieutenant Colonel Belhomme, *Histoire de l'infanterie en France*, 5 vols. (Paris, n.d.), 5:76-77, 122.

8. Ibid., p. 47.

9. E. Hennet de Goutel, ed., *Mémoirs du général Marquis Alphonse d'Hautpoul Pair de France 1789-1865* (Paris, 1906), pp. 145-46.

10. *Ordonnance sur l'exercise et les manoeuvres de l'infanterie du 4 mars 1831*, French Army document (Paris, 1849), pp. i-ii, xiv-xv, xxxiii-xxxiv.

11. H. L. Blackmore, *British Military Firearms, 1650-1850* (London, 1961), pp. 160, 163; H. B. Pollard, *A History of Firearms* (London, 1926), p. 119; L. Winant, *Early Percussion Firearms* (New York, 1959), pp. 4, 33, 112.

12. Blackmore, *British Military Firearms*, pp. 167, 177, 178-82; Pollard, *History of Firearms*, pp. 119, 123.

13. J. Regnault, "Les campagnes d'Algerie et leur influence de 1830 à 1870," *Revue historique de l'Armée* (December, 1953), p. 24. Some sixty-seven line regiments served tours in Algeria between 1830 and 1854.

14. A. Marjoulet, *Historique du 3e régiment de Zouaves* (Paris, 1887), pp. 13-16.

15. Belhomme, *Histoire de l'infanterie*, 5:330-31; G. McClellan, *The Armies of Europe Comprising Descriptions in Detail of the Military Systems of England, France, Russia, Prussia, Austria, and Sardinia* (Philadelphia, 1862), pp. 57-59.

16. J. R. Maréchal Bugeaud, *Aperçus sur quelques détails de la guerre* (Paris, 1846), pp. 119-20, 148-50.

17. Ibid., pp. i-x.

18. *Ordonnance du Roi 22 juillet 1845 sur l'exercise et les manoeuvres des battalions de chasseurs à pied*, French Army document (Paris, 1845), pp. 3, 95, 102-5.

19. Ibid., pp. 5, 19.

20. Ibid., p. 199.

21. Ibid., p. 170 ff.

22. Pollard, *History of Firearms*, p. 123.

23. Colonel Decker, *Les trois armes ou tactique divisionnaire* (Paris, 1851), pp. 13, 26.

24. Belhomme, *Histoire de l'infanterie*, 5:316.

25. Thoumas, *Les Transformations*, 2:451; C. A. Fay, *Souvenirs de la Guerre de Crimée, 1854-1856* (Paris, 1889), pp. 56, 131; Marjoulet, *Historique du 3e Régiment de Zouaves*, pp. 41-42.

26. E. M. Lloyd, *A Review of the History of Infantry*, (London, 1908), pp. 241-42.

27. C. L. baron de Bazancourt, *La Compagne de Italie de 1859*, 2 vols. (Paris, 1859), 1:134-37.

28. Ibid., pp. 175, 179-82.

29. H. C. Wylly, *The Campaign of Magenta and Solferino, 1859* (London, 1907), p. 106.

30. Bazancourt, *La Campagne d'Italie*, 1:262-64, 269-70, 309; A. Duquet, *La Guerre d'Italie (1859)* (Paris, 1882), pp. 71, 91-92, 96-97; G. Berthoffer, *Historique du 52e régiment d'infanterie* (Paris, 1890), p. 188.

31. Bazancourt, *La Campagne d'Italie*, 2:60-63.

32. Ibid., pp. 204, 212-16; Wylly, *Campaign of Magenta and Solferino*, p. 207; Duquet, *La Guerre d'Italie*, pp. 153, 264.

33. Thoumas, *Les Transformations*, 2:455; *Instruction sur l'exercice et les manoeuvres de l'infanterie* French Army document (Paris, 1860).

34. Thirty, *Histoire de la tactique*, p. 12.

35. L. J. Trochu, *L'Armée française en 1867* (Paris, 1867), pp. 208-14.

36. Ibid., pp. 216, 222-23.

37. E. M. Earle, ed., *The Makers of Modern Strategy* (Princeton, 1943), pp. 206-8.

38. A. du Picq, *Battle Studies: Ancient and Modern Battle*, trans. J. N. Greeley and R. C. Cotton (Harrisburg, Pa., 1946), pp. 97, 104, 109-12.

39. Ibid., p. 12.

40. Ibid., pp. 116, 122.

41. Ibid., pp. 126-27, 146-51.

42. Ibid., p. 153.

43. Ibid., pp. 158, 162-64, 166.

44. J. Luvaas, *The Education of an Army: British Military Thought, 1815-1940* (Chicago, 1964), pp. 3, 20-21, 37-38.

45. Blackmore, *British Military Firearms*, pp. 189, 223.

46. J. W. Fortescue, *A History of the British Army*, 13 vols. (London, 1910-30). Volumes 11,12, and 13, describe British champaigns in the post-1815 decades.

47. F. S. Bajwa, *Military System of the Sikhs* (Delhi, 1964), pp. 63, 67, 78-79, 243, 253, 270; G. Bruce, *Six Battles for India: The Anglo-Sikh Wars, 1845-6, 1848-9* (London, 1969), pps. 15, 50, 53-54.

48. Bruce, *Six Battles*, pp. 114, 131, and D. Featherstone, *At Them with the Bayonet: The First Sikh War* (London, 1968), pp. 54-58.

49. Bruce, *Six Battles*, p. 167.

50. Ibid., pps. 238, 289-291, and H. Cook, *The Sikh Wars: The British Army in the Punjab 1845-1849* (London 1975), pp. 169-76.

51. P. Gibbs, *The Battle of the Alma* (Liverpool, 1963), p. 70; W. B. Pemberton, *Battles of the Crimean War* (New York, 1962), pp. 46, 54-55; C. Hibbert, *The Destruction of Lord Raglan* (Baltimore, Md., 1963), pp. 84, 91, 107; W. H. Russell, *The British Expedition to the Crimea* (London, 1877), p. 109.

52. Pemberton, *Battles of the Crimean War*, pp. 48-49, 56-59.

53. Ibid., pp. 117, 130-34; Hibbert, *Destruction of Lord Raglan*, p. 204.

54. R. A. Dixon, "The Rifle—Its Probable Influence on Modern Warfare," *Journal of the United Service Institution* 1 no. 2 (1857), pp. 95-120.

55. T. Harvey, "The Progressive and Possible Development of Infantry Drill and manoeuvres," in *Journal of the Royal United Service Institution* 8 (1865), pp. 292-301.

56. J. S. Curtiss, *The Russian Army under Nicholas I, 1825-1855* (Durham, N.C., 1965), p. 107.

57. Ibid., pp. 112, 119, 121, 123; P. von Wahlde, "A Pioneer of Russian Strategic Thought: G. A. Leer, 1829-1940," *Military Affairs* 35, no. 4 (December 1971), :149.

58. Curtiss, *Russian Army*, pp. 108, 126; McClellan, *Armies of Europe*, pp. 211, 223, 240; B. Renard, *Considerations sur la tactique de l'infanterie en Europe* (Paris, 1857), p. 114.

59. Curtiss, *Russian Army*, pp. 66-67.

60. A. W. Kinglake, *The Invasion of the Crimea* (London, 1899), pp. 153, 163, 171-73; F. Canonge, *Histoire et art militaires*, 2 vols. (Paris, 1901), 2:25; C. à Court, "Russian Infantry Tactics," *Journal of the Royal United Service Institution* 32 (1888):976-978.

61. C. M. Wilcox, *Evolutions of the Line as practiced by the Austrian Infantry and Adopted in 1853* (New York, 1860), pp. 10-11.

62. Ibid., pp. 28, 130.

63. Ibid., pp. 19-21, McClellan, *Armies of Europe*, pp. 63-64; Renard, *Considerations sur la tactique*, pp. 109, 149.

64. Duquet, *La Guerre d'Italie*, pp. 67-68.

65. Bazancourt, *La Campagne d'Italie*, 2:174-75, 244, 251, 262-63.

66. G. A. Craig, *The Battle of Königgrätz: Prussia's Victory over Austria, 1816* (New York, n.d.) p. 9.

67. G. B. Johnson and H. B. Lockhaven, *International Armament*, vols. (Cologne, 1965), 1:180; McClellan, *Armies of Europe*, pp. 76-77.

68. Renard, *Considerations sur la tactique*, pp. 208-9.

69. C. C. Chesney, "The Study of Military Science in Time of Peace," *Journal of the Royal United Service Institution* 15 (1872): 265-66.

70. Craig, *Battle of Königgrätz*, pp. 53-54, 60-64.

71. C. Shuttle, "Military Maxims," *Journal of the Royal United Service Institution* 14(1871): 214-15; M. Heintz, *Conference sur la tactique de l'infanterie prussienne pendant la campagne de 1866* (Paris, 1869), pp. 9-10, 16, 30.

72. Craig, *Battle of Königgrätz*, pp. 105-8, 145-49, 159, 166; W. Rüstow, *Tactique générale*, trans. Savin de Larclause (Paris, 1872), pp. 267, 283.

73. Renard, *Considerations sur la tactique*, p. vi.

74. McClellan, *Armies of Europe*, p. 82; Duquet, *La Guerre d'Italie*, pp. 293-94; Bazancourt, *LaCampagne d'Italie*, 2:272-73.

75. A. Marmont, *Memoires du Duc Maréchal Marmont de Raguse de 1792 à 1832*, 9 vols. (Paris, 1857), 9:273-78.

76. A. Hasbrouck, *Foreign Legionnaires in the Liberation of Spanish South America* (New York, 1928), pp. 124, 134-35.

77. Ibid., pp. 206, 229.

78. Ibid., pp. 319, 338, 396.

79. S. E. Ambrose, *Duty, Honor, Country: A History of West Point* (Baltimore, Md., 1966), pp. 66, 100, 101; R. F. Weigley, *Towards an American Army: Military Thought from Washington to Marshall* (New York 1962), p. 76.

80. D. H. Mahan, *An Elementary Treatise on Advanced-Guard, Out-Post, and Detachment Service of Troops and the Manner of Posting and Handling Them in the Presence of an Enemy* (New York, 1861), pp. 34, 49, 50-51.

81. Ambrose, *Duty, Honor, Country*, pp. 138, 200.

82. C. W. Elliott, *Winfield Scott: The Soldier and The Man* (New York, 1937), pp. 147, 190.

83. W. Scott, *Infantry Tactics or Rules for the Exercise and Manoeuvres of the United States Infantry*, 3 vols. (New York, 1854), 1:9, 69-70, 100-103.

84. T. Ransom, *Military Tactics and Instructions for the Use of Volunteers and Militia of the United States* (Concord, Mass., 1838), pp. 83, 89.

85. E. J. Nichols, *Zach Taylor's Little Army* (New York, 1963), pp. 74-75, 164; N. C. Brooks, *A Complete History of the Mexican War* (Philadelphia, 1849), pp. 127-28, 140, 177, 212-15; J. H. Smith, *The War with Mexico*, 2 vols. (New York, 1919), 1:156-57; H. Hamilton, *Zachary Taylor, Soldier of the Republic* (New York, 1941), pp. 182-83, 187.

86. W. J. Hardee, *Rifle and Light Infantry Tactics*, 2 vols. (Louisville, Ky., 1861).

87. S. Casey, *Infantry Tactics, 2 vols., (New York, 1862), 1:5.*

88. *Hardee, Rifle and Light Infantry Tactics*, 1:174-75; Casey, *Infantry Tactics*, 1:181-223.

89. Casey, *Infantry Tactics*, 1:117-19.

90. G. T. Beauregard, "The Campaign of Shiloh," in *Battles and Leaders of the Civil War*, ed. R. U. Johnson and C. C. Buel, (1884-87; reprinted., New York, 1956), 1:584.

91. J. D. Cox, "Battle of Antietam," in *Battles and Leaders*, 2:638-39, 643, 645.

92. L. McLaws, "The Confederate Left at Fredericksburg," in *Battles and Leaders*, 3:93.

93. Bruce Catton, *Glory Road* (Garden City, N.Y., 1952), p. 337; E. Rice, "Repelling Lee's Last Blow at Gettysburg," in *Battles and Leaders*, 3:387; N. Hall, "Report," in *Battles and Leaders*, 3:390.

94. A. L. Wagner, *Organization and Tactics* (Kansas City, Mo., 1906), pp. 268-69.

95. J. K. Mahon, "Civil War Infantry Assault Tactics," *Military Affairs*, 25(1961): 62-63.

96. Wagner, *Organization and Tactics*, p. 265.

97. Ibid., p. 270; S. E. Ambrose, *Upton and the Army* (Baton Rouge, La., 1964), pp. 31-33; D. L. Thompson, "With Burnside at Antietam," in *Battles and Leaders*, 2:661; G. N. Galloway, "Hand to Hand Fighting at Spottsylvania," in *Battles and Leaders*, 4:171-173.

98. F. J. Porter, "Hanover Court House and Gaines Mill," in *Battles and Leaders*, 2:324, 331, 333, 335.

99. J. Longstreet, "The Battle of Fredericksburg," in *Battles and Leaders*, 3:79;

Catton, *Glory Road,* pp. 338-43; E. B. Coddington, *The Gettysburg Campaign* (New York, 1968), 509-11.

100. B. Catton, *A Stillness at Appomattox* (Garden City, N.Y., 1953) pps. 68, 85, 113, 319; G. Davis, L. Perry, and J. Kirkley, eds., *The War of the Rebellion: A Compilation of the Official Records of the Union and Confederate Armies,* 1st. ser., 53 vols. (Washington, D.C., 1894), 46:231, 242, 244.

101. W. T. Sherman, *Memoirs of General William T. Sherman written by Himself* (Bloomington, Ind., 1957), 2:45.

102. Ibid., pp. 93, 395-97.

103. J. M. Schofield, *Forty-Six Years in the Army* (New York, 1897), p. 145.

6

Conclusion

During the eighteenth and early nineteenth century, European armies faced a similar set of tactical problems. Within the constraints imposed by the social and economic order and technology, armies had to obtain adequate firepower and mobility.

The socioeconomic milieu gave rise to small, long-service armies led by the aristocracy. The enlisted ranks came from the lower orders. Since the common soldiers lacked patriotic motivation and were prone to desertion, rigid discipline, even at the expense of flexibility, was necessary simply to keep the troops with their regiments. The slow-firing, inaccurate smoothbore musket imposed additional requirements for discipline. To obtain a satisfactory volume of firepower, troops had to be treated like cogs in a machine. The delivery of ordered volleys was more important than individual initiative.

The French Revolution eliminated the social constraints on tactical flexibility, but technological problems remained. French Revolutionary armies were able to place great emphasis on open order techniques. Skirmishing became an integral part of battlefield tactics. The French also encouraged greater initiative on the part of junior officers. Revolutionary and Imperial armies no longer had to fight in rigid linear formations. Commanders could wage encounter battles and maneuver units during an engagement to respond rapidly to changing tactical circumstances. The ability of the infantryman to fight either as a skirmisher or as a member of a close order formation greatly enhanced the French army's tactical flexibility.

Close order formations, however, remained vital. Weapons had not changed from the days of the Old Regime. It was therefore still necessary to use deployed lines for fire action and columns for maneuver and assaults. Other armies, to a greater or lesser degree, copied French tactics, and by 1815 European armies had increased their tactical flexibility but, like the French, remained constrained by the nature of infantry weapons.

In the aftermath of the Napoleonic Wars, military men concentrated on perfecting and refining the tactical doctrines that evolved during the previous wars. Improvements in infantry weaponry, however, both enabled and compelled additional changes in tactical doctrine. As weapons became more effective, armies began to increase the number of troops able to function as light infantrymen and followed the British by adopting the two-rank line. Battalion columns began to give way to company columns, and the battlefield role of the column became more and more restricted, until by the late 1860s the column was little more than a maneuver element.

Firepower in the form of individual aimed fire became of increasing importance in battle. The American Civil War demonstrated the increasing difficulty of executing frontal assaults against an entrenched enemy armed with muzzle-loading rifled weapons. The Austro-Prussian War provided a devastating example of the effectiveness of breech-loading rifles. The Franco-Prussian War, the first conflict in which both sides were equipped with breech-loading rifles, again demonstrated the increasing effectiveness of individual aimed fire and the futility of employing close order formations on a modern battlefield.

The American and European combats of the 1860s convinced most military men of the need to use open order formations. The Franco-Prussian War made it abundantly clear that the skirmish order was the only effective battle order. Light infantry no longer paved the way for and supported close order formations. Light infantry methods became the only mode of combat; the skirmish line *was* the line of battle.

Between 1871 and 1914 weapons continued to improve. Magazine rifles, smokeless powder, and the advent of the machine-gun all contributed to the increased ability of soldiers to maintain defensive positions against superior numbers. Military men, therefore, sought to devise tactics to enable them to conduct offensive operations. The initial solution was to emphasize turning maneuvers and enveloping attacks, but it soon became apparent that defenders could easily refuse a wing or create a new flank and force the assailant into a situation where he was again compelled to mount a frontal assault.

Given the power of modern weapons, military men by 1914 were unable to solve the problem of delivering an effective assault without sustaining excessive casualties. They concluded that offensive operations were desirable and necessary both strategically and tactically. They also recognized that attacks would at least initially be very costly. Nevertheless, the professional soldiers sought to devise tactics to make assaults possible. They emphasized artillery support, individual and small unit flexibility, and the need to attain fire superiority before launching the final assault. Still, by 1914 the problem remained unsolved. The First World War provided near catastrophic proof that modern infantry weapons gave tremendous advantages to defensive warfare. Only the advent of armored fighting vehicles and close air support would restore tactical mobility and the ability to launch effective attacks.

More recently, the introduction of guided antiarmor weapons and antiaircraft missiles has raised anew doubts about the effectiveness of offensive operations. Still, the search for tactical flexibility based upon fire and maneuver continues.

Bibliography

PRIMARY SOURCES

UNPUBLISHED DOCUMENTS

National Archives, Paris, France

AFII Carton 9, Section 55.
AFII Carton 27, Section 217.
AFII Carton 77, Section 571.
AFII Carton 212, Section 1807.
AFII Carton 214A, Section 1835.
AFII Carton 214B, Section 1839.
AFIII Carton 149, Dossier 699.
AFIII Carton 149, Dossier 702.
AFIII Carton 150A.
AFIII Carton 151A.
AFIII Carton 151B.
AFIII* Carton 14G

Army Archives, Paris, France

Ministère de la guerre état-major de l'armée archives historiques.

Armées du Nord et des Ardennes correspondance, 1-15 septembre 1793, Carton B^{1}18.

Armées du Nord et des Ardennes correspondance, 16-30 septembre 1793, Carton B^{1}19.

Armées du Nord et des Ardennes correspondance, 1-19 octobre 1793, Carton B^{1}20.

Armées du Nord et de Sambre et Meuse correspondance, 1-13 juin 1794, Carton B^{1}33.

Registre de l'état-major général, 18 août 1793, continuée jusqu'au 1 octobre suivant, Carton B¹110.

Armées de la République situations générales, 1791-1802, Carton B¹244.

Armées de la République situations générales, 1792-1800, Carton B¹245.

Armées de Mayence et d'Helvétie correspondance, janvier 1799, Carton B²69.

Armées d'Italie et de Naples situations 1792-1801, Carton B³381.

Armées de Naples correspondance de Macdonald, mai-octobre 1799, Carton B³*322*.

Rapports du ministre de la guerre au Directoir Executif, 12 ventôse an 7-3 vendémiaire an 8, Carton B¹²*37.

Correspondance du Ministère avec la Convention et le Comité de Salut Public du 6 octobre 1792 au 10 août 1794, Carton B¹²53.

Grande Armée correspondance, 1-15 decembre 1805, Carton C²9.

Grande Armée situations, Carton C²522.

Grande Armée situations, 1805-1806, Carton C²724.

Iᵉʳ Empire situations 1809, Carton C²736.

Ordres de bataille des armées en campagne 1792-1815, Carton Xᴾ3.

Infanterie organization générale 1790-1815, Carton Xᴾ5.

Diverses sur les armées de la République, Carton Xᴾ81.

Organisation générale de l'armée 1793, Carton Xˢ4.

Conseil de'administration de la guerre Consuiat Empire, Carton Xˢ6.

Relation de la bataille de Fleurs livrée le 8 messidor an 2 (26 juin 1794) in Mémoires historiques 274.

Journal de la campagne de l'an IV sous le commandement du général en chef Jourdan in Mémoires historiques 287.

Grouchy, General, "Précis des opérations de l'Armée d'Italie depuis l'affaire de l'Adda jusqu'à la bataille de Novi," in Mémoires historiques 443.

Mémoires Militaires du Maréchal Jourdan in Mémoires historiques 608[2] Campagne de 1794.

Récit de la bataille de Preussich-Eylau in Mémoires historiques 647.

Campagnes de Prusse et de Pologne 1806-1807 in Mémoires historiques 659.

Campagne de 1813 in Mémoires historiques 690.

Relation sur la bataille près Wagram in Mémoires historiques 672.

Campagne de 1813 in Mémoires historiques 688.

Campagne de France 1814 in Mémoires historiques 715.

Retraite des armées françaises d'Espagne et bataille de Vitoria in Mémoires historiques 774 (1813, by a French officer in Spain).

Notice sur la campagne de Portugal en 1810 et 1811 in Mémoires historiques 748 (by Pelet, who was Massena's ADC).

Campagne de 1815 in Mémoires historiques 900[bis2].

Lutzen et Bautzen mai 1813 in Mémoires historiques 902[2] (Pelet Papers)

Bataille de Wagram in Mémoires historiques 910[3].

Journal historique de la campagne de Portugal (15 septembre 1810- 12 mai 1811) in Mémoires historiques 916.

Foreign Office Archives, Paris, France

Archives des Affaires Étrangères Mémoires et Documents 321.

Archives des Affaires Étrangères Correspondance Politique 651.

PUBLISHED DOCUMENTS

Albrecht and William, Archdukes, eds. *Ausgewählte Schriften des Erzherzogs Carl von Oesterreich.* 5 vols. Vienna, 1893-94.

Auszug aus dem Exercier Reglement für die k.k. Infanterie vom Jahr 1807. Austrian Army document. Vienna, 1807.

Balderrabano, A. *Instruccion de guerrilla por el Sr. d. Felipe de San Juan.* Santiago, 1823.

Berthèzene, P. *Souvenirs militaires.* 2 vols. Paris, 1855.

Berthier, A. *Relation des campagnes du général Bonaparte en Égypte et en Syrie.* Paris, 1800.

Beulay, H. *Mémoires d'un grenadier de la grande Armée (18 avril 1808-15 octobre 1815).* Paris, 1907.

Bugeaud, J. R. Maréchal. *Aperçus sur quelques détails de la guerre.* Paris, 1846.

Bunbury, T. *Reminiscences of a Veteran.* 3 vols. London, 1861.

Casey, S. *Infantry Tactics.* 2 vols. New York, 1862.

Cathcart, G. *Commentaries on the War in Russia and Germany in 1812 and 1813.* London, 1850.

Charavany, E. *Correspondance générale de Carnot, 4 novembre 1793-mars 1795.* Paris, 1908.

Clausewitz, K. von. *La campagne de 1812 en Russie.* Translated by M. Bégouën. Paris, 1900.

Coppée, H. *The Field Manual of Evolutions of the Line.* Philadelphia, 1862.

Correspondance de Napoléon Ier. 32 vols. Paris, 1858-69.

Costello, Edward, *The Peninsular and Waterloo Campaigns.* Edited by A. Brett-James. London, 1967.

Davout, Général, ed. *Opérations du 3e corps 1806-1807. Raport du Maréchal Davout Duc d'Auerstaedt.* Paris, 1896.

Decker, Colonel. *Les trois armes ou tactique divisionnaire.* Paris, 1851.

Dixon, R. A. "The Rifle—Its Probable Influence on Modern Warfare." *Journal of the United Service Institution,* no. 2 (1857):95-120.

Eckert, G. *Von Valmy bis Leipzig Quellen und Dokumente zur Geschichte der preussischen Heeresreform.* Hannover, 1955.

Espoz y Mina, F. *Memorias del General don Francisco Espoz y Mina: Biblioteca de autores españoles,* vol. 146. Madrid, 1962.

Fabry, G. *Journal des opérations des IIIe et V^e corps en 1813.* Paris, 1902.

Fain, Baron. *Manuscrit de Mil Huit Cent Treize.* 2 vols. Paris, 1829.

Fay, C. A., *Souvenirs de la Guerre de Crimée, 1854-1856*. Paris, 1889.

Gay de Vernon, J. L. C. *Mémoire sur les opérations militaires des généraux-en-chef Custine et Houchard pendant les années 1792 et 1793*. Paris, 1844.

Goltz, F. von der, ed. *Militärische Schriften von Scharnhorst*. Berlin, 1881.

Griess, T. E., and Luvaas, J., eds. *Regulations for the Prussian Infantry. Translated from the original (1759)*. New York, 1968.

Guibert, J. A. H. *Défense du systême de guerre moderne ou réfutation complette du systême de M. de M. . . D. . . 2 vols. Neuchatel, 1779*.

———Essai général de tactique. 2 vols. Liège, 1775.

Hardee, W. J. *Rifle and Light Infantry Tactics*. 2 vols. Louisville, Ky., 1861.

Harvey, T. "The Progressive and Possible Development of Infantry Drill and Manoeuvres." *Journal of the Royal United Service Institution* 8 (1865): 292-301.

Heintz, M. *Conference sur la tactique de l'infanterie prussienne pendant la campagne de 1866*. Paris, 1869.

Henckens, E. F. C. A. *Mémoires*. The Hague, 1910.

Hennet de Goutel, E., ed. *Mémoires du général Marquis Alphonse d'Hautpoul Pair de France 1789-1865*. Paris, 1906.

Histoire de l'Academie Royale des sciences. Paris, 1759, 1767, 1769, 1772.

Instruction sur l'exercice et les manoeuvres de l'infanterie. French Army document. Paris, 1860.

Kincaid, J. *Adventures in the Rifle Brigade*. London, 1830.

Koch, Général, ed. *Mémoires d'André Masséna Duc de Rivoli Prince d'Essling Maréchal d'Empire*. 7 vols. Paris, 1966-67.

Langeron, A. L. A. *Mémoires de Langeron général d'infanterie dans l'armée russe campagnes de 1812, 1813, 1814*. Paris, 1902.

Larchey, L., ed. *Journal de marche du Sergent Fricasse de la 127e Demi-Brigade, 1792-1802*. Paris, 1882.

Lettres d'un officier du corps royale d'artillerie. Paris, 1774.

Lombard, J. *Un volontaire de 1792*. Paris, 1892.

McClellan, G. *The Armies of Europe Comprising Descriptions in Detail of the Military Systems of England, France, Russia, Prussia, Austria, and Sardinia.* Philadelphia, 1862.

Macdonald, A. *Souvenirs du Maréchal Macdonald Duc de Tarente.* Paris, 1892.

Mahan, D. H. *An Elementary Treatise on Advanced-Guard, Out-Post, and Detachment Service of Troops and the Manner of Posting and Handling Them in Presence of an Enemy.* New York, 1861.

Marbot, M. *Mémoires du général Bon Marbot.* 3 vols. Paris, 1892.

Maricourt, A. de, ed. *Mémoires du général Nouges (1777-1853) sur les guerres de l'Empire.* Paris, 1922.

Marmont, A. *Mémoires du maréchal Marmont Duc de Raguse de 1792 à 1832.* 9 vols. Paris, 1857.

Masséna, A. *Rapport fait par le général Masséna au Directoire exécutif sur les opérations du 3 au 18 vendémiaire an 8* Paris, 1799.

Masson, F., and Biagi, G. *Napoléon inconnu papiers inedits (1786-1793).* 2 vols. Paris, 1895.

Maurice, J. F., ed. *The Diary of Sir John Moore.* 2 vols. London, 1904.

Mistler, J., ed. *Les Cahiers du Capitaine Coignet.* Paris, 1968.

Napoleon, *Commentaires de Napléon Premier.* 6 vols. Paris, 1867.

Ney, J. *Memoirs of Marshal Ney.* 2 vols. London, 1833.

Ordonnance du Roi du 22 juillet 1845 sur l'exercise et les manoeuvres des battalions de Chasseurs à pied. French Army document. Paris, 1845.

Ordonnance sur l'exercise et les manoeuvres de l'infanterie du 4 maris 1831. French Army document. Paris, 1849.

Outram, J. *Rough Notes of the Campaign in Sinde and Afghanistan in 1838-39.* Bombay, 1840.

Picq, A. du. *Battle Studies: Ancient and Modern Battle.* Translated by J. N. Greeley and R. C. Cotton. Harrisburg, Pa., 1946.

Ranson, T. *Military Tactics and Instructions for the Use of Volunteers and Militia of the United States.* Concord, Mass., 1838.

Règlement concernant l'exercise et les manoeuvres de l'infanterie du 1ᵉʳ aôut 1791. French army document. Paris, 1808.

Regulations for the Exercise of Riflemen and Light Infantry; and Instructions for their Conduct in the Field. British Army document. London, 1803.

Renard, B. *Considerations sur la tactique de l'infanterie en Europe.* Paris, 1857.

Rilling, Joseph R. *Baron von Steuben and His Regulations.* Philadelphia, 1966.

Rules and Regulations for the Formations, Field-Exercise, and Movements of His Majesty's Forces. British Army document. London, 1798.

Saint-Cyr, G. *Mémoires sur les campagnes des Armées du Rhin et de Rhin-et-Moselle de 1792 jusqu'à la Paix de Campo Formio.* 4 vols. Paris, 1829.

Saxe, M. de. *Lettres et mémoires choisis parmi les papiers originaux du Maréchal de Saxe.* 2 vols. Paris, 1794.

Scott, W. *Infantry Tactics or Rules for the Exercise and Manoeuvres of the United States Infantry.* 3 vols. New York, 1854.

Sherman, W. T. *Memoirs of General William T. Sherman by Himself.* 2 vols. Bloomington, Ind., 1957.

Shuttle, C. "Military Maxims." *Journal of the Royal United Service Institution* 14(1871): 206-29.

Soult, N. *Mémoires du Maréchal-Général Soult Duc de Dalmatie publiés par son fils première partie histoire des guerres de la Révolution.* 3 Vols. Paris, 1854.

Stewart, J. H. *A Documentary Survey of the French Revolution.* New York, 1951.

Surtees, W. *Twenty-five Years in the Rifle Brigade.* London, 1833.

Teil, J. du. *De l'usage de l'artillerie nouvelle dans la guerre de campagne.* Paris, 1778.

Ternay, C. *Traité de tactique.* 2 vols. Paris, 1832.

Trochu, L. J. *L'Armée française en 1867.* Paris, 1867.

U.S. War Department. *U. S. Infantry Tactics for the Instruction, Exercise, and Manoeuvres of the United States Infantry.* Philadelphia, 1863.

Wilcox, C. M. *Evolutions of the Line as Practiced by the Austrian Infantry and Adopted in 1853.* New York, 1860.

Wilson, R. *Brief Remarks on the Character and Composition of the Russian Army and a Sketch of the Campaigns in Poland in the Years 1806 and 1807.* London, 1810.

SECONDARY SOURCES

Allaix, J. *Système d'artillerie de campagne.* Paris, 1827.

Ambrose, S. E. *Duty, Honor, Country: A History of West Point.* Baltimore, Md., 1966.

— — —.*Upton and the Army.* Baton Rouge, La., 1964.

Amiot, C. *Historique du 24ᵉ régiment d'infanterie.* Paris, 1893.

Anderson, M. S. *Europe in the Eighteenth Century, 1713-1783.* New York, 1962.

Arvers, P. *Historique du 82ᵉ régiment d'infanterie de ligne.* Paris, 1876.

Bacquet, L. H. *L'Infantrie au XVIIᵉ siècle.* Paris, 1907.

Bajwa, F. S. *Military System of the Sikhs.* Delhi, 1964.

Barrière, F., ed. *Bibliothèque des mémoires relatif à l'histoire de France pendant le 18ᵉ siècle Dumouriez.* Paris, 1886.

Bauer, K. *The Mexican War, 1846-1848.* New York, 1974.

Bazancourt, C. L. baron de. *La Campagne d'Italie de 1859.* 2 vols. Paris, 1859.

Beauregard, G. T. "The Campaign of Shiloh." In *Battles and Leaders of the Civil War,* Edited by R. U. Johnson and C. C. Buel. 4 vols. 1884-87. Reprint. New York, 1956. Vol. 1.

Becke, A. F. *An Introduction to the History of Tactics, 1740-1905.* London, 1909.

— — —.*Napoleon and Waterloo: The Emperor's Campaign with the Armée du Nord, 1815.* London, 1939.

Belhomme, Lieutenant Colonel. *Histoire de l'infanterie en France.* 5 vols. Paris, n.d.

Bernardo, C. J., and Bacon, E. H. *American Military Policy: It's Development Since 1775.* Harrisburg, Pa., 1955.

Bertaud, J. P. *Valmy la Démocratie en armes.* Paris, 1970.

Berthoffer, G. *Historique du 52ᵉ régiment d'infanterie.* Paris, 1890.

Bertin, G. *La Campagne de 1812 d'après des tèmoins oculaires.* Paris, 1895.

———.*La Campagne de 1813 d'après des témoins oculaires.* Paris, 1896.

Blackmore, H. L. *British Military Firearms, 1650-1850.* London, 1961.

Blair, C. *European and American Arms.* London, 1962.

Bourgue, M. *Historique du 3ᵉ régiment d'infanterie.* Paris, 1894.

Bouvier, F. *Bonaparte en Italie 1796.* Paris, 1899.

Bouvier, J. *Historique du 96ᵉ régiment d'infanterie.* Lyon, 1892.

Brooks, N. C. *A Complete History of the Mexican War.* Philadelphia, 1849.

Bruce, G. *Six Battles for India: The Anglo-Sikh Wars, 1845-6, 1848-9.* London, 1969.

Buat, E. *Étude critique d'histoire militaire 1809 de Ratisbonne à Znaïm.* 2 vols. Paris, 1909.

Caemmerer, Lieutenant General von. *The Development of Strategical Science during the Nineteenth Century.* Translated by K. von Donat. London, 1905.

Canonge, F. *Histoire et Art Militaires.* 2 vols. Paris, 1901.

Carlyle, T. *History of Friedrich II of Prussia Called Frederick the Great.* 10 vols. London, n.d.

Carrias, E. *L'Armée allemande son histoire, son organization, sa tactique.* Paris, 1938.

Carter, S. *Blaze of Glory: The Fight for New Orleans, 1814-1815.* New York, 1971.

Casse, A. du. *Le Général Vandamme et sa correspondance.* 2 vols. Paris, 1870.

Catton, B. *Glory Road.* Garden City, N.Y., 1952.

A Stillness at Appomattox. Garden City, N.Y., 1953.

Chandler, D. G. *The Campaigns of Napoleon.* New York, 1966.

Chaperon, H. *Historique du 46ᵉ régiment d'infanterie.* Paris, 1894.

Charras, J. B. A. *Histoire de la guerre de 1813 en Allemagne.* Leipzig, 1866.

Chavanon, J., and Saint-Yves, G. *Joachim Murat (1767-1815).* Paris, 1905.

Chesney, C. C. "The Study of Military Science in Time of Peace." *Journal of the Royal United Service Institution* 15(1872): 254-68.

Chidsey, D. B. *The Battle of New Orleans.* New York, 1961.

———.*The War with Mexico.* New York, 1968.

Chuquet, A. *Hoche et la lutte pour Alsace (1793-1794).* Paris, 1893.

———.*Hondschoote.* Paris, n.d.

———.*Jemappes et la conquête de la Belgique.* Paris, 1890.

———.*La jeunesse de Napoléon.* 3 vols. Paris, 1897-99.

———.*Wissembourg (1793).* Paris, n. d.

Clement, A. *Historique du 75ᵉ régiment d'infanterie.* Paris, 1891.

Clerc, D. *Historique du 79ᵉ régiment d'infanterie.* Paris, 1896.

Coddington, E. B. *The Gettysburg Campaign.* New York, 1969.

Colin, J. "La Bataille de Montmirail," *Revue des études napoléoniennes* 4(1914).

———.*Campagne de 1793 en Alsace et dans le Palatinat.* Paris, 1902.

———.*Études sur la campagne de 1796-97 en Italie.* Paris, 1898.

———.*L'Infantrie au XVIIIᵉ siècle: la tactique.* Paris, 1907.

———."La Place de Napolèon dans l'histoire militaire." *Revue des études napoléoniennes* 3(1913).

———.*La Tactique et la discipline dans les armées de la Révolution correspondance du général Schauenbourg du 4 avril au 2 aôut 1793.* Paris, 1902.

———.*Les Transformationss de la guerre.* Paris, 1911.

———.*The Transformations of War.* Translated by L. H. R. Pope-Hennessy. London, 1912.

Cook, H. *The Sikh Wars: The British Army in the Punjab 1845-1849.* London, 1975.

Cope, W. H. *The History of the Rifle Brigade.* London, 1877.

Corvisier, A. *L'Armee française de la fin du XVIIᵉ siècle au ministère de Choiseul.* 2 vols. Paris, 1964.

———."Hiérarchie militaire et hiérarchie sociale à la vielle de la Revolution." *Revue internationale d'histoire militaire,* no. 30. (1970).

Coste, E. *Historique du 40ᵉ régiment d'infanterie de ligne.* Paris, 1887.

Court, C. à. "Russian Infantry Tactics." *Journal of the Royal United Service Institution* 32 (1888).

Coutanceau, H., and Jonquière, C. de la. *La Campagne de 1794 à l'Armée du Nord.* 3 vols. Paris, 1907.

Cox, J. D. "Battle of Antietam." In *Battles and Leaders of the Civil War.* Edited by R. U. Johnson and C. C. Buel. 4 vols. 1884-87. Reprint. New York, 1956. Vol. 2.

Craig, G. A. *The Battle of Königgrätz: Prussia's Victory over Austria, 1866.* New York, n. d.

———.*The Politics of the Prussian Army, 1640-1945.* Oxford, 1956.

Cugnac, Capitaine de. *Campagne de l'Armée de Réserve en 1800 deuxieme partie Marengo.* Paris, 1901.

Curtiss, J. S. *The Russian Army under Nicholas I, 1825-1855.* Durham, N. C., 1965.

Dahlmann, G. D. *Historique du 12ᵉ régiment d'infanterie.* Paris, 1877.

Davies, G. *Wellington and His Army.* Oxford, 1954.

Davis, G; Perry, L.; and Kirkley, J., eds. *The War of the Rebellion: A Compilation of the Official Records of the Union and Confederate Armies.* 1st ser. 53 vols. Washington, D. C., 1894. vol. 46.

Delbauve, E. *Historique du 26ᵉ régiment d'infanterie.* Paris, 1889.

Delderfield, R. F. *Imperial Sunset: The Fall of Napoleon, 1813-1814.* New York, 1968,

Denison, G. T. *A History of Cavalry from the Earliest Times with Lessons for the Future.* London, 1913.

Déprez, E. *Les Volontaires nationaux (1791-1793).* Paris, 1908.

Derode, M. *Nouvelle relation de la bataille de Friedland (14 juin 1807).* Paris, 1839.

Diderot, M., ed. "Artillerie." In *Encyclopédie.* Bern, 1781.

Dodge, T. A. *Napoleon.* 4 vols. New York, 1904.

Duchâtelet, A. *Historique du 106ᵉᵐᵉ régiment d'infanterie de ligne.* Chalons-sur-Marne, 1890.

Duffy, C. *Austerlitz 1805.* London, 1977.

The Wild Goose and the Eagle: A Life of Marshal von Browne, 1705-1757. London, 1964.

Dupuis, V. *La Campagne de 1793 à l'Armée du Nord et des Ardennes d'Hondschoote à Wattignes.* Paris, 1909.

———.*La Campagne de 1793 à l'Armée du Nord et des Ardennes de Valenciennes à Hondtschoote.* Paris, 1906.

———.*Opèrations sur la Sambre en 1794 Bataille de Fleurs.* Paris, 1907.

Duquet, A. *La Guerre d'Italie (1859).* Paris, 1882.

Duroisel, G. *Historique du 93ᵉ régiment d'infanterie.* La Roche-sur-Yon, 1893.

Duruy, A. *L'Armée Royale en 1789.* Paris, 1888.

Duruy, V. *Le 1ᵉʳ Régiment de Tirailleurs Algeriéns.* Paris, 1899.

Dussauge, A. *Le Ministère de Belle-Isle Krefeld et Lütterberg (1758).* Paris, 1914.

Dussieux, L. *L'Armée en France histoire et organisation.* 3 vols. Versailles, 1884.

Earle, E. M. *The Makers of Modern Strategy.* Princeton, N.J., 1943.

Edwards, M. *Battles of the Indian Mutiny.* New York, 1963.

Elliott, C. W. *Winfield Scott: The Soldier and the Man.* New York, 1937.

Ergang, R. *The Potsdam Führer: Frederick William I, Father of Prussian Militarism.* New York, 1941.

Fabry, G. *Campagne de Russie.* Paris, n. d. 5 vols.

Faulk, O. B., and Connor, S. V. *North American Divided: The Mexican War, 1846-1848.* New York, 1971.

Favé, I. *Histoire et tactique des trois armes.* Paris, 1845.

Featherstone, D. *At Them with the Bayonet: The First Sikh War.* London, 1968.

Fezensac, R. M. de. *The Russian Campaign, 1812.* Edited and translated by L. B. Kennett. Baton Rouge, La., 1970.

Ford, G. S. *Stein and the Era of Reform in Prussia, 1807-1815.* Princeton, N.J., 1922.

Fortescue, J. W. *A History of the British Army.* 13 vols. London, 1910-30.

Foucart, P. J. *Bautzen une bataile de deux jours 20-21 mai 1813.* Nancy and Paris, 1897.

———.*Campagne de Prusse (1806).* 2 vol. Paris, 1887.

Foucart, P. J., and Finot, J. *La Defénse nationale dans le nord 1792 à 1802.* 2 vols. Lille, 1890.

Foy, M. S. *Histoire de la guerre de la péninsule sous Napoléon.* 4 vols. Paris, 1824.

Fuller, J. F. C. *Armament and History.* New York, 1945.

— — —.*British Light Infantry in the Eighteenth Century.* London, 1925.

— — —.*The Conduct of War 1789-1961.* London, 1961.

— — —.*Sir John Moore's System of Training.* London, 1925.

Gachot, E. *1809, Napoléon en Allemagne.* Paris, 1913.

Gallois, P. M. *L'Art de guerre de Napoléon Ier.* 3 vols. Paris, 1965.

Galloway, G. N. "Hand to Hand Fighting at Spottsylvania." In *Battles and Leaders of the Civil War.* Edited by R. U. Johnson and C.C. Buel. 4 vols. 1884-87. Reprint. New York, 1956. Vol. 4.

Ganoe, W. A. *The History of the United States Army.* New York, 1924.

Gascon, D. *La Provincia de Teruel en la Guerra de la Independencia.* Madrid, 1908.

Gerome, A. C. *Historique du 75e régiment d'infanterie, 1674-1890.* Paris and Limoges, 1891.

Gerthoffer, G. *Historique du 52e régiment d'infanterie.* Paris, 1890.

Gibbs, P. *The Battle of the Alma.* Liverpool, 1963.

Gilbert, G. *The Evolution of Tactics.* London, 1907.

Girod de l'Ain, M. *Vie militaire du général Foy.* Paris, 1900.

Gleig, G. R. *The Campaigns of the British Army at Washington and New Orleans, 1814-1815.* London, 1879.

Glover, M. *Wellington as Military Commander.* London, 1968.

— — —.*Wellington's Peninsular victories.* London, 1963.

Glover, R. *Peninsular Preparation: The Reform of the British Army, 1795-1809.* Cambridge, 1963.

Godechot, J. *Les Commissaires aux armées sous le directoire.* 2 vols. Paris, 1938.

Goltz, C. von der. *Jena to Eylau.* Translated by C. F. Atkinson. London, 1913.

　　Rosbach et Iéna. Translated by Commandant Chabert. Nancy, 1896.

Greene, F. V. *The Revolutionary War and the Military Policy of the United States.* New York, 1911.

Gumtau, C. F. *Die Jäger und Schutzen des Preussischen Heeres.* 3 vols. Berlin, 1834.

Hall, N. "Report." In *Battles and Leaders of the Civil War.* Edited by R.U. Johnson and C.C. Buel. 4 vols. 1884-87. Reprint. New York, 1956. Vol. 3.

Hamilton, H. *Zachary Taylor, Soldier of the Republic.* New York, 1941.

Hamley, E. B. *The Operations of War Explained and Illustrated.* London, 1907.

Hanoteau, J., and Bonnot, E. *Bibliographie des historiques des régiments français.* Paris, 1913.

Hasbrouck, A. *Foreign Legionaires in the Liberation of Spanish South America.* New York, 1928,.

Henderson, E. F. *Blücher and the Uprising of Prussia against Napoleon, 1807-1815.* London, 1911.

Henderson, G. F. R. *The Science of War.* London, 1912.

Hibbert, C. *The Destruction of Lord Raglan.* Baltimore, Md., 1963.

Higginbotham, D. *The War of American Independence: Military Attitudes, Policies, and Practice, 1763-1789.* New York, 1971.

Holborn, H. *A History of Modern Germany, 1648-1840.* New York, 1964.

Home, R. *A Précis of Modern Tactics.* London, 1882.

Horward, D. *The Battle of Bussaco: Masséna vs. Wellington.* Tallahassee, Fla., 1965.

Houssaye, H. *Iéna et la campagne de 1806.* Paris, 1912.

Hozier, H. M. *The Seven Weeks' War.* 2 vols., London, 1867.

Iribarren, J. M. *Espoz y Mina: El Guerrillero.* Madrid, 1965.

Jany, C. *Geschichte der Preussischen Armee.* 4 vols. Osnabrück, 1967.

Johnson, G. B., and Lockhoven, H. B. *International Armament.* 2 vols. Cologne, 1965.

Jomini, A. de. *The Art of War.* Translated by G. H. Mendell and W. P. Craighill. Philadelphia, 1862. Reprint. Westport, Conn., 1971.

— — —.*Histoire critique et militaire des guerres de la Révolution.* 15 vols. Paris, 1820.

Kelly, W. H. *The Battle of the Wavre and Grouchy's Retreat.* London, 1905.

Kennett, L. *The French Armies in the Seven Years' War.* Durham, N.C., 1967.

Kimball, J. "The Battle of Chippawa: Infantry Tactics in the War of 1812." *Military Affairs* 21 (1967-68): 169-86.

Kinglake, A. W. *The Invasion of the Crimea.* London, 1899.

Kluchevsky, V. *A History of Russia.* 5 vols. New York, 1960.

Knox, T. W. *Decisive Battles Since Waterloo.* New York, 1887.

Kriegsgeschichtliche Einzelschriften, vol. 12, Das Nachtgefecht bei Laon am 9 März 1814. Prussia, Grossen Generalstabe. Berlin, 1889.

Kriegsgeschichtliche Einzelschriften, vol. 10, Nachrichten über Preussen in siner grossen Katastrophe. Prussia, General Staff, Historical Section, Berlin, 1888.

Lachouque, H., and Brown, A. *The Anatomy of Glory: Napoleon and His Guard, A Study in Leadership.* Providence, R.I., 1961.

Lanrezac, C. *La Manoeuvre de Lützen 1813.* Paris, 1904.

Latrille, G. *Considerations sur la guerre.* Paris, n. d.

Lauerma, M. *L'Artillerie de campagne française pendant les guerres de la Révolution.* Helsinki, 1956.

Laurencin, P. *Nos Zouaves.* Paris, 1888.

Law, E. M. "From the Wilderness to Cold Harbor," In *Battles and Leaders of the Civil War.* Edited by R. U. Johnson and C. C. Buel. 4 vols. 1884-87. Reprint. New York, 1956. Vol. 4.

Lefebvre de Béhaine, C. *La campagne de France la défense de la ligne du Rhin novembre 1813 à janvier 1814.* Paris, 1933.

Levinge, R. G. A. *Historical Records of the Forty-third Regiment, Monmouthshire Light Infantry* London, 1868.

Liddell Hart, B. H. *The Ghost of Napoleon.* New Haven, Conn., 1933.

Lloyd, E. M. *A Review of the History of Infantry.* London, 1908.

Longford, E. *Wellington: The Years of the Sword.* New York, 1969.

Longstreet, J. "The Battle of Fredericksburg." In *Battles and Leaders of the Civil War*. Edited by R. U. Johnson and C. C. Buel. 4 vols. 1884-87. Reprint. New York, 1956.

Longworth, P. *The Art of Victory: The Life and Achievements of Field-Marshal Suvorov*. New York, 1965.

Lowell, E. J. *The Hessians and the Other German Auxiliaries of Great Britain in the Revolutionary War*. Port Washington, N.Y. 1884.

Luvaas, J. *The Education of an Army: British Military Throught, 1815-1940*. Chicago, 1964.

— — —.*Frederick the Great on the Art of War*. New York, 1966.

Macartney, C. A. *The Hapsburg Empire, 1790-1918*. London, 1968.

McLaws, L. "The Confederate Left at Fredericksburg." In *Battles and Leaders of the Civil War*. Edited by R. U. Johnson and C. C. Buel. 4 vols. 1884-87. Reprint. New York, 1956. Vol. 3.

Macrory, P. A. *The Fierce Pawns*. New York, 1966.

Mahon, J. K. "Civil War Infantry Assult Tactics." *Military Affairs* 25 (1961): 57-68.

Malleson, G. *The Decisive Battles of India from 1746 to 1849 Inclusive*. London, 1885.

Marine, W. M. *The British Invasion of Maryland, 1812-1815*. Hatboro, Pa., 1965.

Marjoulet, A. *Historique du 3ᵉ Régiment de Zouaves*. Paris, 1887.

Marmont, A. *On Modern Armies*. Translated by Captain Lendy. London, 1865.

— — —.*The Spirit of Military Institutions*. Translated by F. Schaller. Columbia, S. C., 1864.

Martin, E. *Le 55ᵉ régiment d'infanterie*. Avignon, 1905.

Martray, G. du. *Le 132ᵉ Demi-Brigade deux ans à l'Armée de Sambre-et-Meuse 1794-1796*. Paris, 1887.

Matloff, M., ed. *American Military History*. Washington, D. C., 1969.

Maude, F. N. *The Jena Campaign, 1806*. London, 1909.

— — —.*The Leipzig Campaign, 1813*. London, 1908.

Maycock, F. W. O. *The Invasion of France, 1814*. London, 1914.

Mention, L. *Le comte de Saint Germain et ses réformes*. Paris, 1884.

Meynier, A. "Levées et pertes d'hommes sous le Consulat et Empire." *Revue des études napoléoniennes* 30(1930).

The Military Exploits etc., etc. of Don Juan Martin Diez, The Empecinado. . . . Translated by a general officer. London, 1823.

Moodie, D. C. F. *The History of the Battles and Adventures of the British, the Boers, and the Zulus, etc. in Southern Africa.* 2 vols. Capetown, 1888.

Morvan, J. *Le Soldat impérial (1800—1814).* 2 vols. Paris, 1904.

Napier, W. F. P. *History of the War in the Peninsula and in the South of France from the Year 1807 to the Year 1814.* 6 vols. Paris, 1839.

Naylor, J. *Waterloo.* London, 1960.

Nicholas, E. J. *Zach Taylor's Little Army.* New York, 1963.

Nolan, L. E. *Cavalry: Its History and Tactics.* Columbia, S. C., 1864.

Norris, J. A. *The First Afghan War, 1838-1842.* Cambridge, 1967.

Oman, C. *A History of the Peninsular War.* 7 vols. Oxford, 1902-30.

Oman, C. W. C. *Wellington's Army,* London, 1968. *1809-1814.* 1912. Reprint.

Pajol, C. *Les Guerres sous Louis XV.* 7 vols. Paris, 1883-91.

Palmer, R. R. *The Age of the Democratic Revolution: A Political History of Europe and America, 1760-1800* 2 vols. Princeton, N.J., 1959.

Paret, P. *Yorck and the Era of Prussian Reform, 1807-1815.* Princeton, N.J. 1966.

Parker, H. T. *Three Napoleonic Battles.* Durham, N.C., 1944.

Parkinson, R. *Clausewitz: A Biography.* New York, 1971.

Pemberton, W. B. *Battles of the Crimean War.* New York, 1962.

Peterson, H. L. *Encyclopedia of Firearms.* New York, 1964.

Petre, F. L. *Napoleon's Last Campaign in Germany, 1813.* London, 1912.

Petrie, C. *King Charles III of Spain.* London, 1971.

Phipps, R. W. *The Armies of the First French Republic.* 5 vols. London, 1926-39.

Picard, E., and Jouan, L. *L'Artillerie française au XVIIIe siècle.* Paris, 1906.

Pichené. R. *Histoire de la tactique et de la stratégie jusqu'à la guerre mondiale.* Paris, 1957.

Piéron, G. *Histoire d'un régiment la 32e Demi-Brigade (1775-1890).* Paris, 1891.

Pollard, H. B. *A History of Firearms.* London, 1926.

Porter, F. J. "Hanover Court House and Gaines Mill." In *Battles and Leaders of the Civil War.* Edited by R. V. Johnson and C. C. Buel. 4 vols. 1884-87. Reprint. New York, 1956. vol. 2.

Pratt, S. C. *A Précis of Modern Tactics. Originally compiled in 1873 by Col. Robert Home.* London, 1892.

Preston, R. A.: Wise, S. F.; and Werner, H. O. *Men in Arms: A History of Warfare and Its Interrelationships with Western Society.* New York, 1962.

Quimby, R. S. *The Background of Napoleonic Warfare.* New York, 1957.

Regele, O. *Feldmarschall Radetzky.* Vienna, 1957.

Regnault, J. "Les campagnes d'Algérie et leur influence de 1830 à 1870." *Revue historique de l'Armée.* (December 1953).

Reimpression de l'Ancien Moniteur. 31 vols. Paris, 1840. Vols. 15, 17.

Revol, J. F. *Histoire de l'armée française.* Paris, 1929.

Rice, E. "Repelling Lee's Last Blow at Gettysburg." In *Battles and Leaders of the Civil War.* Edited by R. U. Johnson and C.C. Buel, 4 vols, 1884-87. Reprint. New York, 1956. Vol. 3.

Ritter, G. *Frederick the Great: A Historical Profile.* Translated by P. Paret. Los Angeles, Calif., 1968.

Robinson, C. W. *Wellington's Campaigns Peninsula—Waterloo 1808-1815.* London, 1907.

Ropp, T. *War in the Modern World.* Durham, N.C., 1959.

Ross, S. T. "The Development of the Combat Division in Eighteenth-Century French Armies." *French Historical Studies,* 4, no. 1 (1965).

Rothenberg, G. "The Hapsburg Army in the Napoleonic Wars." *Military Affairs* 37, no. 1 (February 1973):1-5.

Rousseau, F. *Règne de Charles III d'Espagne.* 2 vols. Paris, 1907.

Rousset, C. *La Grande Armée de 1813.* Paris, 1892.

————.*Les Volontaires, 1791-1794.* Paris, 1870.

Russell, W. H. *The British Expedition to the Crimea.* London, 1877.

Rüstow, W. *L'Art militaire au XIX siècle.* Translated by Savin de Larclause. 2 vols. Paris, 1875.

————.*Tactique générale.* Translated by Savin de Larclause. Paris, 1872.

Schofield, J. M. *Forty-six Years in the Army* New York, 1897.

Shanahan, W. O. *Prussian Military Reforms, 1786-1813.* New York, 1945.

Simon, P., and Simon E. *historique du 89ᵉ régiment d'infanterie.* Paris, 1899.

Simond, E. *Historique des nouveaux régiments crées par la loi du 25 juillet 1887.* Paris, 1889.

Simond, J. G. E. *Le 28ᵉ de Ligne historique du régiment.* Rouen, 1889.

Six, G. *Les Généraux de la Révolution et de l'Empire.* Paris, 1947.

Skrine, F. H. *Fontenoy and Great Britain's Share in the War of the Austrian Succession, 1741-48.* London, 1906.

Smith, J. H. *The War with Mexico.* 2 vols. New York, 1919.

Soboul, A. *Les Soldats de l'an.* 2 vols. Paris, 1959.

Tarragon, M. *Historique du 15ᵉ régiment d'infanterie.* Paris-Limoges, 1895.

Thiry, Commandant. *Histoire de la tactique de l'infanterie française de 1791 à 1905.* Paris, 1905.

Thompson, D. L. "With Burnside at Antietam." In *Battles and Leaders of the Civil War.* Edited by R. U. Johnson and C. C. Buel. 4 vols. 1884-87. Reprint. New York, 1956. Vol. 2.

Thoumas, Général. *Les Transformations de l'armée française.* 2 vols. Paris, 1887.

Tournes, R. *Lützen étude d'une manoeuvre napoléonienne.* Paris, 1931.

Tucker, G. *Poltroons and Patriots.* 2 vols. New York, 1954.

Upton, E. *The Military Policy of the United States.* Washington, D.C., 1917.

Vigier, H. *Davout Maréchal d'Empire duc d'Averstadt Prince d' Eckmühl (1770-1823).* 2 vols. Paris, 1898.

Waddington, R. *La Guerre de Sept Ans.* 3 vols. Paris, n. d.

Wagner, A. L. *Organization and Tactics.* Kansas City, Mo., 1906.

Wahle, P. von. "A Pioneer of Russian Strategic Thought: G. A. Leer, 1829-1904." *Military Affairs* 35, no. 4 (December 1971): 148-53.

Wallon, H. *Les Représentants du peuple en mission et la justice revolutionnaire dans les départements.* 5 vols. Paris, 1889.

Ward, C. *The War of the Revolution.* 2 vols. New York, 1952.

Wartenburg, Yorck von. *Napoleon as a General.* 2 vols. London, 1897, 1955.

Weigley, R. F. *Towards an American Army: Military Thought from Washington to Marshall.* New York, 1962.

Weil, M. H. *La Campagne de 1814.* 4 vols. Paris, 1891.

Weller, J. *Wellington at Waterloo.* New York, 1967.

White, J. M. *Marshal of France: The Life and Times of Maurice Comte de Saxe (1696-1750).* London, 1962.

Wilkinson, S. *The French Army Before Napoleon.* London, 1915.

— — — . *The Rise of General Bonaparte.* Oxford, 1930.

Williams, B. *The Whig Supremacy, 1714-1760.* London, 1962.

Winant, L. *Early Percussion Firearms.* New York, 1959.

Wirth, J. *Le maréchal Lefebvre duc de Danzig.* Paris, 1904.

Wylly, H. C. *The Campaign of Magenta and Solferino, 1859.* London, 1907.

Index